T0253677

Getting Started with Istio Service Mesh

Manage Microservices in Kubernetes

Rahul Sharma
Avinash Singh

Apress®

Getting Started with Istio Service Mesh

Rahul Sharma
Delhi, India

Avinash Singh
Gurgaon, Haryana, India

ISBN-13 (pbk): 978-1-4842-5457-8
https://doi.org/10.1007/978-1-4842-5458-5

ISBN-13 (electronic): 978-1-4842-5458-5

Copyright © 2020 by Rahul Sharma, Avinash Singh

This work is subject to copyright. All rights are reserved by the Publisher, whether the whole or part of the material is concerned, specifically the rights of translation, reprinting, reuse of illustrations, recitation, broadcasting, reproduction on microfilms or in any other physical way, and transmission or information storage and retrieval, electronic adaptation, computer software, or by similar or dissimilar methodology now known or hereafter developed.

Trademarked names, logos, and images may appear in this book. Rather than use a trademark symbol with every occurrence of a trademarked name, logo, or image we use the names, logos, and images only in an editorial fashion and to the benefit of the trademark owner, with no intention of infringement of the trademark.

The use in this publication of trade names, trademarks, service marks, and similar terms, even if they are not identified as such, is not to be taken as an expression of opinion as to whether or not they are subject to proprietary rights.

While the advice and information in this book are believed to be true and accurate at the date of publication, neither the authors nor the editors nor the publisher can accept any legal responsibility for any errors or omissions that may be made. The publisher makes no warranty, express or implied, with respect to the material contained herein.

Managing Director, Apress Media LLC: Welmoed Spahr
Acquisitions Editor: Nikhil Karkal
Development Editor: Matthew Moodie
Coordinating Editor: Divya Modi

Cover designed by eStudioCalamar

Cover image designed by Freepik (www.freepik.com)

Distributed to the book trade worldwide by Springer Science+Business Media New York, 233 Spring Street, 6th Floor, New York, NY 10013. Phone 1-800-SPRINGER, fax (201) 348-4505, e-mail orders-ny@springer-sbm.com, or visit www.springeronline.com. Apress Media, LLC is a California LLC and the sole member (owner) is Springer Science + Business Media Finance Inc (SSBM Finance Inc). SSBM Finance Inc is a **Delaware** corporation.

For information on translations, please e-mail rights@apress.com, or visit www.apress.com/rights-permissions.

Apress titles may be purchased in bulk for academic, corporate, or promotional use. eBook versions and licenses are also available for most titles. For more information, reference our Print and eBook Bulk Sales web page at www.apress.com/bulk-sales.

Any source code or other supplementary material referenced by the author in this book is available to readers on GitHub via the book's product page, located at www.apress.com/978-1-4842-5457-8. For more detailed information, please visit www.apress.com/source-code.

Printed on acid-free paper

To my wife Neha and my daughter, Avyanna, without whom this book would never have been completed.

—*Avinash Singh*

Table of Contents

About the Authors...xi

About the Technical Reviewer xiii

Acknowledgments xv

Chapter 1: Quick Tour of Kubernetes 1

K8s Architecture/Components 2

   Kubernetes Master 3

   Kubernetes Workers 5

Kubernetes Terminology 9

Set Up a Kubernetes Cluster 11

   Set Up VirtualBox..11

   Install Kubectl...11

   Set Up Minikube 12

   Set Up Docker...13

   Set Up Python 15

   Set Up Java..15

Our First Kubernetes Cluster...15

Run an Application on Kubernetes 17

   Application Details..17

   Deploy the Application 19

   Kubernetes Service 24

   Kubernetes Is Self-Healing..30

Add a Microservice 32

    Application Setup 32

    Release and Deployment..34

Readiness Probes 37

Summary..45

Chapter 2: Introduction to the Service Mesh.............................47

Microservice Architecture 47

    Agility...51

    Innovation 52

    Scalability 52

    Maintainability 53

    Challenges 53

    Language Libraries 62

Service Mesh 77

    Traffic Control 78

    Security 79

    Analytics 80

Sidecar Pattern 82

Envoy, the Sidecar Provider 84

    Configuring Envoy...88

    Verifying the Service 95

Summary..98

Chapter 3: Installing Istio 99

Istio Service Mesh...99

Istio Architecture 102

    Data Plane 103

    Control Plane 104

Mixer 106

Pilot 111

Citadel 114

Galley..114

Setting Up Istio...114

Installation Using Helm...115

Demo Installation Without Helm 118

GKE Installation 120

Verifying the Installation...120

Istio Services 122

Working with Istio 123

Using the Istio CLI 124

authn 124

deregister 124

register 125

experimental...125

kube-inject 128

proxy-config bootstrap|cluster|endpoint|listener|route 135

validate 135

Summary..136

Chapter 4: Istio VirtualService...137

Request Routing...137

Kubernetes Practices 141

Naming Service Ports..142

Pods with Version Labels...143

Declared Pod Ports..144

Destination Rules 146

    Connection Pool 148

    Load Balancing 151

    Outlier Detection 151

VirtualService 153

    Forwarding 154

    Rewrite 156

    HTTP Attributes Lookup 158

    Weighted Distribution 160

Canary Releases 163

Summary 168

Chapter 5: Istio Gateway 169

Ingress 169

Secure Sockets Layer 176

    Configure istio-ingressgateway-certs 178

    Configure istio-ingressgateway-ca-certs 181

External Service Access 182

    Service Entry 185

    Egress 188

Summary 192

Chapter 6: Service Resiliency 193

Application Setup 195

Load Balancing 201

Retry Requests 205

Timeout Requests 212

Circuit Breaker 219

Connection Pool Circuit Breaker 222

Load Balancer Circuit Breaker 229

Resiliency 231

Summary 232

Chapter 7: Application Metrics 233

Application Monitoring 233

Istio Mixer 236

Prometheus 237

Installation 238

Prometheus Dashboard 240

Custom Metrics 245

Grafana 249

Installation 249

Grafana Dashboard 251

Grafana Alert 253

Summary 258

Chapter 8: Logs and Tracing 259

Distributed Tracing 259

Application Logs 266

Mixer 271

Handler 273

Instance 274

Rules 278

Summary 279

Chapter 9: Policies and Rules **281**

Authentication 281

    Transport Authentication 282

    User Authentication 289

Authorization 297

Rules 301

Summary 304

Chapter 10: Troubleshooting **305**

Configmaps 305

Proxy 307

Routes 309

Summary 313

Index **315**

About the Authors

Rahul Sharma is a seasoned Java developer with more than 14 years of industry experience. During his career, he has worked with companies of various sizes, from enterprises to startups, and has developed and managed microservices on the cloud (AWS/GCE/DigitalOcean) using open source software. He is an open source enthusiast and shares his experience at local meetups. He is also the co-author of *Java Unit Testing with JUnit 5* (Apress, 2017).

Avinash Singh is an IIT-Kanpur alumnus with more than ten years of experience in architecture, design, and developing scalable and distributed cloud applications. He has hands-on experience in technologies such as AWS Cloud, J2EE, ROR, MySQL, MongoDB, Spring, and Hibernate. Avinash has a strong understanding of SOA and microservices architecture, with a good handle on resource capacity planning.

About the Technical Reviewer

 **Harish Oraon** is an experienced professional from Bangalore, India, with almost a decade of experience developing scalable and distributed systems. He has worked with multiple technologies and stacks. Currently, he is leading the technology arm at a startup. Previously he was associated with Edureka, an ed-tech company, and played a key role in shaping the technology and infrastructure. He has also been associated with these giants: Roofandfloor by the Hindu Media, Koovs Fashion, and Sportskeeda.

Harish holds a UG degree from BIT Mesra, a premier institute in India. When he is not working, he loves to contribute to the open source community. He writes articles on Medium.com and answers questions on Stack Overflow and Google Groups. In his spare time, he loves spending time with his family.

Acknowledgments

This book would not have been possible without the support of my family. I want to thank my parents, my loving and supportive wife Swati, and my son, Rudra. They are a constant source of encouragement and inspiration. Thanks for providing the time and for listening to my gibberish when things were not going according to plan. I would also like to thank my co-author, Avinash Singh, for his knowledge and support. Your experience and willingness has made this a successful project.

I am grateful to Nikhil Karkal for believing in me and providing this wonderful opportunity. I would also like to thank Divya Modi and her editorial team for the constant push throughout the process. It would have been difficult to finish the project without her support. I would like to thank Harish Oraon and Matthew Moodie for sharing valuable feedback. Your advice has helped me to deliver my ideas in a better manner.

—Rahul Sharma

CHAPTER 1

Quick Tour of Kubernetes

Kubernetes originated from the Greek word κυβερνήτης, meaning "governor," "helmsman," or "pilot." That's what the founders Joe Beda, Brendan Burns, and Craig McLuckie had in mind. They wanted to "drive a container ship" leading to the creation of a container orchestration platform, which these days is becoming the de facto standard for running microservices in the cloud.

In late 2013, the declarative configuration of IaaS started to gain strength over bash scripts for cloud infrastructure. Though companies like Netflix were popularizing immutable infrastructures, that came with the cost of heavyweight virtual machine images. Docker became a savior by offering a lightweight container. It allowed a simple way to package, distribute, and deploy applications on a machine as compared to heavyweight VM images. But running Docker containers on a single machine was not a solution for scaling applications, which required deploying Docker containers across multiple machines. This created a need for an orchestrator.

Kubernetes development started by focusing on the key features of an orchestrator, such as replication of an application with load balancing and service discovery, followed by basic health checks and repair features to ensure availability. Kubernetes was also released as an open source version of Borg, a large-scale cluster manager at Google running hundreds of thousands of jobs for different applications across clusters, with each cluster

© Rahul Sharma, Avinash Singh 2020
R. Sharma and A. Singh, *Getting Started with Istio Service Mesh*,
https://doi.org/10.1007/978-1-4842-5458-5_1

having tens of thousands of machines. In the middle of 2015, Kubernetes was committed to GitHub and opened for developers to start contributing. In no time, big players like Microsoft, Red Hat, IBM, Docker, Mesosphere, CoreOS, and SaltStack joined the community and started contributing. In time, multiple modules were developed in and on Kubernetes, ensuring the basic orchestrator was intact and optimized over time.

With the increasing popularity of Kubernetes in the developer community, developers started making the deployment process even simpler. Helm, a package manager for Kubernetes, was launched in early 2016, aimed at simplifying how one defines, installs, and upgrades complex Kubernetes applications. Sometime in the middle of 2016, Minikube was released; Minikube brought the Kubernetes environment to a developer's local system. We will be using Minikube later in the chapter for our example Kubernetes application. One of the popular applications featuring Kubernetes in production was *PokemonGo*. At the time, it was one of the largest Kubernetes deployments on Google Container Engine. They released a case study explaining how Kubernetes helped the company scale when the traffic on the application was way beyond expectations.

Later, in 2017 and early 2018, cloud players like AWS and DigitalOcean made room for Kubernetes on their stacks. Kubernetes today is a portable, extensible, open source platform for managing containerized applications. It has micro components taking care of the basic features of the orchestrator. Let's start by taking a look at what K8s, an abbreviation for the word *Kubernetes*, consists of.

K8s Architecture/Components

Kubernetes follows a client-server architecture where the master is installed on a machine and nodes are distributed across multiple machines accessible via the master. Figure 1-1 shows the building blocks of the Kubernetes architecture. The K8s master and K8s workers are part of the Kubernetes control plane, whereas the container registry may lie outside of the control plane.

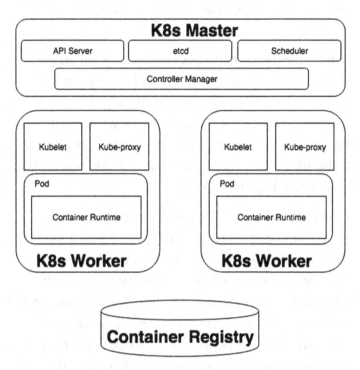

Figure 1-1. Kubernetes architecture overview

Kubernetes Master

The Kubernetes master is the main node responsible for managing the entire cluster. The orchestration of the K8s workers is handled by this node. This node is replicable to avoid any single point of failure. The control panel accesses the master only to make modifications to the cluster. The master comprises four major components.

- **API server:** This is the front end of a Kubernetes control plane. It maintains RESTful web services to define and configure a Kubernetes cluster.

3

- **etcd**: This is a highly available component maintaining a record of all the objects running in the system. Any changes in the configuration of Kubernetes are stored here, and the changes are allowed to be watched for immediate action.

- **Scheduler**: This schedules workloads on Kubernetes workers in the form of pods. We will cover pods in the next section. The scheduler reads through the resource requirements of each pod and distributes the pods throughout the cluster based on availability. By default, it also tries to distribute pod replicas to different nodes to maintain high availability.

- **Controller manager**: This runs controllers in the background that are responsible for different important tasks in the cluster. Controllers keep watch on etcd for configuration changes and take the cluster to the desired state; on the other end, the control loops watch for the changes in the cluster and work to maintain the desired state as per etcd. Let's visit a few controller examples to understand what controllers do in the cluster.

  - **Node controller**: This monitors the nodes in the cluster and responds when a node comes up or goes down. This is important so the scheduler can align pods per the availability of a node and maintain state per etcd.

  - **Endpoint controller**: This joins services and pods by creating endpoint records in the API, and it alters the DNS configuration to return an address pointing to one of the pods running the service.

- **Replication controller**: Replication is a general practice to maintain the high availability of an application. The replication controller makes sure the desired number of pod replicas/copies is running in the cluster.

We will be looking at these controllers in action later in this chapter. In addition, there is a cloud controller manager, which allows cloud providers to integrate with Kubernetes easily by using plugins.

Kubernetes Workers

It might be clear by now that the actual application runs on worker nodes. Earlier these were also referred to as *minions*. The terms *minions* and *nodes* are still used interchangeably in some documentation. Each node has three major components.

- **Kubelet**: Kubelet is the primary *node agent* running on each node and monitoring that the containers on the node are running and healthy. Kubelet takes a set of PodSpecs, which is a YAML or JSON object describing a pod, and monitors the containers described in those specs only. Note that there can be other containers, other than the containers listed in PodSpecs, running on the node, but Kubelet does not monitor these containers.

- **Kube-proxy**: The Kubernetes master scheduler usually runs multiple services on a node. Kube-proxy creates a network proxy and load balancer for these services. It can do simple TCP, UDP, and SCTP stream forwarding or round-robin TCP, UDP, and SCTP forwarding across a set of back ends. It also allows, if configured, nodes to be exposed to the Internet.

- **Pods**: A pod is the smallest unit of the Kubernetes object model that can be created, deployed, or destroyed. A Kubernetes pod usually has a single container but is allowed to contain a group of tightly coupled containers as well. A pod represents a running process on a cluster. It can be used in two broad ways.

    a. **Single-container pod**: This was the most common Kubernetes use case, also called *one container per pod*. The pod wraps the container and provides an abstract layer to Kubernetes to access or modify the container.

    b. **Multiple-container pod**: There are scenarios when an application requires multiple tightly coupled containers that are sharing resources. In such scenarios, a pod builds a wrapper on these containers and treats them as a single service. An example would be one container serving REST APIs to end users, with a *sidecar* counting the number of requests implementing the API limitation. The containers inside a pod share the same IP that was given to the pod and share the same set of storage. In the following chapters, we will be looking at sidecars in action with Istio.

Containers, as stated earlier, deployed inside each pod run the service. The container packaging and storage depend on the container runtime and registry.

- **Container runtime**: To understand this, let's try to understand what a container is. A container is a unit of code packaged with its dependencies that creates an artifact that can run quickly on different computing environments. The container runtime lets someone run containers by providing a basic set of resources and libraries, which combined with the container's package boots up an application. An application in a container has the liberty of its own environment including storage, network, etc., with the restriction of how much of each resource can be used. The container runtime also manages container images on a node. There are multiple container runtimes available, so let's go through a couple of them.

  a. **Rocket**: Rocket, also referred to as *rkt*, is a container runtime provided by coreOS. Rkt uses a few similar terms as Kubernetes. A pod is the core execution unit of Rkt. Please note, though, that this pod is different from a Kubernetes pod. Rocket allows a container configuration at a more granular level; in other words, one may set the memory limit of an application running inside the pod. Rocket follows the app container specification in its containers but supports Docker images as well. The main difference brought in by Rocket is that it runs in daemon-less mode; the containers launched don't run under the umbrella of a daemon but are given separate process IDs on the base machine. This allows it to run multiple processes inside the same container and restart any of them without killing the parent container.

b. **Docker**: Docker is one of the most popular
    container runtimes these days. As stated earlier,
    its solution to provide lightweight containers
    was the reason orchestration was required,
    which led to the need for Kubernetes. The
    Docker community is vast because one may
    easily get any common package available as a
    Docker image in the registry.

Which container runtime to choose is a matter
of personal preference and also depends on how
complex your codebase is and the kind of resources
it depends on. Using Rocket, you may be able to
pass on file descriptors from one process to another
with the file descriptions still listening. Though
these kinds of scenarios are not common, they
are important ones to consider before choosing a
container runtime. In this book, we will be using
Docker as our container runtime.

- **Container registry**: Each container generation
  requires code development, adding libraries from
  different package managers and creating the basic
  environment to run the code. A container can be built
  every time when deploying, but getting the latest code,
  getting new libraries, and preparing the environment
  every time is time-consuming. To simplify this,
  developers store their once-created container and
  use it whenever required. The container registry is the
  place that allows developers to save their container
  images and use them as and when required. Individual

providers such as Azure, Docker, and Google have their own container registries that host images in a highly available environment with access-level restrictions.

Kubernetes uses the Container Runtime Interface (CRI) to interact with the container runtime. Since Kubernetes 1.5, container runtimes are expected to implement CRI, which acts as a bridge between Kubernetes Kubelet and the container runtime. CRI provides an abstraction between Kubernetes and the container runtimes and enables Kubernetes to run independent of the container runtimes.

Now that you understand the architecture of Kubernetes, let's try to understand a few important terminologies used in Kubernetes.

Kubernetes Terminology

There are a few terms that we may be using frequently throughout this book. Let's go through a few of them to avoid any confusion in future references.

- **Deployment**: A deployment is an abstract unit built on pods. To deploy an application or a microservice, one needs to run it inside a pod. To do so, a deployment configuration is created where one states what needs to be deployed along with the number of replicas of the application. On submitting this configuration to Kubernetes, a set of pods is spawned by the deployment controller deploying the application with the configured replicas.

- **Image**: An image is the software/container that will be deployed on the cluster. In this book, we will be using *image* interchangeably with Docker *image*.

- **Kubectl**: This is a CLI to interact with a Kubernetes cluster. We will be using this to deploy clusters, check the status of them, and update our clusters.

- **Namespace**: As the name suggests, this is used to group multiple virtual clusters on the same Kubernetes instance or organize the resources within the same cluster. It allows each resource to be identified uniquely.

- **Replicaset**: This is the same as a replication controller with an additional support of a set-based selector rather than an equality-based selector. This will be clearer in the example later in this chapter.

- **Service**: This is a description of how an application deployed on one or multiple pods can be accessed internally or externally. Since pods are not permanent and Kubernetes may relocate pods from time to time based on availability, relying on direct access to pods is not recommended. The service discovers the application running in pods and provides access to them via ports, load balancers, or other mechanisms.

- **StatefulSet**: This is similar to a deployment managing the ordering and uniqueness of the pods. In other words, if a pod dies, a new pod is spawned by the StatefulSet controller with the same identity and resources as the dead pod.

These are not all the terms used in this book, but the list should be sufficient to get us started on creating our first Kubernetes cluster. Before we do that, we need to set up the Kubernetes environment.

Set Up a Kubernetes Cluster

As mentioned, Minikube is a tool to run a Kubernetes cluster locally. Since it's local, it provides a single-node Kubernetes cluster. Minikube starts a server of its own on a hypervisor. For simplicity, we will use VirtualBox as a hypervisor, which is available for Windows, Linux, and macOS.

Set Up VirtualBox

Before starting, make sure AMD-v or VT-x virtualization is enabled in your system BIOS. This allows you to run VirtualBox instances on the machine. Download and install VirtualBox by following the steps at `https://www.virtualbox.org/wiki/Downloads`. Once the installation is complete, let's install Kubectl.

Install Kubectl

Kubectl, as stated earlier, is the CLI to interact with a Kubernetes cluster. Setting up Kubectl across different platforms is a bit different on each one. Let's go through them one by one.

Linux Installation

The latest release of Kubectl can be downloaded with this:

```
curl -LO https://storage.googleapis.com/kubernetes-release/
release/$(curl -s https://storage.googleapis.com/kubernetes-
release/release/stable.txt)/bin/linux/amd64/kubectl
```

Make the downloaded file executable and move it to your PATH.

```
chmod +x ./kubectl
sudo mv ./kubectl /usr/local/bin/kubectl
```

macOS Installation

Installation on macOS is similar to the Linux setup.

```
curl -LO https://storage.googleapis.com/kubernetes-release/
release/$(curl -s https://storage.googleapis.com/kubernetes-
release/release/stable.txt)/bin/darwin/amd64/kubectl
```

Make the downloaded file executable and move it to your PATH.

```
chmod +x ./kubectl
sudo mv ./kubectl /usr/local/bin/kubectl
```

Windows Installation

Download the latest release using the following:

```
curl -LO https://storage.googleapis.com/kubernetes-release/
release/v1.14.0/bin/windows/amd64/kubectl.exe
```

Add the binary EXE file to the PATH in Windows.

Set Up Minikube

Installing Minikube requires different steps on different OSs.

Linux Installation

The latest release of Kubectl can be downloaded using this:

```
curl -Lo minikube https://storage.googleapis.com/minikube/
releases/latest/minikube-linux-amd64
```

Make the downloaded file executable and move it to your PATH.

```
chmod +x minikube
sudo mv ./minikube /usr/local/bin/minikube
```

macOS Installation

Installation on macOS is similar to the Linux setup.

```
curl -Lo minikube https://storage.googleapis.com/minikube/
releases/latest/minikube-darwin-amd64
```

Make the downloaded file executable and move it to your PATH.

```
chmod +x minikube
sudo mv ./minikube /usr/local/bin/minikube
```

Windows Installation

For Windows, it's better to use a package manager to take care of the installation overhead. A popular package manager for Windows is Chocolatey (https://chocolatey.org). It allows quick installation of Minikube. After Chocolatey is installed, run choco as an administrator.

```
choco install minikube kubernetes-cli
```

That's it.

Set Up Docker

Installing Docker on your local system allows Minikube to access images from your local system. Similar to Minikube, the Docker setup is a little different for different OSs.

Linux Installation

We will install Docker using a Ubuntu repository. For other Linux installations, please visit https://docs.docker.com/install/linux/docker-ce/centos/.

1. Update the local repository.

   ```
   sudo apt-get update
   ```

2. Install the dependency packages.

```
> sudo apt-get install \
    apt-transport-https \
    ca-certificates \
    curl \
    gnupg-agent \
    software-properties-common
```

3. Add Docker's GPG key.

```
> curl -fsSL https://download.docker.com/linux/ubuntu/
gpg | sudo apt-key add -
```

4. Add the repository to apt.

```
> sudo add-apt-repository \
    "deb [arch=amd64] https://download.docker.com/linux/
    ubuntu \
    $(lsb_release -cs) \
    stable"
```

5. Update the local repository to pull the Docker package.

```
> sudo apt-get update
```

6. Install Docker using the following command:

```
> sudo apt-get update
```

7. Install docker-ce and cli.

```
> sudo apt-get install docker-ce docker-ce-cli
containerd.io
```

macOS Installation

The simplest way to install on macOS is by downloading and installing the DMG file, available here:

`https://hub.docker.com/editions/community/docker-ce-desktop-mac`

Windows Installation

Similar to macOS, Docker provides an installer, available here:

`https://hub.docker.com/editions/community/docker-ce-desktop-windows`

We will be developing and deploying a few applications in Java and Python. Therefore, we will be needing the SDK for both languages.

Set Up Python

The Python setup can be easily done by following the steps at `https://www.python.org/downloads/`.

Set Up Java

Similar to Python, the Java setup can be easily done by following the steps at `https://www.oracle.com/technetwork/java/javase/downloads/jdk8-downloads-2133151.html`.

Our First Kubernetes Cluster

Once the setup is done, let's start our first Kubernetes server. For simplicity, we will be showing the output from the Ubuntu terminal.

```
> minikube start
Starting local Kubernetes v1.13.2 cluster...
Starting VM...
Getting VM IP address...
Moving files into cluster...
Setting up certs...
Connecting to cluster...
Setting up kubeconfig...
Stopping extra container runtimes...
Starting cluster components...
Verifying kubelet health ...
Verifying apiserver health ...
Kubectl is now configured to use the cluster.
Loading cached images from config file.
Everything looks great. Please enjoy minikube!
```

This will spawn a new virtual machine on VirtualBox with a few network settings, allowing it to be accessible by the base system. The Kubernetes cluster will be limited to this virtual machine. At any time during development and deployment, if the cluster seems to be slow or your local system starts consuming more than the expected resources, you can shut down the VM using this:

```
> minikube stop
```

Further, you can tweak the resources used by this virtual machine from the VirtualBox UI. Please note for the scope of this book, it is advisable to allow this virtual machine to use a minimum of two CPU cores and 4 GB of RAM.

You can look at the brief of Kubernetes cluster by running the following command:

```
> minikube dashboard
Enabling dashboard ...
Verifying dashboard health ...
```

```
Launching proxy ...
Verifying proxy health ...
Opening http://127.0.0.1:58969/api/v1/namespaces/kube-system/
services/http:kubernetes-dashboard:/proxy/ in your default
browser...
```

Figure 1-2 shows the Minikube dashboard. If you are able to see the dashboard, your cluster is up and running and ready to deploy an application.

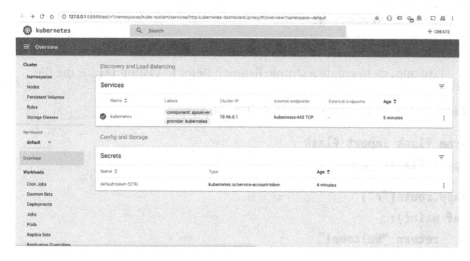

Figure 1-2. *Minikube dashboard*

Run an Application on Kubernetes

We have our Kubernetes cluster ready, so let's try to deploy an application on it and understand how it happens.

Application Details

Let's start by creating a simple web application in Python using Flask. `pip` is a package manager for Python. It can be installed with this:

```
> curl https://bootstrap.pypa.io/get-pip.py | python
```

17

Once pip is installed, Flask can be installed with this:

```
> pip install flask
```

Let's create a project called WebApp with app.py inside to handle web requests. The app structure should look like this:

```
.
|____WebApp
| |____app.py
| |____requirement.txt
| |____Dockerfile
```

Edit app.py to create a simple listener. Refer to Listing 1-1 for the file.

Listing 1-1. Web Requests Handler: app.py

```
from flask import Flask
app = Flask(__name__)

@app.route("/")
def main():
    return "Welcome!"

if __name__ == "__main__":
    app.run(host='0.0.0.0')
```

Let's create a Dockerfile to containerize the application. Listing 1-2 explains the container creation.

Listing 1-2. Dockerfile to Containerize the Application

```
FROM ubuntu:18.04
RUN apt-get update -y && apt-get install -y python-pip python-dev
COPY ./requirement.txt /app/requirement.txt
WORKDIR /app
```

```
RUN pip install -r requirement.txt
COPY . /app
ENTRYPOINT [ "python" ]
CMD [ "app.py" ]
```

The Docker environment and images stored are different for Minikube. Instead of storing images to our local environment, sending them to the registry, and bringing them back on Minikube, we will be storing the container image directly on the Minikube instance.

```
> eval $(minikube docker-env)
```

Build the WebApp application container with the name web-app and assign version 1.0.

```
> docker build -t web-app:1.0 .
```

Figure 1-3 shows the new container image created.

REPOSITORY	TAG	IMAGE ID	CREATED	SIZE
web-app	1.0	87d178fd42b6	About an hour ago	473MB
ubuntu	18.04	d131e0fa2585	5 days ago	102MB
k8s.gcr.io/kube-proxy	v1.13.2	01cfa56edcfc	3 months ago	80.3MB
k8s.gcr.io/kube-controller-manager	v1.13.2	b9027a78d94c	3 months ago	146MB
k8s.gcr.io/kube-apiserver	v1.13.2	177db4b8e93a	3 months ago	181MB
k8s.gcr.io/kube-scheduler	v1.13.2	3193be46e0b3	3 months ago	79.6MB
k8s.gcr.io/kubernetes-dashboard-amd64	v1.10.1	f9aed6605b81	4 months ago	122MB
k8s.gcr.io/coredns	1.2.6	f59dcacceff4	5 months ago	40MB
k8s.gcr.io/etcd	3.2.24	3cab8e1b9802	7 months ago	220MB
k8s.gcr.io/kube-addon-manager	v8.6	9c16409588eb	14 months ago	78.4MB
k8s.gcr.io/pause	3.1	da86e6ba6ca1	16 months ago	742kB
k8s.gcr.io/metrics-server-amd64	v0.2.1	9801395070f3	16 months ago	42.5MB
gcr.io/k8s-minikube/storage-provisioner	v1.8.1	4689081edb10	18 months ago	80.8MB

Figure 1-3. *Images available on Minikube server after creation of web-app*

Deploy the Application

Let's create our first deployment configuration. This tells Kubernetes to create a container for our application. Listing 1-3 shows the webapp-deployment.yaml file for our webapp.

Listing 1-3. webapp-deployment.yaml File for Web App

```
apiVersion: extensions/v1beta1
kind: Deployment
metadata:
  name: webapp-deployment
  labels:
    app: webapp
spec:
  replicas: 1
  selector:
    matchLabels:
      app: webapp
  template:
    metadata:
      labels:
        app: webapp
    spec:
      containers:
      - name: webapp
        image: web-app:1.0
        imagePullPolicy: Never
        ports:
        - containerPort: 5000
```

Let's try to understand the YAML file.

- apiVersion: This is the API version used to create this object.

- kind: This explains that we are creating a Kubernetes deployment.

- `metadata`: This specifies the name of deployment (a must-have key) and optional labels one may want to put on the deployment.

- `replicas`: This specifies the number of pods to be created for this deployment.

- `selector`: This is how the deployment manages to locate the pods.

- `template.metadata`: The pods created from this deployment will be named from these labels.

- `containers`: This specifies the containers that need to be deployed in this pod. In our case, we are deploying one container with the image we created in the previous section. Since we made sure in the previous section that the image is available to the Kubernetes cluster, we haven't uploaded the image to any registry, and therefore `imagePullPolicy` is set to `Never`.

- `ports`: This is the port of the container exposed to the cluster.

Let's deploy the application on the cluster using this:

```
> kubectl apply -f webapp-deployment.yaml
```

The previous command applies the configuration defined in YAML on the Kubernetes cluster. In other words, it creates a deployment named `webapp-deployment`. Figure 1-4 shows all the deployments on the cluster with their status and the number of running and active replicas.

```
avinashsingh$ kubectl get deployments
NAME                READY   UP-TO-DATE   AVAILABLE   AGE
webapp-deployment   1/1     1            1           2s
avinashsingh$ █
```

Figure 1-4. *Deployments running on the Kubernetes cluster*

The figure shows there is a pod running the WebApp application. The deployment spawns a ReplicaSet, which tries to maintain the state of having one pod running at all times. Figure 1-5 and Figure 1-6 show the running ReplicaSets and pods on the cluster.

```
avinashsingh$ kubectl get replicaset -o wide
NAME                             DESIRED   CURRENT   READY   AGE   CONTAINERS   IMAGES
  SELECTOR
webapp-deployment-7946f7db77     1         1         1       15m   webapp       web-app:1.0
  app=webapp,pod-template-hash=7946f7db77
```

Figure 1-5. *Replicaset started from deployment*

```
avinashsingh$ kubectl get pods -o wide
NAME                              READY   STATUS    RESTARTS   AGE     IP          NODE
  NOMINATED NODE    READINESS GATES
webapp-deployment-7946f7db77-gtsbg  1/1   Running   0          6m36s   172.17.0.7  minikube
  <none>            <none>
```

Figure 1-6. *Pods running on the cluster*

The pod details include an IP address. The pod is accessible to the internal network using this IP address, but as stated earlier, accessing pods directly via IP addresses is discouraged since pods are expendables and a new pod might have a different IP address. It is clear from the IP address that though the pod is accessible through this IP address inside the Kubernetes network, one may not be able to access it from the host machine. Kubectl provides a way to use a proxy for the pod and access the application from the host machine.

> kubectl port-forward webapp-deployment-7946f7db77-gtsbg 5000:5000

webapp-deployment-7946f7db77-gtsbg is our pod name (refer to Figure 1-6), and 5000 is the port exposed on the pod to access the application. Figure 1-7 shows the output of port forwarding.

```
avinashsingh$ kubectl port-forward webapp-deployment-7946f7db77-gtsbg 5000:5000
Forwarding from [::1]:5000 -> 5000
Forwarding from 127.0.0.1:5000 -> 5000
```

Figure 1-7. *Port forwarding the host port to the pod port*

Now the application is accessible from the host machine. Figure 1-8 shows the application running on the host machine browser.

Figure 1-8. *Application port forwarded to the host machine and accessible in the browser*

The application logs can be accessed from the pod using this:

```
> kubectl log -f webapp-deployment-7946f7db77-gtsbg 5000:5000
```

Figure 1-9 shows the output of the pod logs.

```
avinashsingh$ kubectl log -f webapp-deployment-7946f7db77-gtsbg
log is DEPRECATED and will be removed in a future version. Use logs instead.
 * Serving Flask app "app" (lazy loading)
 * Environment: production
   WARNING: Do not use the development server in a production environment.
   Use a production WSGI server instead.
 * Debug mode: off
 * Running on http://127.0.0.1:5000/ (Press CTRL+C to quit)
127.0.0.1 - - [14/May/2019 04:55:15] "GET / HTTP/1.1" 200 -
127.0.0.1 - - [14/May/2019 04:55:15] "GET /robots.txt HTTP/1.1" 404 -
127.0.0.1 - - [14/May/2019 04:55:15] "GET /favicon.ico HTTP/1.1" 404 -
127.0.0.1 - - [14/May/2019 04:55:19] "GET / HTTP/1.1" 200 -
127.0.0.1 - - [14/May/2019 04:55:30] "GET / HTTP/1.1" 200 -
127.0.0.1 - - [14/May/2019 05:01:22] "GET / HTTP/1.1" 200 -
```

Figure 1-9. *Pod logs visible via log -f*

Kubernetes Service

Kubernetes pods are expendable. ReplicaSet creates and destroys pods in the process of scaling up and down; therefore, accessing the pods via an IP address is not a reliable solution. Then how do microservices inside Kubernetes communicate with other microservices? The answer is *Kubernetes services*. Let's try to understand the concept of services.

Kubernetes services provide a virtual IP-based bridge to access the pods. One may access a single pod or may refer to a group of pods at the same time. There can be two types of interactions.

- Pods accessing services

- Services exposed publicly

Before explaining this, let's expose our web application via a service. Listing 1-4 shows a simple service with the selector pointing to our webapp.

Listing 1-4. webapp-service.yaml File for Our Web App

```
apiVersion: v1
kind: Service
metadata:
  name: webservice
spec:
  selector:
    app: webapp
  ports:
  - protocol: TCP
    port: 80
    targetPort: 5000
```

The service is named webservice and points to the deployments with a selector as app:webapp. The service is exposed on port 80 and proxies the request to port 5000 of the result pods. Apply the service using this:

```
> kubectl apply -f webapp-service.yaml
```

Verify that the service is created successfully using this:

```
> kubectl describe service webservice
```

Figure 1-10 shows a description of the created service.

```
avinashsingh$ kubectl describe service webservice
Name:              webservice
Namespace:         default
Labels:            <none>
Annotations:       kubectl.kubernetes.io/last-applied-configuration:
                     {"apiVersion":"v1","kind":"Service","metadata":{"annotations":{},"r
Selector:          app=webapp
Type:              ClusterIP
IP:                10.107.243.100
Port:              <unset>  80/TCP
TargetPort:        5000/TCP
Endpoints:         172.17.0.7:5000
Session Affinity:  None
Events:            <none>
```

Figure 1-10. *Service created pointing to pods with selector app:webapp*

The service is assigned a cluster IP address of 10.107.243.100. Any microservice inside the cluster will be able to access the service using this IP address via port 80.

Now, let's try to understand the two types of service interactions possible in a Kubernetes cluster.

Pods Accessing Services

Any microservices architecture requires a service to access multiple microservices within the private network. The access to other services is possible either through their IP address or through a DNS request. Kubernetes supports both of them.

- **Environment variables**: When a pod is launched in a node,
  Kubectl declares all the running services to be accessed
  as environment variables for the pod. But this forces a
  sequence to be followed; if new service is defined after the
  first service is booted, the first one doesn't get access to the
  new service. Try to log in to the Docker container of the
  webapp pod and check the environment variables. The new
  service is not visible. If the developer deletes the existing
  deployment and re-creates the deployment, the service is
  visible in the environment variables. Figure 1-11 shows the
  environment variables for the second case.

```
root@webapp-deployment-7946f7db77-hq4gg:/app# env
LS_COLORS=rs=0:di=01;34:ln=01;36:mh=00:pi=40;33:so=01;35:do=01;35:bd=40
31:*.arj=01;31:*.taz=01;31:*.lha=01;31:*.lz4=01;31:*.lzh=01;31:*.lzma=0
zo=01;31:*.xz=01;31:*.zst=01;31:*.tzst=01;31:*.bz2=01;31:*.bz=01;31:*.t
e=01;31:*.zoo=01;31:*.cpio=01;31:*.7z=01;31:*.rz=01;31:*.cab=01;31:*.wi
.pgm=01;35:*.ppm=01;35:*.tga=01;35:*.xbm=01;35:*.xpm=01;35:*.tif=01;35:
5:*.webm=01;35:*.ogm=01;35:*.mp4=01;35:*.m4v=01;35:*.mp4v=01;35:*.vob=0
5:*.dl=01;35:*.xcf=01;35:*.xwd=01;35:*.yuv=01;35:*.cgm=01;35:*.emf=01;3
6:*.ogg=00;36:*.ra=00;36:*.wav=00;36:*.oga=00;36:*.opus=00;36:*.spx=00;
WEBSERVICE_PORT=tcp://10.107.243.100:80
HOSTNAME=webapp-deployment-7946f7db77-hq4gg
WEBSERVICE_PORT_80_TCP_PORT=80
WEBSERVICE_PORT_80_TCP_ADDR=10.107.243.100
KUBERNETES_PORT_443_TCP_PROTO=tcp
KUBERNETES_PORT_443_TCP_ADDR=10.96.0.1
KUBERNETES_PORT=tcp://10.96.0.1:443
PWD=/app
HOME=/root
KUBERNETES_SERVICE_PORT_HTTPS=443
KUBERNETES_PORT_443_TCP_PORT=443
KUBERNETES_PORT_443_TCP=tcp://10.96.0.1:443
WEBSERVICE_PORT_80_TCP=tcp://10.107.243.100:80
TERM=xterm
WEBSERVICE_SERVICE_HOST=10.107.243.100
WEBSERVICE_SERVICE_PORT=80
SHLVL=1
KUBERNETES_SERVICE_PORT=443
PATH=/usr/local/sbin:/usr/local/bin:/usr/sbin:/usr/bin:/sbin:/bin
KUBERNETES_SERVICE_HOST=10.96.0.1
WEBSERVICE_PORT_80_TCP_PROTO=tcp
_=/usr/bin/env
```

Figure 1-11. *Environment variables with the service endpoints defined*

- **DNS**: Though this is not a default setup, it is an optional but recommended add-on for Kubernetes. As the name says, each service registers a DNS record for itself as soon as it is created. The DNS record follows the pattern *<service-name>.<namespace>*. Any pod in the same namespace can access the service directly via *<service-name>*, whereas pods outside the namespace must include *.<namespace>* to access the service.

Services Exposed Publicly

There are multiple ways to expose a service to external world. Kubernetes provides multiple ways of achieving this.

ClusterIP

This allows a service to be exposed via a cluster's internal IP. As shown earlier, a cluster's internal IP address is exposed and can be accessed by the pods inside the cluster.

NodePort

This allows a service to be exposed at the node IP address on a specific port. This allows the service to be accessed via the *<NodeIP>:<PORT>* address. Internally Kubernetes creates a ClusterIP service that acts as a connection between the node IP and the actual service. The port number can be between 30000 and 32767. Each node proxies the selected port to the service pod.

LoadBalancer

This creates a public IP on top of NodePort. So, the service is accessible via a public IP, which is routed to NodePort and then is further routed to ClusterIP. Its implementation varies between cloud providers. A small addition to the configuration creates a LoadBalancer type. Listing 1-5 shows the addition of a LoadBalancer type in the service.

Listing 1-5. webapp-service-loadbalancer.yaml File for Our Web App

```
apiVersion: v1
kind: Service
metadata:
  name: webservice
spec:
  type: LoadBalancer
  selector:
    app: webapp
  ports:
  - protocol: TCP
    port: 80
    targetPort: 5000
```

Once a service is created using this configuration, a developer can check the external IP address of the service using this:

```
> kubectl get service webservice
```

Figure 1-12 shows our example. We do not get the external IP address since we are running our application on Minikube. On the cloud, the external IP is populated with a value.

```
avinashsingh$ kubectl get service webservice
NAME        TYPE          CLUSTER-IP       EXTERNAL-IP   PORT(S)       AGE
webservice  LoadBalancer  10.107.243.100   <pending>     80:30516/TCP  45h
```

Figure 1-12. *LoadBalancer type service deployed*

ExternalName

This simply maps the service to an address using a CNAME record. These are typically used when using an external service from within a cluster and abstracting out the actual link of the external service. Listing 1-6 shows a simple service with the type `ExternalName`.

Listing 1-6. database-external-name.yaml Showing ExternalName Configuration

```
apiVersion: v1
kind: Service
metadata:
  name: db1
spec:
  type: ExternalName
  externalName: mysql01.database.test.com
```

When internal pods look for the service `db1`, they receive a CNAME record of `mysql01.database.text.com`. There is no forwarding involved; only a single redirection happens at the DNS level.

`ExternalName` also allows a developer to add a custom IP address to a service through which the service can be accessed by clients. The IP assignment is the sole responsibility of the cluster manager; it doesn't come from Kubernetes. Listing 1-7 shows an example of an external IP assignment to a service.

Listing 1-7. External IP Assigned to a Service

```
apiVersion: v1
kind: Service
metadata:
  name: externalIpAssignedService
spec:
  selector:
    app: externalIpService
  ports:
  - name: http
    protocol: TCP
    port: 80
    targetPort: 9000
  externalIPs:
  - 70.34.1.23
```

Kubernetes, as defined earlier, is a self-healing platform. Let's try to play around a bit with the cluster and see the role of Kubernetes services in it.

Kubernetes Is Self-Healing

In any application, it's difficult to assure 100 percent uptime or availability of a single node. Kubernetes provides a means to create replicas of a service and also ensures the number of replicas are intact. Let's modify our deployment and increase the number of replicas.

```
> kubectl scale --replicas=2 deployment webapp-deployment
> kubectl get deployments
```

Figure 1-13 shows the result of the deployment

```
avinashsingh$ kubectl get deployments
NAME                READY   UP-TO-DATE   AVAILABLE   AGE
webapp-deployment   2/2     2            2           47h
```

Figure 1-13. *Deployment State After Increasing the Replicas*

> kubectl get pods

Figure 1-14 shows the running pods.

```
avinashsingh$ kubectl get pods
NAME                                   READY   STATUS    RESTARTS   AGE
webapp-deployment-7946f7db77-hq4gg     1/1     Running   1          47h
webapp-deployment-7946f7db77-1519w     1/1     Running   0          11m
```

Figure 1-14. *Deployment state after increasing the replicas*

If one tries to kill any of the pods, the replication controller tries to reinstate the state and spawn a new pod. Let's try killing one of the pods to see the state of the application. Figure 1-15 shows the deletion of a pod.

```
avinashsingh$ kubectl get pods
NAME                                   READY   STATUS    RESTARTS   AGE
webapp-deployment-7946f7db77-hq4gg     1/1     Running   1          47h
webapp-deployment-7946f7db77-1519w     1/1     Running   0          17m
avinashsingh$ kubectl delete pod webapp-deployment-7946f7db77-hq4gg
pod "webapp-deployment-7946f7db77-hq4gg" deleted
```

Figure 1-15. *A pod is forcefully deleted from the cluster*

Figure 1-16 shows how a new pod is autospawned to match the replication number.

```
avinashsingh$ kubectl get pods
NAME                                   READY   STATUS        RESTARTS   AGE
webapp-deployment-7946f7db77-hq4gg     1/1     Terminating   1          47h
webapp-deployment-7946f7db77-1519w     1/1     Running       0          18m
webapp-deployment-7946f7db77-x597s     1/1     Running       0          21s
```

Figure 1-16. *A new pod is spawned while the deleted pod is terminating*

Through this, Kubernetes tries to keep the service available at all times.

Add a Microservice

Now you have seen how to deploy and run a microservice on Kubernetes, and you have seen the theory of how microservices interact with each other. Let's create a new microservice that consumes a response from the webapp and renders it to the UI. Let's call this app istio-frontend. We have already created a Docker file.

Application Setup

istio-frontend is a Java application that makes a request to the webapp service and populates its web page with the received data. In case the data is not received or the web-app service is not available, it populates ERROR RECEIVED as a response. We have created a Docker file with the tag frontend-app:1.0. Let's follow the same approach as the previous application and create a deployment and service for the application. Listing 1-8 and Listing 1-9 show the deployment and service file.

Listing 1-8. frontend-deployment.yaml Configuration

```
apiVersion: apps/v1
kind: Deployment
metadata:
  name: frontend-deployment
  labels:
    app: frontend
spec:
  replicas: 1
  selector:
    matchLabels:
      app: frontend
```

```
template:
  metadata:
    labels:
      app: frontend
  spec:
    containers:
    - name: frontend
      image: frontend:1.0
      imagePullPolicy: Never
      ports:
      - containerPort: 8080
```

Listing 1-9. frontend-service.yaml Configuration

```
apiVersion: v1
kind: Service
metadata:
  name: frontendservice
spec:
  selector:
    app: frontend
  ports:
  - protocol: TCP
    port: 80
    targetPort: 8080
```

Figure 1-17 shows the new services available. Let's try to proxy to the new service to get the app running.

```
avinashsingh$ kubectl get services
NAME             TYPE          CLUSTER-IP       EXTERNAL-IP   PORT(S)        AGE
frontendservice  ClusterIP     10.97.67.167     <none>        80/TCP         4m28s
kubernetes       ClusterIP     10.96.0.1        <none>        443/TCP        34d
webservice       LoadBalancer  10.107.243.100   <pending>     80:30516/TCP   5d
```

Figure 1-17. New front-end service available

33

Figure 1-18 shows the output page.

Figure 1-18. *Output of proxy port to the front-end pod*

Reducing the replica count to 0 for the webapp service gives the state shown in Figure 1-19 and Figure 1-20.

```
avinashsingh$ kubectl get deployments
NAME                      READY    UP-TO-DATE    AVAILABLE     AGE
frontend-deployment       1/1      1             1             13h
webapp-deployment         2/2      2             2             5d13h
avinashsingh$ kubectl scale --replicas=0 deployment webapp-deployment
deployment.extensions/webapp-deployment scaled
avinashsingh$ kubectl get pods
NAME                                    READY    STATUS        RESTARTS    AGE
frontend-deployment-758d68bf4b-1dpxh    1/1      Running       0           13h
webapp-deployment-7946f7db77-1519w      1/1      Terminating   1           3d14h
webapp-deployment-7946f7db77-x597s      1/1      Terminating   1           3d13h
avinashsingh$ kubectl port-forward frontend-deployment-758d68bf4b-1dpxh 8080:8080
Forwarding from 127.0.0.1:8080 -> 8080
Forwarding from [::1]:8080 -> 8080
```

Figure 1-19. *Replicas of webapp reduced to 0*

Figure 1-20. *Front end shows error if unable to communicate with back-end service*

Release and Deployment

In a large organization, any application going to production requires regular development and maintenance. With new methodologies like agile firmly in place, release frequency has increased to multiple releases a day and so have release rollbacks. The traditional process of shutting down an application, redeploying, and restarting results in downtime. In the world of 99.99 percent availability, the scope of downtime means one minute or less in a seven-day period, so a single release a week violates the agile methodology.

To minimize downtime, multiple deployment techniques are used, such as blue-green, canary, and rolling deployments. We will cover these techniques in later chapters. Kubernetes by default follows a rolling deployment. In other words, it creates two identical environments, and once the new environment is up, traffic is routed to the new environment, and later the old environment is terminated.

Let's upgrade our webapp to 2.0 and see the deployment on Kubernetes in action. Listing 1-10 shows the changes in the file. We will simply add time to the welcome message.

Listing 1-10. Updated Web Requests Handler: app.py

```python
from flask import Flask
import datetime

app = Flask(__name__)

@app.route("/")
def main():
    currentDT = datetime.datetime.now()
    return "Welcome user! current time is " + str(currentDT)

if __name__ == "__main__":
    app.run(host='0.0.0.0')
```

Create a new container by following the same process as stated earlier. Listing 1-11 shows the modified deployment file with the upgraded container details.

Listing 1-11. Updated webapp-deployment-v2.yaml for webapp 2.0

```
apiVersion: apps/v1
kind: Deployment
metadata:
  name: webapp-deployment
  labels:
    app: webapp
spec:
  replicas: 1
  selector:
    matchLabels:
      app: webapp
  template:
    metadata:
      labels:
        app: webapp
    spec:
      containers:
      - name: webapp
        image: web-app:2.0
        imagePullPolicy: Never
        ports:
        - containerPort: 5000
```

Let's deploy the application on a cluster using this:

```
> kubectl apply -f webapp-deployment-v2.yaml
```

A new pod is spawned, and the earlier one is terminated once the new pod is ready. Figure 1-21 shows the output of the newly deployed application.

Figure 1-21. *Front end showing the new response from the back-end service*

What has happened in the background is a new environment with a single machine and version 2.0 is spawned while the webapp service was still pointing to the old environment. Once the new spawned pods returned the running status, the webapp service pointed the traffic to the new environment, and the earlier pods were terminated.

Here's the catch: what happens when a new pod is spawned but the application inside is still deploying and not yet up? The pod at this point returns a *running* status, but the application is still down, and at the same time the service starts directing traffic to the new environment. This adds downtime to the service until the application is up and running. To solve this issue, Kubernetes uses a readiness probe.

Readiness Probes

Updating deployments with new ones can result in downtime as old pods are replaced by new ones. If for some reason the new deployment is misconfigured or has some error, the downtime continues until the error is detected. When a readiness probe is used, the service doesn't forward traffic to new pods until the probe is successful. It also ensures that the old pods are not terminated until the new deployment pods are ready. This ensures that the deployment with the error doesn't receive any traffic at all.

To incorporate a readiness probe, we need to add a health link to our webapp. Listing 1-12 shows the change in the app.py code. A /health link is added, which will be available once the app is up and running. A delay of 60 seconds has been added in the code, which will help demonstrate this behavior of Kubernates.

Listing 1-12. Addition of Health Link to app.py

```python
from flask import Flask
import datetime
import time

time.sleep(60)
app = Flask(__name__)

@app.route("/")
def main():
    currentDT = datetime.datetime.now()
    return "Welcome user! current time in v3 is " + str(currentDT)

@app.route("/health")
def health():
    return "OK"

if __name__ == "__main__":
    app.run(host='0.0.0.0')
```

Create a new container with the tag web-app:3.0 and add it to the deployment file, as shown in Listing 1-13.

Listing 1-13. Updated webapp-deployment-v3.yaml for web-app 3.0

```yaml
apiVersion: apps/v1
kind: Deployment
metadata:
  name: webapp-deployment
  labels:
    app: webapp
```

```
spec:
  replicas: 1
  selector:
    matchLabels:
      app: webapp
  template:
    metadata:
      labels:
        app: webapp
    spec:
      containers:
      - name: webapp
        image: web-app:3.0
        imagePullPolicy: Never
        ports:
        - containerPort: 5000
        readinessProbe:
          httpGet:
            path: /health
            port: 5000
          initialDelaySeconds: 40
```

The readiness probe initializes with an initial delay of 40 seconds.
If one already knows that an application deployment takes some time,
this can be stated in initialDelaySeconds to avoid unnecessary checks
on the application. After the initial delay, Kubelet does regular checks
on the /health link, and when the link is up, the pod is moved to a
ready state to accept traffic. Figure 1-22 shows the status of deployment
at different times.

```
avinashsingh$ kubectl get deployments
NAME                    READY  UP-TO-DATE   AVAILABLE   AGE
frontend-deployment     1/1    1            1           41h
webapp-deployment       1/1    1            1           6d16h
avinashsingh$ kubectl apply -f webapp-deployment-v3.yaml
deployment.apps/webapp-deployment configured
avinashsingh$ kubectl get deployments
NAME                    READY  UP-TO-DATE   AVAILABLE   AGE
frontend-deployment     1/1    1            1           41h
webapp-deployment       1/1    1            1           6d16h
avinashsingh$ kubectl get pods
NAME                                      READY   STATUS        RESTARTS   AGE
frontend-deployment-758d68bf4b-ldpxh      1/1     Running       0          41h
webapp-deployment-64c5c78954-4srdh        0/1     Running       0          11s
webapp-deployment-f8c4549fb-pdp4z         1/1     Running       0          5m27s
avinashsingh$ kubectl get pods
NAME                                      READY   STATUS        RESTARTS   AGE
frontend-deployment-758d68bf4b-ldpxh      1/1     Running       0          41h
webapp-deployment-64c5c78954-4srdh        0/1     Running       0          41s
webapp-deployment-f8c4549fb-pdp4z         1/1     Running       0          5m57s
avinashsingh$ kubectl get pods
NAME                                      READY   STATUS        RESTARTS   AGE
frontend-deployment-758d68bf4b-ldpxh      1/1     Running       0          41h
webapp-deployment-64c5c78954-4srdh        1/1     Running       0          67s
webapp-deployment-f8c4549fb-pdp4z         1/1     Terminating   0          6m23s
```

Figure 1-22. *Deployment with readiness state checks*

Let's see what happened in the background.

1. Checked the available deployments. A frontend-deployment and a webapp-deployment are working, each having one available pod in a ready state.

2. Applied the new version 3 configuration.

3. The ready pods number remains the same.

4. On getting the pod's details, we can see two webapp-deployment pods. The old one is ready, and the latest one is *running* but still not ready to accept traffic.

5. At 40 seconds, no request to the readiness probe is triggered by Kubernetes; therefore, the pod remains in a ready-pending state. By default the health check is done every 10 seconds.

6. After 60 seconds of deployment, the new pod upgrades to a *ready* state, and the old pod is moved to a *terminating* state.

This ensures that until the new deployment becomes ready, the earlier deployment is not scrapped, and the traffic is routed to the older one. This is helpful when an application is being upgraded or when a new application is deployed. But this isn't useful after the deployment is complete and the old deployment pods are terminated. If after that the deployment pods fail for known/unknown reasons, the readiness probe fails, and the traffic is not sent to the pod. This, on one hand, ensures that the application is not down, but the number of pods available to serve the traffic goes down. A corner case would be if the same issue happens to all the pods in the deployment; your complete application may go down.

There is no ideal way to deal with such issues, but Kubernetes provides a common solution of restarting the application if the application becomes irresponsive. The liveness probe, similar to the readiness probe, keeps a check on the application, and in case the application stops responding, it restarts the pod.

Let's make a small change in our application to kill the application in 60 seconds and see the behavior of the liveness probe. Listing 1-14 shows the change.

Listing 1-14. Autostopping the Application After Some Time in app.py

```
from flask import Flask
import datetime
import time
import threading
import os
```

```
time.sleep(60)
app = Flask(__name__)

@app.route("/")
def main():
    currentDT = datetime.datetime.now()
    return "Welcome user! current time is " + str(currentDT)

@app.route("/health")
def health():
    return "OK"

def exit_after():
    time.sleep(60)
    os._exit(1)

exit_thread = threading.Thread(target=exit_after)
exit_thread.start()

if __name__ == "__main__":
    app.run(host='0.0.0.0')
```

Create a new container with the tag web-app:4.0 and add it to deployment file, as shown in Listing 1-15.

Listing 1-15. Updated webapp-deployment-v4.yaml for web-app 4.0

```
apiVersion: apps/v1
kind: Deployment
metadata:
  name: webapp-deployment
  labels:
    app: webapp
```

```
spec:
  replicas: 1
  selector:
    matchLabels:
      app: webapp
  template:
    metadata:
      labels:
        app: webapp
    spec:
      containers:
      - name: webapp
        image: web-app:4.0
        imagePullPolicy: Never
        ports:
        - containerPort: 5000
        readinessProbe:
          httpGet:
            path: /health
            port: 5000
          initialDelaySeconds: 40
        livenessProbe:
          httpGet:
            path: /health
            port: 5000
          initialDelaySeconds: 120
```

The liveness probe initializes with a delay of 120 seconds. Since we already know the application bootup time takes 60 seconds, it's no use to restart the app before it even boots up. The same process as redinessProbe is followed to check the health of the application. Let's see the changes in action in Figure 1-23.

```
avinashsingh$ kubectl get deployments
NAME                    READY   UP-TO-DATE   AVAILABLE   AGE
frontend-deployment     1/1     1            1           42h
webapp-deployment       1/1     1            1           6d18h
avinashsingh$ kubectl apply -f webapp-deployment-v4.yaml
deployment.apps/webapp-deployment configured
avinashsingh$ kubectl get deployments
NAME                    READY   UP-TO-DATE   AVAILABLE   AGE
frontend-deployment     1/1     1            1           42h
webapp-deployment       1/1     1            1           6d18h
avinashsingh$ kubectl get pods
NAME                                      READY   STATUS        RESTARTS   AGE
frontend-deployment-758d68bf4b-ldpxh      1/1     Running       0          42h
webapp-deployment-6594fdbbd7-r9kqj        0/1     Running       0          8s
webapp-deployment-f8c4549fb-w2jnx         1/1     Running       0          71s
avinashsingh$ kubectl get pods
NAME                                      READY   STATUS          RESTARTS   AGE
frontend-deployment-758d68bf4b-ldpxh      1/1     Running         0          42h
webapp-deployment-6594fdbbd7-r9kqj        1/1     Running         0          67s
webapp-deployment-f8c4549fb-w2jnx         1/1     Terminating     0          2m10s
avinashsingh$ kubectl get pods
NAME                                      READY   STATUS      RESTARTS   AGE
frontend-deployment-758d68bf4b-ldpxh      1/1     Running     0          42h
webapp-deployment-6594fdbbd7-r9kqj        0/1     Running     1          2m6s
avinashsingh$ kubectl get pods
NAME                                      READY   STATUS      RESTARTS   AGE
frontend-deployment-758d68bf4b-ldpxh      1/1     Running     0          42h
webapp-deployment-6594fdbbd7-r9kqj        1/1     Running     1          3m15s
```

Figure 1-23. *Deployment with readiness and liveliness state checks*

Assuming our application fails at some point after the deployment, this is how Kubernetes tries to recover it:

1. When the application goes down, the readiness probe fails.

2. Kubernetes stops the traffic on that pod and restrains itself to the rest of the replicas. In our case, since we have only one replica, the application is bound to have downtime.

3. The liveness probe goes down since it's on the same health link.

4. Kubernetes tries to restart the pod and restore the application state.

5. After restarting, the application comes up, and the readiness probe is successful.

6. Traffic is restored to this pod.

Summary

In this chapter, we went through a brief history of Kubernetes. You now understand its basic components and learned the terminology used in it. We set up Kubernetes locally with Minikube and the Docker container runtime. We also created an example application and showed how application deployment happens in a cluster and how the Kubernetes application heals itself.

In the next chapter, we will go through the microservice architecture, its challenges, and how they can be solved using a service mesh.

## CHAPTER 2

Introduction to the Service Mesh

In the previous chapter, we took a quick tour of Kubernetes, the container orchestration engine. Leveraging such an infrastructure effectively requires the adoption of a microservice-based application architecture. But this type of architecture imposes a new set of development and operational challenges. In this chapter, we will discuss how a service mesh helps to mitigate these challenges.

Microservice Architecture

Monolith architectures have been the development model traditionally used. In a monolith architecture, the complete software is a unified, self-contained application. The application has discrete subsystems/ capabilities that are tightly coupled with the rest of the application. Changes to one part of the application require a complete release of the software. See Figure 2-1.

© Rahul Sharma, Avinash Singh 2020
R. Sharma and A. Singh, *Getting Started with Istio Service Mesh*,
https://doi.org/10.1007/978-1-4842-5458-5_2

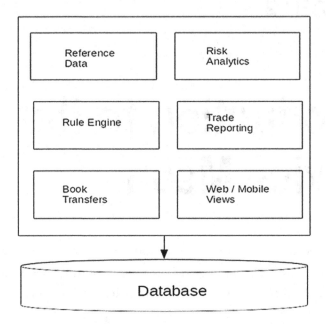

Figure 2-1. *Monolith architecture*

An example of such a system is a trading application that takes care of the following functions:

- A trade capture system using a desktop client. These clients are also known as *application views*. There can be a web view enabling traders to use a browser-based user interface. The system is responsible for running a few validations and then booking a trade in the system. These validation are expressed and executed using a rule engine.

- A mobile app and a browser-based trade blotter. The blotters shows the current set of booked trades. Additionally, the application can have a mobile view that can be used to view the available reports.

- Trade risk analytics reports shown in a browser. The risk subsystem shows the near-real-time risk exposure after a trade booking.

- A book transfer system used to transfer money from one account to another account in the system.

- An asset allocation system used to allocate money across different investment instruments currently available.

- An instrument and market golden source (known as *reference data*) used to define which financial instruments are used by the application. This helps in directly selecting an instrument/market with an alias rather providing complete details every time.

Besides this set of major functions, there are other features such as risk alerts, book validations, and so on. All this functionality is compiled and deployed as a single software application.

A monolith application starts small. Everything is quick to develop in the early stages because the complete application has high cohesion. The complete application is easier to deploy and test because it is one single unit.

But as the application grows organically, it becomes harder to maintain and operate. Over time such an application is usually maintained by multiple development teams. These teams are responsible for each of the subsystems of the application. These subsystems get highly coupled, and over a period of time there is an interdependence of development teams for making new features available. But because of a single unit, each team faces the following set of issues:

- **Quick feature roll-out**: The teams are dependent, so they can rarely release features independently. Usually such application releases are one big coordinated effort, which can be done only a couple of times in a quarter.

- **Deprecated stack**: Since the technologies are widely used, a team can rarely independently change/update a subsystem. It often requires a complete rewrite of multiple subsystems, which is risky to the business.

- **Steep learning curve**: Since the complete system is tightly coupled, none of the developers can work without understanding other subsystems. This leads to a steep learning curve for the new developers. Often such applications have a large codebase, and a developer is interested in only a particular subset. This causes an overall slow development cycle.

- **Scaling issues**: A monolith application can be scaled only vertically. If there is load on a particular subsystem by a large number of requests, it is impossible to deploy more units of the subsystem or scale the particular subsystem only. It is an all-or-none scenario with a monolith application, and this is often a very costly affair.

Often these challenges require organizations to look at other paradigms. A microservice architecture is an alternative to a monolith architecture. It often requires breaking the application into various independent, loosely coupled units. The aim is to have independent business services with well-defined interfaces and operations. Each of these services has its own independent context. These services can interact with other services to perform the required task. Looking back at our trade processing application, individual services can be built for risk computing, trade transfers, and golden data sources. Additionally, there can be reporting services that consume data from each of the basic services for delivering the correct reports. The reports can be rendered to the Web and mobile devices using another set of services. Thus, the complete monolith can be broken into different components, as shown in Figure 2-2.

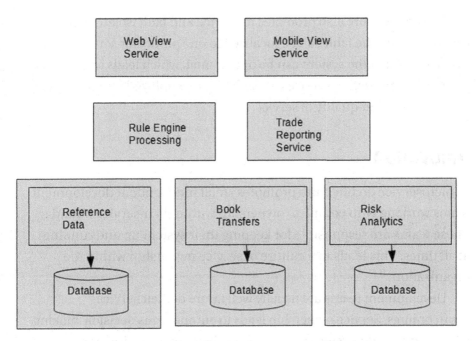

Figure 2-2. Microservice architecture

Adopting such an architecture not only requires a change in software design but also requires a change in organization interaction. Teams reap the following benefits of such an application design.

Agility

Agility is one of the biggest driving factors for an organization to adopt the microservice architecture. The loose coupling offered by the architecture allows accelerated development. The model dictates small independent development teams working within their defined boundaries. Each team can work with complete freedom within their context. This speeds up development.

The architecture also promotes resilience and fault isolation. In the case of failures, the fault can be localized to one particular service. As a result, the rest of the system can be operational, which leads to improved uptime. The particular service can be fixed and deployed independently, leading to a better quality of service.

Innovation

A microservice architecture promotes small independent development teams working with complete ownership within their service boundary. These teams are responsible for keeping their system up and running at all times. This leads to a culture of service ownership within the organization.

Development teams are usually well aware of their service shortcomings. Service ownership leads to autonomous decision-making with regard to addressing service issues. They can fix the issues and deploy the improved service as per their service milestones. They are fully empowered to select the appropriate tools and framework for this. This ultimately leads to an improved technical stack and innovation with the organization.

Scalability

In a monolith system, as load increases, not all subsystems get proportional increased traffic. It is often the case that some parts of the system get more traffic, which affects the service performance. Often it is a subset of the services that govern the performance of the overall system. Thus, the growth in load on the overall system is not linear across all of its subsystems. But when a monolith system is under load, the system can be scaled by adding more hardware. This will often result in under-utilization of the additional hardware as we need to add more hardware for the complete software rather than only for the subsystem under load.

The decoupling offered by microservices enables the organization to understand the traffic that each microservice is serving. Developers can make decisions isolated to the service in demand and make it more efficient. They can adopt appropriate programming languages and frameworks, fine-tuned with the best possible configuration and deployed to production. Moreover, in times of load, it is a matter of scaling the underlying hardware of the service on demand rather than scaling the entire ecosystem.

Maintainability

As discussed earlier, there is steep learning curve while working with monolith software. Often there are parts that no one on the current team will understand, and the team will be uncomfortable to work on them. This is often termed *technical debt*. Addressing technical debt in a monolith architecture is difficult because people can fear breaking one of the working features. There have been cases where unwanted dead code was made alive by addressing technical debt in a particular monolith architecture.

The microservice architecture can help to mitigate the problem by following the principle of divide and conquer. The benefits can be correlated to object-oriented application design where a system is broken into objects. Each object has a defined contract that leads to improved maintenance of the overall system. A developer can unit test each of the objects being refactored to validate the correctness of it. Similarly, a microservice created around a business context has a defined contract. Developers can address the technical debt of the service while validating the service contract.

Challenges

Microservices solve a number of existing issues with monolith architecture, but they also bring new challenges to the table. It is important to be aware of these challenges. A microservice breaks a single system into a distributed system. A distributed architecture needs to be modeled carefully. Care must be taken for various points of failures, and a microservice is no exception. In the late 1990s, James Gosling compiled a list of false assumptions that can make a distributed system inefficient, insecure, and harder to maintain. Let's cover them in context of a microservices architecture.

The Network Is Reliable

According to Murphy's law, "Anything that can go wrong will go wrong."

In a distributed architecture, there are many moving parts, and it is highly probable that one of the services could fail at any time. The failure can be caused by a software issue, a hardware fault like a network switch, or a DNS issue. This would result in failed delivery of the consumer service and could lead to a stale state of the system. As software designers, we need to be prepared to handle such scenarios by putting enough redundancy into the system.

Specifically, for cloud-native microservices, Kubernetes provides an out-of-the-box solution for this challenge. We usually deploy services to the Kubernetes cluster with a replication factor. Kubernetes makes sure that a service is deployed with the specified redundancy, and in the case of failures, all service calls are routed to the secondary service deployed in the cluster. Meanwhile, Kubernetes tries to bring in a new instance, and it maintains the replication factor for the said service. Let's look at a sample Kubernetes configuration.

```
---
apiVersion: extensions/v1beta1
kind: Deployment
metadata:
  name: spring-gs
spec:
  replicas: 1
```

```
template:
  metadata:
    labels:
      app: spring-gs
      version: v0.1.0
  spec:
    containers:
    - name: spring-gs
      image: k8s-sample /spring-gs:0.1.0
      imagePullPolicy: IfNotPresent
      ports:
      - containerPort: 8080
---
```

In the previous configuration, we have specified `replicas : 1`. This
will make sure that Kubernetes deploys at least two instances of the
service. This mechanism is a server-side solution for recovering from an
application crash. On the client side, we need to add a retry mechanism to
handle network failures. A request must be sent a couple of times before
the client can drop it completely. This way, an application will be able
to handle transient failures. This is just one example; as microservice
architecture adopters, we need to add required resilience patterns while
building our services.

Latency Is Zero

Nowadays each language generates stubs for web service/remote
invocations. The generated clients mask the boilerplate logic required
to invoke the function calls. But at the same time, developers
sometimes assume the client invocation is on par with local service
invocations. This is not true; a call over a network is much slower than
a local call. If not handled properly, it can block an application for a

large amount of time. Service outages are extreme scenarios that occur rarely. A much more common scenario is that services are responding slowly because of load. Testing for service response delays is quite difficult. In a unit test case, most external dependencies are mocked; thus, building a test for this involves a certain level of developer maturity. In an acceptance environment where there is not enough load replicating, this is quite difficult.

The Circuit Breaker pattern, proposed by Michael Nygard, is aimed at handling these scenarios. The pattern is all about encapsulating the remote function call in an object that keeps track of failures. If there are more failures, then the service no longer invokes the external call; instead, it returns immediately with an error code. The circuit breaker keeps track of the connection in the following three states (see Figure 2-3):

- **Closed**: This is the state when external service calls are working fine without any reported failures. The circuit breaker keeps track of failures. This makes the circuit breaker more resilient against service performance blips. But when the number of failures exceeds a threshold, the breaker trips, and it goes into the Open state.

- **Open**: In this state, the circuit breaker returns an error without invoking the external call.

- **Half-Open**: After a configured time interval, the circuit breaker goes into a half-open state and validates if the external invocation still fails. If a call fails in this half-open state, the breaker is once again tripped. If it succeeds, the circuit breaker resets to the normal, closed state.

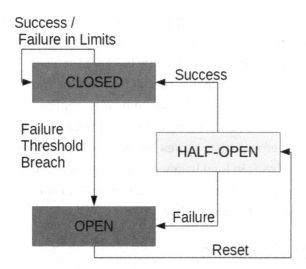

Figure 2-3. *Circuit breaker states*

An efficient circuit breaker strategy is also essential for releasing new versions of existing services. Upgrading the entire system at one time is a futile exercise. It often leads to a large amount of overhead. Instead, it is much more effective to have periodic rolling updates for existing services, but this is possible only if the dependent services handle failures in an effective manner. Teams adopting a microservice architecture need to embrace outages and must not regard them as extreme scenarios. If unaddressed, these failures can have a cascading effect in the complete ecosystem. This would lead to an avalanche of unnecessary service spikes.

Caching application data is another manner in which we can handle failures. This is applicable to situations where we can operate with stale data. Applications can cache the last response they have received. Next invocations either can get new data or can serve the older cached data.

Bandwidth Is Infinite

In a microservice architecture, we have exponential growth in the number of services deployed in production. Usually whenever we are addressing a new use case, we question if we need a new service or the function can be built in an existing one. In greenfield cases, more often we reach a conclusion of building it as a new service. But this has a cost on the existing deployed services. Let's say there is an SSO service; if every new service invokes the SSO validation, the SSO team starts running into issues if there is a single rogue service. To overcome this, applications need to have a mechanism of quota allocation and consumption tracking.

The explosive growth also creates issues for server-side load balancers. A large number of calls in load balancers often saturate them with traffic and thereby degrade their performance. Client-side load balancing is often a good approach when facing such situations.

The Network Is Secure

In distributed architectures like microservices, the onus of security is on every team. First, there are many technical choices, so teams need to keep track of bug fixes/issues in each of them. Each of these technologies must be configured correctly to avoid any security concerns. Second, interservice communication needs to be controlled. Service-level authorization is a must to filter out rouge or unknown service connections. Moreover, applications performing plain-text exchanges are exposing sensitive data. Thus, the communication needs to happen using a secured protocol.

Topology Doesn't Change

Agility is one of the reasons for adopting a microservice architecture. Agility means being able to quickly build, release, and deploy. This means a low coupling between dependent services. This is easier said than done. Let's say because of load, a new instance of an existing service is deployed in production. Other services must connect to this new dynamically added instance. This in turn means that services can no longer have hard-coded/fixed address locations of their dependencies. There needs to be an effective service resolution mechanism that can help determine the current location of services.

Adding the capabilities of service discovery also enables the overall system resilience. In production there are unexpected failures. Systems go down, and topology changes happen. Service discovery enables all running services to discover each of these changes, rather than painfully making configuration changes to each of them.

There Is One Administrator

Operations is another area of concern while working with distributed systems like microservices. Traditionally there was a single system that could be monitored and administrated by a couple of people. But this model fails as soon as there is an explosive growth of microservices. It is next to impossible for a handful of people to have complete operational knowledge for all microservices running in the ecosystem. Microservices aim to make teams autonomous. So, each team is responsible for maintaining and administrating their own services. This asks for providing production system access for each team member. Thus, to be successful in this approach, there needs to be efficient role-based access, which can be federated in development teams.

Transport Cost Is Zero

In microservices, we make lots of calls to dependent services. It is important to note that the data exchange incurs a cost. Data must be serialized at one end and deserialized at the other end. Thus, the cost is in terms of CPU resources consumed and amount of data transferred. The protocol of communication has an impact on our service performance. Traditional protocols like SOAP/XML exchange are highly inefficient. JSON is considered a better choice than SOAP. But binary protocols like protocol buffers have outperformed JSON. Considering that the information exchange is occurring between applications, it is better to select a binary protocol for the complete ecosystem.

The Network Is Homogeneous

A network would be classified as homogeneous if it had the same set of hardware running on all the systems and all the applications are communicating on a standard protocol. Running the same hardware on all the systems is next to impossible, but with Kubernetes we can limit the resources so that every time an application container is deployed, it gets the same amount of resources.

```
apiVersion: v1
kind: Pod
metadata:
  name: frontend
spec:
  containers:
  - name: gs
    image: istio-ks/spring-gs
    resources:
      requests:
        memory: "64Mi"
        cpu: "250m"
      limits:
        memory: "128Mi"
        cpu: "500m"
```

In the previous code, the `spring-gs` application container asks for a specified number of CPU and memory resources. It has also defined an upper bound of the CPU and memory consumed.

Similarly, it is not possible to run a single communication protocol for the entire ecosystem. This idea is futile for the microservice philosophy of independent autonomous teams.

James pointed out that building a distributed system without explicitly handling these issues is a setup for failures. Enterprise-grade systems are always going to have issues in all these areas. Thus, mitigating these challenges is essential to a successful adoption of microservice architecture. Besides the earlier generic distributed system challenges, microservices have their own set of issues. These issues are due to the philosophy of agility and autonomous teams.

Infrastructure

A microservice architecture is much more complex than a monolith architecture. There are many moving parts, and each is dependent on one or more microservices. Since each team can choose the technology behind their microservice, it is challenging to support all these infrastructure requirements.

The infrastructure team first needs to find ways to provision the infrastructure on-demand in a cost-effective manner. On the microservice adoption journey, the hardware demand increases as we deploy more services. The granularity dictated by microservices enable us to scale individual services in times of load. For this to happen, infrastructure should be available when required. Infrastructure can no longer be the bottleneck as was the case with monolith versions.

Provisioning hardware is not just about making it available. It is also about getting the correct set of libraries and frameworks. The wide choice of technology makes it challenging to support the new needs without breaking existing services. There needs to be much closer collaboration between the development and infrastructure teams.

Monitoring and Debugging

Monitoring microservices is completely different from monitoring a monolith architecture. The techniques used to monitor a monolith architecture do not work for microservices. There are many moving parts for one functionality. Thus, it needs to be more automated. Capturing effective metrics is also an important aspect. This influences how a service is scaled up or scaled down. As services are scaled up or scaled down, the monitoring should discover them and take relevant actions.

Traditional log handling mechanisms do not work well with microservices. First, there is much more logging done by the entire system. An effective log archiving is required as the system will quickly run out of space. Second, we must be able to quickly look up and correlate logs between multiple services. In times of a production outage, we do want to be in a position where it is hard to connect the dots between two interdependent services.

Until this point we have discussed major operational challenges. We will look at ways to address issues. There are other challenges like a service testing approach, knowledge distribution, etc. These challenges are beyond the scope of this book. If we inspect closely, then all the operational challenges are related to the mismatch between the federated application architecture and the traditional approaches to application management. Implementing a container orchestrator like Kubernetes helps to address some challenges related to infrastructure. Teams can provision resources quickly using Kubernetes. It can help services to scale on demand. But it cannot solve the remaining concerns. More tooling is required to address each of these challenges in an effective manner.

Language Libraries

In the early 2010s, companies like Netflix and Twitter started adopting a microservices architecture for their solutions. They faced all the previously discussed challenges. Each of these companies started building tools and infrastructure libraries for solving the challenges. The libraries are made up of the technologies used in each of these companies; for example, Netflix services are mostly based on Java, so Netflix created the following Java libraries to address the concerns:

- **Eureka**: This tool is aimed at service discovery. It consists of two components: a service registry and a service client. Services at bootstrap register them with the Eureka server using the service client. The service client is also used by the applications to discover the instances of their dependencies.

- **Hystrix**: This tool is a Java library providing fault tolerance between service interactions.

- **Ribbon**: This tool is a Java library supporting client-side load balancing.

- **Zuul**: This tool is an application gateway that supports dynamic routing based on service discovery.

These solutions were open sourced around 2012 and were adapted by developers. Over time Spring Boot was released, and these projects were combined with it as Spring Cloud Netflix.

Let's now build a simple microservice example with these libraries.

Hands-on Examples

This book follows a hands-on approach where you will learn by working through an example. We have chosen a simple example to understand the takeaways from the previously discussed issues. In-depth details of the libraries are beyond the scope of the book.

We will build a simple greetings service. The service has a simple offering. We can invoke the service using a userName, and it will respond with a greeting for the specified user. Thus, as a contract, users can invoke the following HTTP GET call: http://localhost:8080/greeting/Rahul. The service will respond with the following response:

```
Hello ! Rahul
```

To get the solution working, we will have to do some basic setup. Install the following on your machine:

1. **Java**: We need Java 8 or above. Please download the latest update of Java from the official Oracle web site at `http://www.oracle.com/technetwork/java/javase/downloads/index.html`. At the time of writing, the latest Java version is 12.01. You can check your Java version by running the following command:

```
$ java --version
openjdk 11.0.3 2019-04-16
OpenJDK Runtime Environment (build 11.0.3+7-Ubuntu-
1ubuntu218.04.1)
OpenJDK 64-Bit Server VM (build 11.0.3+7-Ubuntu-
1ubuntu218.04.1, mixed mode, sharing)
```

2. **IDE**: The code in this chapter is built using IntelliJ. But you can use any Java IDE of your choice.

3. **Maven**: Maven is a popular build tool in the JVM ecosystem. It is used for dependency management and running automated tasks. You don't need to install Maven on your local machine. Download the latest version of Apache Maven from `https://maven.apache.org/`. To learn more about Maven, you can refer to the Maven documentation. You can check the Maven version by using the following command:

```
$ mvn -version
Apache Maven 3.6.0 (97c98ec64a1fdfee7767ce5ffb2091
8da4f719f3; 2018-10-25T00:11:47+05:30)
Maven home: /home/home/Tools/apache-maven-3.6.0
```

```
Java version: 1.8.0_201, vendor: Oracle Corporation,
runtime: /usr/lib/jvm/java-8-oracle/jre
Default locale: en_IN, platform encoding: UTF-8
OS name: "linux", version: "4.15.0-50-generic", arch:
"amd64", family: "unix"
```

Now, that we have all the prerequisites, let's create a Maven project using the following command:

```
$ mvn archetype:generate greeting-rest-service
```

Now update POM.xml to add the Spring Boot dependencies.

```xml
<project xmlns="http://maven.apache.org/POM/4.0.0"
xmlns:xsi="http://www.w3.org/2001/XMLSchema-instance"
    xsi:schemaLocation="http://maven.apache.org/POM/4.0.0
    https://maven.apache.org/xsd/maven-4.0.0.xsd">
    <modelVersion>4.0.0</modelVersion>

    <groupId>com.example</groupId>
    <artifactId>eureka-client</artifactId>
    <version>0.0.1-SNAPSHOT</version>
    <packaging>jar</packaging>

    <parent>
        <groupId>org.springframework.boot</groupId>
        <artifactId>spring-boot-starter-parent</artifactId>
        <version>2.1.4.RELEASE</version>
        <relativePath/> <!-- lookup parent from
        repository -->
    </parent>

    <properties>
        <project.build.sourceEncoding>UTF-8
        </project.build.sourceEncoding>
```

```
        <java.version>1.8</java.version>
    </properties>

    <dependencies>
        <dependency>
            <groupId>org.springframework.boot</groupId>
            <artifactId>spring-boot-starter-web
            </artifactId>
        </dependency>

    </dependencies>

    <build>
        <plugins>
            <plugin>
                <groupId>org.springframework.boot
                </groupId>
                <artifactId>spring-boot-maven-
                plugin</artifactId>
            </plugin>
        </plugins>
    </build>

</project>
```

In the POM file, we have done the following:

- Added `spring-boot-starter-parent:20104.RELEASE` as our parent. This makes sure we get correct versions of the required Spring Boot dependencies.

- Added `spring-boot-starter-web` as a starter to make sure we have the required dependencies for creating a REST-based service.

- Added `spring-boot-maven-plugin`, which can enable
  us to run our project from the command line as an
  executable by using `mvn spring-boot:run`.

Now let's add a REST controller for our functionality in the following
manner:

```
@RestController
class ApplicationRestController {

  @RequestMapping("/greeting/{user}")
  public String greeting(@PathVariable String user) {
    return "Hello! " + user;
  }
}
```

In the previous code, we have done the following:

- Created an `ApplicationRestController` and
  annotated it with `RestController` to provide REST API
  endpoints.

- Added a greeting method to handle a `"/greeting/
  {user}"` location and send back a `String` response to it.

To run this application, we need to add the following main class:

```
@SpringBootApplication
public class ApplicationMain {

  public static void main(String[] args) {
    SpringApplication.run(ApplicationMain .class, args);
  }
}
```

In the previous code, we have done the following:

- Annotated `ApplicationMain` with the `SpringBootApplication` annotation. It will bootstrap Spring with the required configuration.

- The main method invokes `SpringApplication` using the annotated main class.

Let's now run this in an IDE (Eclipse/IntelliJ). Validate in the browser by looking up `http://localhot:8080/greeting/Rahul`. See Figure 2-4.

Figure 2-4. *Greeting service output*

Now we have a simple REST service in place that can be used to get some experience with the various Netflix libraries.

Enable the Circuit Breaker

Now, let's build a service that can be one of the clients for our web service.

```
@Service
class GreetingService {
  private final RestTemplate restTemplate;
  public GreetingService(RestTemplate rest) {
    this.restTemplate = rest;
  }
```

```java
public String greet(String username) {
  URI uri = URI.create("http://localhost:8080/greeting/"
  +username);
  return this.restTemplate.getForObject(uri, String.class);
}

}
```

In the previous code, we have done the following:

- Added a GreetingService that is making a REST call to our greeting{User} location.

- The greet() method abstracts the REST call, making it appear as a local invocation to other components.

The method can be invoked in a test as follows:

```java
@Test
public void testGreetingService() {
  String response = greetingService.greet("user");
  then(response).contains("Hi! User");
}
```

In the previous test case, we are invoking greetingService and validating the response. But if the greeting service is unavailable or facing performance issues, this test would fail with the following error:

```
I/O error on GET request for "http://localhost:8080/greeting/
user": Connection refused (Connection refused); nested
exception is java.net.ConnectException: Connection refused
(Connection refused)

    at org.springframework.web.client.RestTemplate.doExecute
    (RestTemplate.java:744)
    at org.springframework.web.client.RestTemplate.execute
    (RestTemplate.java:710)
```

```
at org.springframework.web.client.RestTemplate.
getForObject(RestTemplate.java:329)
at hello.GreetingService.greet(RestTemplateClientTest.
java:87)
```

Let's now configure the Hystrix circuit breaker to handle these common production issues. Before we can proceed, we need to add the spring-cloud-starter-netflix-hystrix dependencies. To do so, update the POM.xml file as follows:

```xml
<dependencyManagement>
    <dependencies>
        <dependency>
            <groupId>org.springframework.cloud</groupId>
            <artifactId>spring-cloud-dependencies</artifactId>
            <version>Finchley.SR2</version>
            <type>pom</type>
            <scope>import</scope>
        </dependency>
    </dependencies>
</dependencyManagement>

<dependencies>
.....
<dependency>
    <groupId>org.springframework.cloud</groupId>
    <artifactId>spring-cloud-starter-netflix-hystrix</artifactId>
</dependency>
...
</dependencies>
```

In the previous code, we have done the following:

- Added the spring-cloud-dependencies BOM that configures the right versions of the spring-cloud dependencies.

- Added the spring-cloud-starter-netflix-hystrix dependency.

Now let's configure the Hystrix circuit breaker for our GreetingService.

```
@HystrixCommand(fallbackMethod = "fallbackGreeting",
commandProperties = {
        @HystrixProperty(name = "execution.isolation.thread.
        timeoutInMilliseconds", value = "1000")
})
public String greet(String username) {
  URI uri = URI.create("http://localhost:8080/greeting/"
  +username);
  return this.restTemplate.getForObject(uri, String.class);
}
public String fallbackGreeting(String username) {
  return "Hi! there";
}
```

In the previous code, we have configured the Hystrix circuit breaker in the following manner:

- We enabled the circuit breaker by using the HystrixCommand annotation.

- The fallbackGreeting method is used to provide the fallback method for failures. It is configured by using the fallbackMethod attribute of HystrixCommand.

- We configured a timeout by using the `execution.
  isolation.thread.timeoutInMilliseconds` property.

Now when we run the test case, we no longer see the exception. We get a response from the `fallbackGreeting` method instead of the original greet method.

Enable Service Discovery

Now let's configure service discovery using Netflix Eureka. As a first step, we need to run the Eureka server. This is accomplished by adding the `spring-cloud-starter-netflix-eureka-server` dependency.

```
<dependencies>
....
<dependency>
    <groupId>org.springframework.cloud</groupId>
    <artifactId>spring-cloud-starter-netflix-eureka-server</artifactId>
</dependency>
....
</dependencies>
```

Now, the Eureka server can be started from the Spring Boot application in the following manner:

```
@EnableEurekaServer
@SpringBootApplication
public class EurekaServiceApplication {

    public static void main(String[] args) {
        SpringApplication.run(EurekaServiceApplication.class,
        args);
    }
}
```

- The `EnableEurekaServer` annotation starts the Eureka service.

- The server can be configured with the following additional application properties:

server.port=8761
eureka.client.register-with-eureka=false

Let's run the application and look up `http://localhost:8671/`. See Figure 2-5.

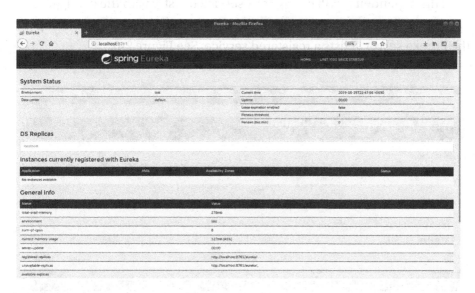

Figure 2-5. *Eureka server for service discovery*

Now we need to configure the previously created REST service to use this Eureka server for service registry and then use service discovery for our `greetingService`. To enable service registry, add the `spring-cloud-starter-netflix-eureka-client` dependency.

\<dependencies\>

. . . .

   \<dependency\>

      \<groupId\>org.springframework.cloud**\</groupId\>**

      \<artifactId\>spring-cloud-starter-netflix-eureka-
client**\</artifactId\>**

   \</dependency\>

. . .

\</dependencies\>

This dependency will configure a service registry with the configured
spring.application.name property name. Start the service and look up
the Eureka server. It lists a registered service. See Figure 2-6.

Figure 2-6. *Service registered with the Eureka server*

Now, let's use `service-discovery` in our `greeting-rest-service`. There are many ways we can configure it. Spring Boot provides a native EurekaClient to interact with the Eureka server. Alternatively, if we are using restTemplate, the same thing can be achieved by enabling client-side load balancing using Netflix Ribbon.

```
@Bean
@LoadBalanced
public RestTemplate restTemplate() {
  return new RestTemplate();
}
// Rest removed for Brevity
public String greet(String username) {
  URI uri = URI.create("http://A-BOOTIFUL-CLIENT/greeting/"+username);
  return this.restTemplate.getForObject(uri, String.class);
}
```

In the previous code, we have done the following:

- Annotated the RestTemplate configuration with the LoadBalancer annotation. This will enable the Ribbon if spring-cloud-starter-netflix-ribbon is in our classpath.

- Used the service name to connect to the service instead of a host and port address. The service name is first looked into the Eureka server to determine the address of the registered service.

In the previous section, we discovered how Netflix OSS solved the various issues with the microservice architecture. Similarly, other companies like Google and Twitter have built stacks around their frameworks like Stubby and Finagle.

But there are problems while working with the infrastructure libraries. First the application code gets coupled with its infrastructure. This makes services dependent on infrastructure components. Also, since every call is fine-tuned in the application, the team must collaborate with the operations teams to tweak and fine-tune timeouts.

Potentially, infrastructure libraries make it difficult for application teams to update their frameworks. Also, these frameworks are language-oriented. The Netflix stack is Java based, while Twitter is based in Scala. Each of these stacks offers a different set of features. If we are looking for a feature not available in the stack of choice, we can't change it. Thus, in a nutshell, if we truly want the flexibility of selecting our choice of technologies, then we cannot get bound to any of these frameworks. Lastly, building services around each of these frameworks requires a learning curve for developers. See Figure 2-7.

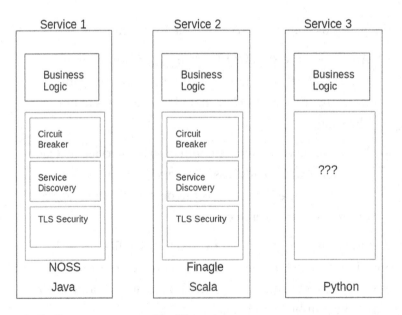

Figure 2-7. *Language-specific libraries*

Service Mesh

Previously, we discussed the challenges faced while adopting a microservice architecture. If we deep dive into each of these challenges, we'll find they are not related to microservices business logic but to the way services interact with each other. In a cloud-native ecosystem like Kubernetes, these challenges can be addressed by deploying a service mesh.

A service mesh is defined as a distributed system to address the microservice networking challenges in an integrated way. The complete system provides functions that are complementary to Kubernetes. It is built on the foundation of a dedicated layer that controls all service interaction in a Kubernetes cluster. The layer is usually composed of lightweight network proxies deployed along with the service, without the service knowing about it. See Figure 2-8.

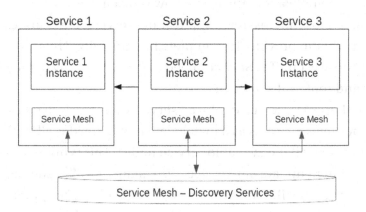

Figure 2-8. *Service mesh*

The aim of deploying a service mesh is to have an integrated platform that can actively monitor all service traffic. In doing so, a service mesh can address concerns related to fault tolerance, service security, and application monitoring. As discussed in the previous section, there are independent libraries that can solve these issues. But a service mesh provides a new nonobtrusive way of doing things efficiently in a cloud-native environment. Compared to language-specific frameworks, a service mesh addresses the challenges outside of the services. The services are not aware that they are working with a service mesh.

Service meshes are protocol-agnostic and operate on layer 5. This way, they can be deployed in a polygot environment. This abstraction allows developers to focus on their application business logic and allows system engineers to efficiently operate the infrastructure. This is a win-win situation for both of them. Overall, a service mesh addresses concerns about these challenges and adds the following benefits.

Traffic Control

In a monolith application, the traffic flow is in a north-to-south direction. But in a microservice application, services communicate with each other to provide the complete functionality. Thus, there is more east-to-west traffic. Services need to discover newly deployed services and route calls to them.

In a Kubernetes cluster, deployed services can be resolved using DNS. Kubernetes also acts as a load balancer and divides all traffic equally between all the available service nodes. This is quite useful when we want to update our service. We can update all instances by doing one at a time. But Kubernetes does not allow a fine-grained traffic control mechanism, where traffic can be routed using various other means. See Figure 2-9.

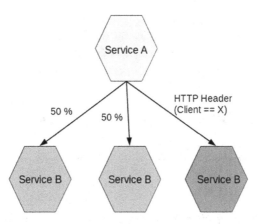

Figure 2-9. *Service mesh traffic routing*

On the other hand, a service mesh allows us to fine-tune traffic flow to each of the deployed instances of a service. A server mesh enables lookup of layer 7 request headers and then routes a request to a particular service instance. This process of dark launch/cannery deployment can be used to release the service for a subset of users. The process allows us to gain confidence in a new version before releasing it to the entire user base. This creates a smooth release process from one version to another, with automated rollback if a new version creates new errors or issues.

Security

Service-level security is another key benefit of having a service mesh in a Kubernetes cluster. Applications deployed in a Kubernetes cluster perform an SSL-based handshake before proceeding. The SSL protocol validates the service identity and authorizes it accordingly. Security issues are well beyond the scope of Kubernetes, which aim to have maximum service uptime. See Figure 2-10.

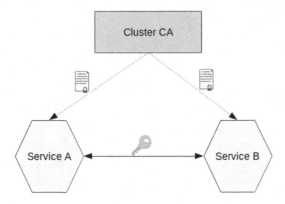

Figure 2-10. *TLS security*

We can also apply a fine-grained policy that can look for application user attributes. Since a service mesh is built on L4 communication, it can apply all security policies without understanding the service protocol. A service mesh also allows us to configure rate limits so as to limit a rogue service user.

Analytics

A service mesh allows us to systematically track and correlate interactions between various services. It presents this information in the form of request timelines. This capability is called *tracing*. Tracing enables us to debug how a request flows from one service to another. In a monolith application, we used to have a request log that could point to the request being a service. But in a service mesh where each service is calling the next one, it is hard to debug a request lifecycle. Tracing enables us to reconstruct a request flow and determine performance issues in our application. See Figure 2-11.

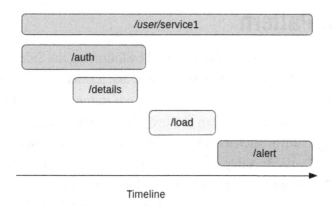

Timeline

Figure 2-11. *Distributed tracing*

Microservices in a service mesh achieve this by forwarding tracing context headers. This way, distributed tracing can help to visualize interservice dependencies. A service mesh also captures metrics around request volumes and failure rates.

Another important aspect is service log handling. In a traditional application, there is often one log file that is logging everything. In a microservice architecture, where we have a number of services logging, we need to look up all of them to understand the applicable behavior. A service mesh provides centralized logging and graphical dashboards built over logs. The aim there is to provide operational visibility within the microservices.

In summary, a service mesh allows us to decouple the infrastructure from the application code. It also simplifies the underlying network topology as the network is just providing the physical connection. All firewalls, load balancers, and subnets can be removed as they do not want to control any service interaction. Instead, all such things can be configured using the service mesh.

Sidecar Pattern

The service mesh is usually implemented by following the Sidecar pattern. As discussed previously, a separate process, aka a sidecar, is deployed along with the application code. This pattern is named Sidecar because it resembles a sidecar attached to a motorcycle. The sidecar is responsible for providing features such as networking, monitoring, tracing, logging, and so on. The sidecar is dependent on the parent application. It has the same lifecycle as that of the parent application. This way we can extend applications across different technology stacks, including legacy applications that offer no extensibility.

In a Kubernetes cluster, a sidecar runs alongside every service running in the cluster. The sidecar proxies all traffic to and from the service. The sidecar communicates with other sidecars and is managed by the Kubernetes framework. See Figure 2-12.

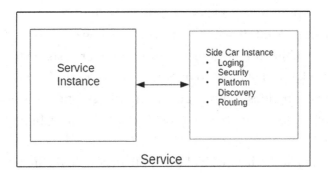

Figure 2-12. *Sidecar pattern*

It is important to note that the pattern is applicable to application cross-cutting concerns without any consideration to performance overhead. If performance is a consideration, then network overhead by the pattern will make it not suitable. Since the sidecar has the same lifecycle as that of the parent, it is scaled up along with the parent application. The pattern does not allow scaling up the sidecar in isolation. In a service mesh, the sidecar proxy performs the following tasks:

- **Service discovery**: The proxy determines the list of upstream and downstream service instances that are available.

- **Health checks**: The proxy checks whether the upstream service instances returned by service discovery are healthy and ready to accept network traffic. These checks can include lookup to the /health endpoint. It could also be based on service failure rates (e.g., using three consecutive 5xx values as an indication of an unhealthy state).

- **Routing**: Given a REST request for /foo from a service of the service mesh, the proxy determines to which cluster it should route the request.

- **Load balancing**: Once an upstream service cluster has been selected during routing, to which upstream service instance should the request be sent? The proxy is also responsible for applying a circuit breaker (maybe with a timeout) and retrying.

- **Authentication and authorization**: It validates service interactions by using mTLS or any other mechanism.

- **Observability**: For each request, detailed statistics, logging, and distributed tracing data are generated so that operators can understand distributed traffic flow and debug problems as they occur.

All of the previous items are responsibilities of the service mesh sidecar. Said another way, the sidecar is responsible for conditionally translating, forwarding, and observing every network packet that flows to and from a service instance. The sidecar is also known as a service mesh data plane.

Envoy, the Sidecar Provider

The network should be transparent to applications. When network and application problems do occur, it should be easy to determine the source of the problem.

—Envoy design goal

Now that we understand the role of sidecar, let's create one using Envoy. Envoy is a high-performance L7 proxy and communication bus written in C++. It has been battle-tested in large, modern, service-oriented architectures. The Envoy architecture offers the following benefits:

- Highly optimized out-of-process service proxy written in a native language

- Pluggable at L3/L4 to perform various tasks on the TCP messages received

- Pluggable at HTTP L7 to perform tasks such as request routing, rate limiting, and so on

- Versatile application observability, enabling it to capture and report statistics across all components

- Support for various applications like MongoDB, DynamoDB, MySQL, Thrift, and so on

Since its release, Envoy has gained popularity among the community and has become the de facto standard for application sidecars. At its core, the Envoy architecture consists of the following components:

- **Port listener**: The listener allows Envoy to listen to network traffic at a specified address. Envoy supports only TCP-based listeners. As a practice, it is recommended to run a single instance of Envoy configured with multiple listeners.

- **Filters**: Filters enable Envoy to perform various operations such as routing, translating protocols, generating statistics, etc., on a received message. Each port listener configures its own set of filters. All these filters are combined for a filter chain, which is invoked for every TCP message. Envoy has a large set of out-of-the-box filters. These filters can be broadly classified as follows:

  - **Listener filters**: Listener filters are invoked as part of a handshake in a connection request. These are responsible for things like TLS inspection or service remote destination, etc. These filter access raw data and manipulate the metadata of L4 connections during the initial phase.

  - **Network filters**: Network filters are invoked in for every TCP message after a connection. They perform a wide array of tasks such as application authorization, rate limiting, TLS authentication, etc. They are not limited to generic things. There are filters for application-specific protocols like MySQL and MongoDB, which are invoked to gather statistics, perform role-based access, etc.

- **HTTP filters**: Envoy comes bundled with a large set of HTTP filters. The filters can do various things like gzip compression, grpc to JSON translation, etc. These filters can manipulate HTTP requests received by the Envoy proxy. These filters are created by the HTTP network connection manager network filter.

- **Cluster**: A cluster is defined as a group of logically similar hosts that Envoy connects to. Envoy clusters can be defined as static configuration, or they can be generated dynamically using the built-in service discovery.

Figure 2-13 summarizes the Envoy components for each service.

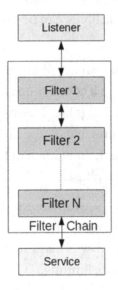

Figure 2-13. *Envoy filter chain*

It is important to note that these components are defined statically in a configuration file. Alternatively, Envoy can be configured with a dynamic service configuration. The configuration gets generated by the following components:

- **Endpoint Discovery Service (EDS)**: Envoy can add/ remove services to/from a cluster by using this service. The service offers alternative to DNS and can be used to address DNS bottlenecks.

- **Cluster Discovery Service (CDS)**: The service enables Envoy to dynamically discover application clusters that are used in routing. After discovering a cluster, Envoy gracefully adds, updates, and removes it to/from the configuration.

- **Route Discovery Service (RDS)**: The service enables Envoy to dynamically build a filter chain to the HTTP connection manager filter.

- **Listener Discovery Service (LDS)**: The service enables Envoy to dynamically build a complete listener chain to the HTTP connection manager filter.

- **Secret Discovery Service (SDS)**: The service enables Envoy to discover application secrets like TLS certificates, private keys, etc. The service is also responsible for providing client's public certificate.

Now that we have a brief understanding of how Envoy works, let's try to configure it for our Spring Boot greeting service.

Configuring Envoy

Before we can work with Envoy, we need to install it on our box. At the time of this writing, 1.10.0 is the latest version. Envoy is an open source application; it needs to be compiled and built for a particular system. It can be built using the instructions at https://www.envoyproxy.io/docs/envoy/latest/install/building.

Alternatively, we can work with Docker images published by the Envoy project. To do that, we need to make sure Docker is installed, as shown here:

```
$ docker --version
Docker version 18.09.6, build 481bc77
```

Download the latest version of Docker at https://docs.docker.com/install.

Official release versions of Envoy are also published as Docker images. These images are available in the following repositories:

envoyproxy/envoy: Contains an Envoy binary on top of an Ubuntu Xenial base

envoyproxy/envoy-alpine: Contains an Envoy binary on top of a glibc alpine base

envoyproxy/envoy-alpine-debug: Contains an Envoy binary with debug symbols on top of a glibc alpine base

---

Once we have Docker installed, let's download the Envoy proxy alpine image.

```
$ docker run -it envoyproxy/envoy-alpine envoy –version

envoy version: e95ef6bc43daeda16451ad4ef20979d8e07a5299/1.10.0/
Clean/RELEASE/BoringSSL
```

Envoy has a command-line interface that can be used to configure it. Let's look at some of the commonly used options.

- **--version**: This describes the released version of the Envoy.

- **-c**: This provides the configuration file used for Envoy. The configuration can be provided as YAML or YSON.

- **--mode**: Envoy can be involved to start a proxy server or validate a proxy configuration. This is accomplished by invoking validate mode. Envoy runs in server mode by default.

- **-l, --log-level**: This is used to set the Envoy logging level. There are additional options that can be used to configure the log path and log format.

- **--service-node**: This defines the local service node where Envoy is running.

- **--service-cluster**: This defines the local cluster node where Envoy is running.

The Envoy CLI has a large number of options. Most of them are optional values. We have discussed only the ones that are quite often used. You should read the official documentation to get to know each of them in detail.

Let's now configure Envoy to proxy our greeting service. To do so, let's first run our greeting service and verify it by looking up `http://localhost:8080/greeting/Rahul`. See Figure 2-14.

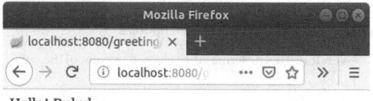

Figure 2-14. *Spring Boot greeting service*

Now, let's configure Envoy using the following configuration:

```
static_resources:
  listeners:
  - address:
      socket_address:
        address: 0.0.0.0
        port_value: 80
    filter_chains:
    - filters:
      - name: envoy.http_connection_manager
        typed_config:
          "@type": type.googleapis.com/envoy.config.filter.
          network.http_connection_manager.v2.HttpConnection
          Manager
          codec_type: auto
          stat_prefix: ingress_http
          route_config:
            name: local_route
            virtual_hosts:
            - name: service
              domains:
              - "*"
```

```
            routes:
            - match:
                prefix: "/greeting"
              route:
                cluster: greeting_service
          http_filters:
          - name: envoy.router
            typed_config: {}
  clusters:
  - name: local_service
    connect_timeout: 0.25s
    type: strict_dns
    lb_policy: round_robin
    load_assignment:
      cluster_name: greeting_service
      endpoints:
      - lb_endpoints:
        - endpoint:
            address:
              socket_address:
                address: 172.17.0.1
                port_value: 8080
  admin:
    access_log_path: "/dev/null"
    address:
      socket_address:
        address: 0.0.0.0
        port_value: 8081
```

There are many parts in this configuration, as covered here:

- The listeners section specifies that Envoy is listening
  to port 80 of our container.

- The listener is associated with a `filter_chain`. The filter chain has a layer 7 HTTP filter.

- The filter has a route configuration, which matches all domain names that are going to the `/greeting` location. The configuration routes all such requests to a `greeting_service`.

- The `greeting_service` location is defined by *clusters*. It can be used to define multiple instances of a service and the possible load balancing mechanism between them. In the previous configuration, we are running the service on port 8080. The IP address of the machine specifies the address of the Docker gateway. We can determine the Docker gateway address with the following command:

```
$ docker network inspect bridge
[
    {
        "Name": "bridge",
        "Id": "93196df71406f690bf83ba65d7556
        a4ba9fae676b828e578c53832f8b59608ef",
        "Created": "2019-05-30T07:42:54.43279813+05:30",
        "Scope": "local",
        "Driver": "bridge",
        "EnableIPv6": false,
        "IPAM": {
            "Driver": "default",
            "Options": null,
            "Config": [
```

```
        {
            "Subnet": "172.17.0.0/16",
            "Gateway": "172.17.0.1"
        }
    ]
  },
  // Removed for Brevity
}
]
```

- Lastly, Envoy has an admin service that can be used to get stats, configure the proxy, etc. In the above-configuration, the admin service runs on 8081 port of the container.

Now run Envoy with the previous configuration by using the following Docker commands:

```
$ docker run -v /home/rahul/Projects/envoy-conf:/envoy-conf -p
80:80 -p 8081:8081 -it envoyproxy/envoy-alpine envoy -c /envoy-
conf/service-envoy.yaml
```

```
[2019-05-30 06:03:17.152][1][info][main] [source/
server/server.cc:205] initializing epoch 0 (hot restart
version=10.200.16384.127.options=capacity=16384, num_slots=8209
hash=228984379728933363 size=2654312)
[2019-05-30 06:03:17.152][1][info][main] [source/server/server.
cc:207] statically linked extensions:
[2019-05-30 06:03:17.152][1][info][main] [source/server/server.
cc:209]    access_loggers: envoy.file_access_log,envoy.http_
        grpc_access_log
[2019-05-30 06:03:17.152][1][info][main] [source/server/
server.cc:212]    filters.http: envoy.buffer,envoy.cors,envoy.
ext_authz,envoy.fault,envoy.filters.http.grpc_http1_reverse_
```

```
bridge,envoy.filters.http.header_to_metadata,envoy.filters.
http.jwt_authn,envoy.filters.http.rbac,envoy.filters.http.
tap,envoy.grpc_http1_bridge,envoy.grpc_json_transcoder,envoy.
grpc_web,envoy.gzip,envoy.health_check,envoy.http_dynamo_
filter,envoy.ip_tagging,envoy.lua,envoy.rate_limit,envoy.
router,envoy.squash
[2019-05-30 06:03:17.152][1][info][main] [source/server/server.
cc:215]    filters.listener: envoy.listener.original_dst,envoy.
           listener.original_src,envoy.listener.proxy_
           protocol,envoy.listener.tls_inspector
[2019-05-30 06:03:17.152][1][info][main] [source/server/server.
cc:218]    filters.network: envoy.client_ssl_auth,envoy.
           echo,envoy.ext_authz,envoy.filters.network.dubbo_
           proxy,envoy.filters.network.mysql_proxy,envoy.
           filters.network.rbac,envoy.filters.network.
           sni_cluster,envoy.filters.network.thrift_
           proxy,envoy.filters.network.zookeeper_proxy,envoy.
           http_connection_manager,envoy.mongo_proxy,envoy.
           ratelimit,envoy.redis_proxy,envoy.tcp_proxy
[2019-05-30 06:03:17.152][1][info][main] [source/server/server.
cc:220]    stat_sinks: envoy.dog_statsd,envoy.metrics_
           service,envoy.stat_sinks.hystrix,envoy.statsd
[2019-05-30 06:03:17.152][1][info][main] [source/server/server.
cc:222]    tracers: envoy.dynamic.ot,envoy.lightstep,envoy.
           tracers.datadog,envoy.zipkin
[2019-05-30 06:03:17.152][1][info][main] [source/server/server.
cc:225]    transport_sockets.downstream: envoy.transport_
           sockets.alts,envoy.transport_sockets.tap,raw_
           buffer,tls
```

```
[2019-05-30 06:03:17.152][1][info][main] [source/server/server.
cc:228]   transport_sockets.upstream: envoy.transport_sockets.
        alts,envoy.transport_sockets.tap,raw_buffer,tls
[2019-05-30 06:03:17.152][1][info][main] [source/server/server.
cc:234] buffer implementation: old (libevent)
[2019-05-30 06:03:17.160][1][info][main] [source/server/server.
cc:281] admin address: 0.0.0.0:8081
```

In the previous Docker command, we are doing the following:

- -v /home/rahul/Projects/envoy-conf:/envoy-conf:
  The -v option mounts the /home/rahul/Projects/
  envoy-conf location in the host to the /envoy-conf
  location in the container.

- -p 80:80 -p 8081:8081: The -p option binds the ports
  80 and 8081 in the container to the host.

- envoy -c /envoy-conf/service-envoy.yaml: This
  Envoy command runs the configuration specified in
  the configuration file.

The command runs the Envoy proxy on port 80 and binds it to the
localhost port 80.

Verifying the Service

Let's verify the service by looking up http://localhost/greeting/rahul.
See Figure 2-15.

Figure 2-15. *Greeting service via Envoy proxy*

Envoy is now the proxy for our service. It is monitoring all requests made to our greetings service. If we shut down the greeting service and look up http://localhost/greeting/rahul, we get a 503 error instead of 404. See Figure 2-16.

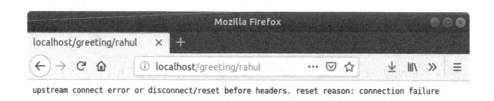

Figure 2-16. *Envoy service 503*

Now let's do a lookup for the Envoy admin UI on port 8081, as in http://localhost:8081/. The interface enables us to not only view the state of the proxy but also modify it. See Figure 2-17.

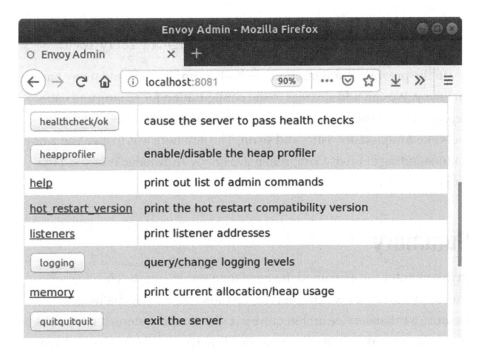

Figure 2-17. Envoy admin UI

We can find service stats under the /stats location. We can also find circuit-breaker stats being reported. The stats are in Prometheus format, which can be injected into the Prometheus server for detailed monitoring.

```
cluster.local_service.bind_errors: 0
cluster.local_service.circuit_breakers.default.cx_open: 0
cluster.local_service.circuit_breakers.default.cx_pool_open: 0
cluster.local_service.circuit_breakers.default.rq_open: 0
cluster.local_service.circuit_breakers.default.rq_pending_open: 0
cluster.local_service.circuit_breakers.default.rq_retry_open: 0
cluster.local_service.circuit_breakers.high.cx_open: 0
cluster.local_service.circuit_breakers.high.cx_pool_open: 0
cluster.local_service.circuit_breakers.high.rq_open: 0
```

```
cluster.local_service.circuit_breakers.high.rq_pending_open: 0
cluster.local_service.circuit_breakers.high.rq_retry_open: 0
```

In the previous configuration, we built a simple front-end proxy based on Envoy. We can add services to the configuration for scaling and canary deployment. Envoy is a versatile framework that is employed in various tools like Ambassador, Istio, and so on. The aim here was to give you a brief understanding of Envy. Comprehensive Envoy knowledge is beyond the scope of the book.

Summary

In this chapter, we explained the need for a service mesh. The chapter started by covering the microservice architecture and its challenges. Because a microservice architecture is a distributed system, it succumbs to the "fallacies of distributed computing." Enterprises like Netflix and Twitter that have pioneered microservice architecture have built language-specific frameworks to handle the microservice challenges. These frameworks, being language oriented, do not offer a clean solution to the issues at hand. Next, we looked at how Kubernetes with a service mesh can help in handling these challenges in a language-neutral manner. We also looked at the various benefits offered by a service mesh. Going forward in our journey, we looked at the service mesh architecture using the Sidecar pattern. The chapter concluded with a brief tour of Envoy, the de facto sidecar proxy framework. In the next chapter, we will look at the Istio service mesh and configure it for various use cases.

## CHAPTER 3

Installing Istio

In the previous chapter, we went through the microservice architecture and its challenges. You learned how an orchestration engine can solve these challenges, but to make a solution more elegant and reusable, you need a service mesh. In this chapter, we will show you how to set up the Istio environment and understand the basics of Istio.

Istio Service Mesh

As discussed in the previous chapter, when using a microservices architecture, calling services over the network is a little less reliable when you want to provide a response. To streamline the process, clients should be able to discover the services dynamically with the surety of service availability. The service must be discovered in such a way that the calling service agrees to an API version contract of the discovered service. On top of this, the calling service should handle any errors during the network call and retry any failed calls and also time out when necessary. These steps are necessary to create smooth network interactions in a microservices architecture. In addition, an application is required to log the calls and instrument transactions and also limit the access for different services. All this brings additional redundant work to be done inside an application and does not have much to do with the application logic.

© Rahul Sharma, Avinash Singh 2020
R. Sharma and A. Singh, *Getting Started with Istio Service Mesh*,
https://doi.org/10.1007/978-1-4842-5458-5_3

When you look closely, all these issues and challenges are directly or indirectly related to network communication. The Istio service mesh offers an infrastructure layer for service-to-service communication, abstracting away the network complexity and challenges. The following are the core features offered by Istio:

- **Service discovery**: One of the primary needs of an application running in a production environment is to be highly available. This requires one to scale up a service with increasing load and scale down when it's not needed to save costs. Service discovery keeps track of the nodes of a service that are available and ready to pick up new tasks. If a node is unavailable, service discovery removes it from the list of available nodes and stops sending new tasks/requests to the node.

- **Routing**: Istio provides flexibility so one can finely control the traffic among the available nodes of a service. The following list highlights the basic support offered by Istio:

  a. **Load balancing**: Istio allows load balancing based on different algorithms such as round-robin, random, weighted, and least request.

  b. **Health checks**: Istio focuses not just on node availability but also on whether the service is up, running, and still responding, before including it in the available nodes.

  c. **Automatic deployments**: Based on the deployment type used, Istio drives traffic to new nodes in a weighted pattern.

- **Resilience**: Istio removes the need for coding circuit breakers within an application. It also takes care of the timeouts to a service and the retries to be made, without the application knowing about them.

- **Security**: Istio takes care of access control by supporting TLS-based encryption including key management.

- **Telemetry**: Since Istio is an abstraction on the network layer, it can keep track of the network calls, hence tracing calls across multiple services initiated from a single source, and it can also collect the metrics around the calls.

Figure 3-1 gives you a glimpse of what happens between a service and its node using Istio.

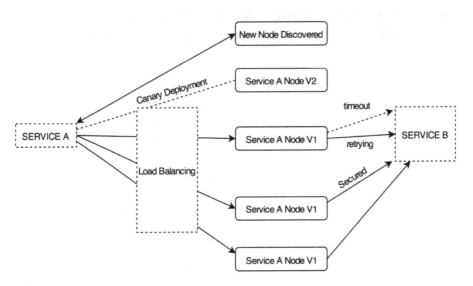

Figure 3-1. *Istio features*

These features are must-haves for an application, and taking this functionality out of the application code makes the code much cleaner and removes unnecessary modules and redundancy across multiple languages. Let's see how Istio achieves this functionality by going through its architecture.

Istio Architecture

The Istio features, as stated, can be implemented inside an application too. Istio uses the Sidecar pattern, which extracts these features out as small components and wraps each service such that any inbound and outbound requests are observed, validated, and accounted for. All of the traffic is directed to the proxy, which follows rules or a policy to decide how, when, or if that traffic should be deployed to the service. Using these rules, it also enables techniques such as fault injections, circuit breaking, and canary deployments without the services worrying about all that.

Figure 3-2 shows the different components of the Istio architecture.

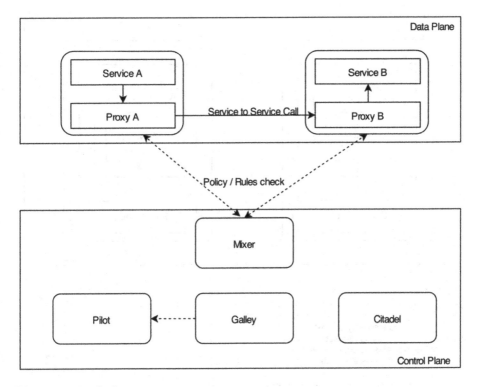

Figure 3-2. *Istio components*

Istio is logically divided into two broad components, the data plane and the control plane.

Data Plane

The data plane is responsible for translating, forwarding, and monitoring every network packet flowing to and from an instance. As the name suggests, it is responsible for gathering metadata in a service mesh. It owns the key features such as health checking, routing, service discovery, load balancing, security, and telemetry. As discussed in the previous chapter, the sidecar takes care of all these key features using the Envoy proxy. Essentially, the data plane can be seen as a sidecar proxy deployed across the service mesh. Figure 3-3 shows an overview of the data plane.

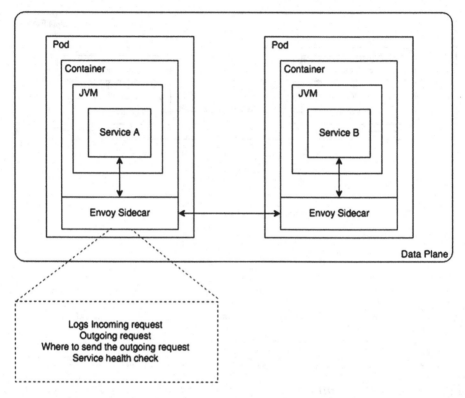

Figure 3-3. *Data plane services with Envoy sidecar*

If the data plane takes care of all the essential items, what does the control plane do?

Control Plane

The data plane is a set of independent nodes interacting with each other, and the control plane creates a distributed system out of them. When a network request is initiated, the proxy doesn't know which other proxy to connect to. The control plane is the one providing this information in the mesh. When a new service is discovered, the control plane populates the existing list of services, which is then used by the proxies to figure out the presence of a new service and direct the traffic. The basic configurations of circuit breaking, load balancing, timeouts, security information, and so on, are stored with the control plane. When a new deployment happens, the data plane has the information when a new node is ready to accept requests, but whether to do blue/green deployment or to shift traffic gradually is defined by the control plane.

The control plane provides policy and configuration to the data plane without touching any network packet in the mesh. Figure 3-4 shows the flow of network packets and metadata in the system. The configurations are referred to from the control plane while all the action happens in the data plane.

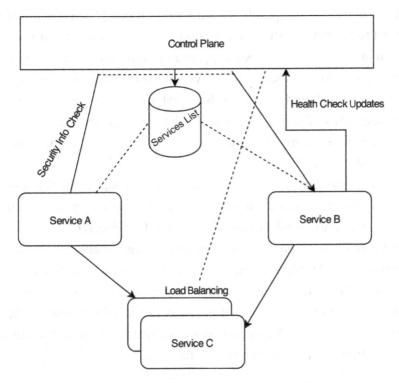

Figure 3-4. *Control plane guiding the requests and receiving metadata from the data plane*

The data plane has always been there in any architecture. Most of the features stated in the data plane are available in popular projects like Nginx, HAproxy, and Envoy, as stated in the previous chapter. But these require configurations to be set up manually or through self-written scripts or by using multiple other tools. Istio clubs all these and provides a single platform, removing boilerplate configurations and offering durability in the solution. Istio uses four major components to simplify these tedious tasks.

Mixer

Mixer is a platform-independent component. It provides a mechanism to collect telemetry for the services and also enforces the authorization policy. It abstracts out the basic support functionalities such as telemetry capture, quota enforcement, billing systems, and so on, provided by infrastructure back ends, from the Istio system. Services usually are tightly bound with the infrastructure back ends to get these details, which leads to following specific protocols and increasing limitations and dependencies.

Consider an example where a service is writing logs to the file system. Since containers are volatile, the service logs may be lost with time. To solve this, one starts sending the logs to a cloud service. A few months later, one wants to introduce a new log capturer that has the ability to search through the logs. Traditionally the service would be modified to send logs to both these log services, but ideally a service should be concerned only about its task and not about the logs. Istio takes the responsibility of collecting this data, and Mixer provides a uniform abstraction for Istio to interact with the infrastructure back ends.

Figure 3-5 shows the topology that Mixer follows. All requests are sent for a policy check, and afterward, the request telemetry data is reported to Mixer. The process is optimized using caching and buffering.

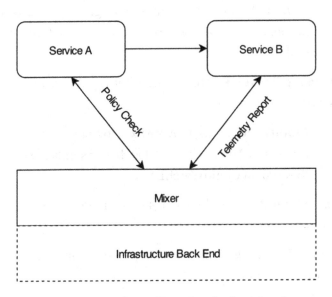

Figure 3-5. *Request sent to be policy checked with telemetry data reported*

The infrastructure back end may depend on infrastructure providers. To make Mixer a modular and extensible component, it would not be correct to bind it to a specific protocol and ask the infrastructure providers to follow that. Instead, Mixer provides general-purpose plug-ins called *adapters.*

Adapters

Adapters allow Mixer to interact with infrastructure back ends and keep the rest of the Istio abstracted from the provider. The adapters to be used are driven through the Mixer configuration to target any infrastructure back end at runtime. Here are a few popular adapters that interact with different back ends:

- **Logging Backends**: This adapter helps process and save logs from services.

    a. **CloudWatch**: This allows Mixer to deliver metrics to Amazon CloudWatch and sends logs to Amazon CloudWatchLogs.

    b. **Fluentd**: This delivers logs to the Fluentd daemon.

- **Quota Backends**: This helps keep track of different endpoint quotas.

    a. **Redis Quota**: This supports the rate-limiting quota for a fixed or rolling window algorithm. As the name suggests, it uses Redis to store data.

- **Authorization Backend**: This helps authorize any request within and outside the Istio mesh.

    a. **List**: This performs simple whitelist and blacklist checks of IP addresses or regex patterns.

- **Telemetry back end**: This helps process telemetry data collected from pods.

    a. **StatsD**: This delivers metric data to a StatsD monitoring back end.

Figure 3-6 depicts the interaction of Mixer with the infrastructure back ends.

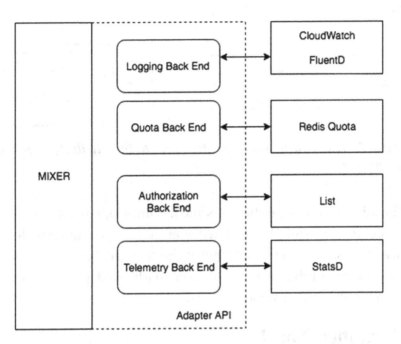

Figure 3-6. *Istio interacting with back-end services via the Mixer adapter*

Since Mixer interacts with different infrastructure back ends, how does it decide which back end to send data to or request data from? Mixer essentially depends on attributes available with it to make this call.

Attributes

Attributes are the smallest data chunk that defines a property of a request. Attributes include the request path, IP address to which a request is directed to, response code, response size, request size, and so on. Mixer processes these attributes and, based on the configuration, triggers calls to different infrastructure back ends. As shown in Figure 3-7, the data flow starts from the data plane and goes to the infrastructure back ends via Mixer.

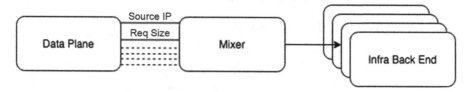

Figure 3-7. *Data plane sending attributes to the attribute processor or Mixer*

The Mixer receives the attributes and has the adapters call the infrastructure back ends, but as stated, there are configurations to define active adapters, how to map the input attributes to adapter attributes, and which instances attributes should be given to which adapters. This comes under the configuration model of Mixer.

Configuration Model

The configuration model is based on adapters and templates. Templates define how attributes are fed into the adapters. Combines, they do three types of configurations.

- **Handlers**: This is responsible for defining the configuration of an adapter. In the case of StatsD, the requests count can be one attribute to be fed into an adapter. This needs to be defined in the configuration.

- **Instances**: This defines how instance attributes should be mapped to adapter inputs. For the request count, an instance configuration metric can define the value to be 1 (i.e., count each request one time).

- **Rules**: Now we know the attributes to be read from an instance and how they can be mapped to adapter attributes. Rules define when to run this flow. Let's assume we want to push a request count for only one service; then that check needs to be placed in the match spec of the configuration, as in `destination.service.name == <Service Name>`.

This provides granular control to operators to know which infrastructure back end to use and add and remove it when required without making any changes to the service, which makes life much easier for developers.

Pilot

Pilot drives the traffic. It figures out the new path, manages traffic, and handles dead ends. In other words, it does the routing, provides service discovery, and facilitates timeouts, retries, circuit breakers, and so on. Pilot separates out the platform-specific way of service discovery from Istio, thus allowing Istio to run on multiple environments such as Kubernetes, Nomad, and so on. Istio uses the Envoy proxy in sidecars in all the pods to handle traffic and configuration. Pilot translates the traffic-related configuration to the Envoy configuration and pushes it to the sidecar at runtime. Figure 3-8 shows the architecture of Pilot and how it works.

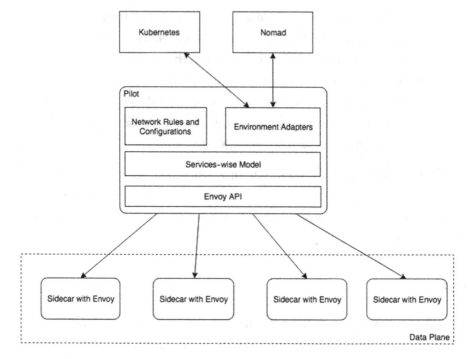

Figure 3-8. *Pilot architecture*

To enable traffic control for each service, the pilot maintains a model for each of them in the mesh. Any update to replicas and service discovery is tracked in the model service-wise. This helps in following a consistent protocol to keep data in models across multiple environments. This also means that environment adapters must act upon the data available through their resources to convert it to the Pilot services model.

Let's consider an example of a mesh deployed on Kubernetes. When a new pod is created by Kubernetes, it informs its adapter, which stores the information about a new replica of the service in a service-specific model. This, as per the network rules and configuration, creates an Envoy-specific configuration, and the Envoy API informs the sidecars of a new service discovery. The important thing here is since the environment adapters are responsible for service discovery, the services may lie in multiple environments, which means Istio can deploy the mesh across multiple environments. Figure 3-9 shows the flow of metadata from the environment to Istio.

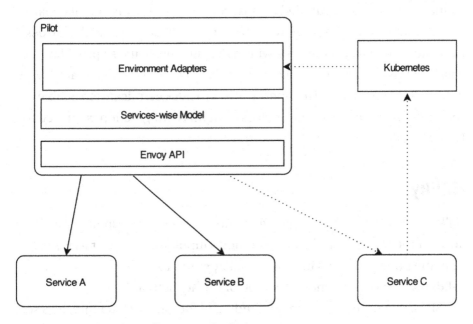

Figure 3-9. *Services discovery in Istio*

Within a service model, Pilot stores the number of replicas and configures Envoy to support different types of load balancing such as round-robin, weighted, random, and so on, which are not available out of the box by the environment providers.

The services are able to call each other, ensuring availability and responsiveness. However, should all the services be able to call other services? Should these services be communicating over unencrypted connections? All these questions are taken care of by Citadel.

Citadel

We saw how bringing in microservices can improve an application's development time and performance, but it also comes with security issues since the network connection becomes part of the application. This connection has to safeguarded against common security issues like man-in-the-middle attacks; therefore, TLS support is needed. Citadel provides the features to encrypt requests within the Istio mesh. It also provides role-based access control for services within the mesh. Please note that Citadel only enables encryption (in other words, provides certificates to enable secure connections between services), but this configuration is pushed to Envoy by Pilot.

Galley

Galley can be considered a management plane. Its core responsibility is to abstract the Istio mesh of a configuration's input from the user as well as from the underlining environment. Galley stores the user configuration, validates it, and then sends it to Pilot for further action.

Since you have a basic understanding of the Istio architecture, let's see how to set up Istio in different environments.

Setting Up Istio

Istio, as stated earlier, is supported in multiple environments like Kubernetes, Nomad, and so on. We will be restricting our setup to Kubernetes. There are two ways to install Istio on a machine; one uses the Helm chart, and the other is a quick demo installation. Let's go through these.

Installation Using Helm

Helm is a package manager running on Kubernetes. It allows us to define the application structure through Helm charts. This installation is the one that should be used for a production environment. It provides flexibility for customizing the data plane and control plane components. Helm helps us to generate the configuration file, which can then be used by the Kubernetes controller to do the installation.

Download the Istio Release

Download the Istio release from GitHub and set up the Istio path.

1. Pull Istio from GitHub and install it. Version 1.2.2 is the latest version as of this writing.

   ```
   curl -L https://git.io/getLatestIstio | ISTIO_
   VERSION=1.2.2 sh -
   ```

2. Add the Istio path to the environment variable. The current Istio folder is istio-1.2.2.

   ```
   export PATH=$PWD/bin:$PATH
   ```

Figure 3-10 shows the output of installing Istio on a Mac machine.

```
avinashsingh$ curl -L https://git.io/getLatestIstio | ISTIO_VERSION=1.2.2 sh -
  % Total    % Received % Xferd  Average Speed   Time    Time     Time  Current
                                 Dload  Upload   Total   Spent    Left  Speed
  0     0    0     0    0     0      0      0 --:--:-- 0:00:01 --:--:--     0
100  2207  100  2207    0     0    720      0  0:00:03  0:00:03 --:--:--  3359
Downloading istio-1.2.2 from https://github.com/istio/istio/releases/download/1.2.2/istio-1.2.2-osx.tar.gz ...  % Total    % Received % X
ferd  Average Speed   Time    Time     Time  Current
                                 Dload  Upload   Total   Spent    Left  Speed
100   612    0   612    0     0    516      0 --:--:-- 0:00:01 --:--:--   516
100 20.1M  100 20.1M    0     0   418k      0  0:00:49  0:00:49 --:--:--  333k
Istio 1.2.2 Download Complete!

Istio has been successfully downloaded into the istio-1.2.2 folder on your system.

Next Steps:
See https://istio.io/docs/setup/kubernetes/install/ to add Istio to your Kubernetes cluster.

To configure the istioctl client tool for your workstation,
add the /Users/avinashsingh/work1/book/istio-1.2.2/bin directory to your environment path variable with:
        export PATH="$PATH:/Users/avinashsingh/work1/book/istio-1.2.2/bin"

Begin the Istio pre-installation verification check by running:
        istioctl verify-install

Need more information? Visit https://istio.io/docs/setup/kubernetes/install/
avinashsingh$ export PATH="$PATH:/Users/avinashsingh/work1/book/istio-1.2.2/bin"
```

Figure 3-10. *Installing the Istio release*

Install Helm

Setting up Helm is different on different platforms but quite straightforward in all cases.

1. **Installation on macOS**: On a Mac, one can use Homebrew to install Helm.

   ```
   brew install kubernetes-helm
   ```

2. **Installation on Ubuntu**: On Ubuntu, use Snap to install Helm.

   ```
   sudo snap install helm --classic
   ```

3. Initialize Helm as a client to fetch the remote repositories.

   ```
   helm init --client-only
   ```

Once Helm is installed, we need to add the istio-release repository to Helm. This will include the charts provided by Istio.

4. Add the Istio repository to Helm.

   ```
   helm repo add istio.io https://storage.googleapis.com/
   istio-release/releases/1.2.2/charts/
   ```

Figure 3-11 shows the installation process.

```
avinashsingh$ helm init --client-only
Creating /Users/avinashsingh/.helm
Creating /Users/avinashsingh/.helm/repository
Creating /Users/avinashsingh/.helm/repository/cache
Creating /Users/avinashsingh/.helm/repository/local
Creating /Users/avinashsingh/.helm/plugins
Creating /Users/avinashsingh/.helm/starters
Creating /Users/avinashsingh/.helm/cache/archive
Creating /Users/avinashsingh/.helm/repository/repositories.yaml
Adding stable repo with URL: https://kubernetes-charts.storage.googleapis.com
Adding local repo with URL: http://127.0.0.1:8879/charts
$HELM_HOME has been configured at /Users/avinashsingh/.helm.
Not installing Tiller due to 'client-only' flag having been set
avinashsingh$ helm repo add istio.io https://storage.googleapis.com/istio-release/releases/1.2.2/charts/

"istio.io" has been added to your repositories
avinashsingh$
```

Figure 3-11. *Installing Helm*

Install Istio

Let's install Istio using Helm. We will be using the Minikube Kubernetes cluster created in Chapter 1. Please ensure that Minikube is up and running. Figure 3-12 shows how to check the status and start Minikube in case it's down.

```
avinashsingh$ minikube status
There is a newer version of minikube available (v1.2.0).  Download it here:
https://github.com/kubernetes/minikube/releases/tag/v1.2.0

To disable this notification, run the following:
minikube config set WantUpdateNotification false
host: Stopped
kubelet:
apiserver:
kubectl:
avinashsingh$ minikube start
Starting local Kubernetes v1.13.2 cluster...
Starting VM...
Getting VM IP address...
Moving files into cluster...
Setting up certs...
Connecting to cluster...
Setting up kubeconfig...
Stopping extra container runtimes...
Machine exists, restarting cluster components...
Verifying kubelet health ...
Verifying apiserver health ....

Kubectl is now configured to use the cluster.
Loading cached images from config file.

Everything looks great. Please enjoy minikube!
```

Figure 3-12. *Starting Minikube Kubernetes*

1. We will create a namespace called `istio-system` under which the Istio services will be deployed.

   `kubectl create namespace istio-system`

2. Istio comes with 23 custom resource definitions (CRDs) that can be used when configuring Istio. Let's install them using `kubectl`. Make sure you are inside the `istio` folder since the `install` folder is expected in the current location.

```
helm template install/kubernetes/helm/istio-init
--name istio-init --namespace istio-system |
kubectl apply -f -
```

3. Verify if all the CRDs are installed correctly.

```
kubectl get crds | grep 'istio.io\|certmanager.
k8s.io' | wc -l
```

4. There are multiple profiles available in the install
   folder. Check out install/kubernetes/helm/istio.
   We will be using the demo profile, which allows us
   to experiment with most of the Istio features.

```
helm template install/kubernetes/helm/istio --name
istio --namespace istio-system \
    --values install/kubernetes/helm/istio/values-
istio-demo.yaml | kubectl apply -f -
```

Figure 3-13 shows the installation output.

```
avinashsingh$ kubectl create namespace istio-system
namespace/istio-system created
avinashsingh$ helm template install/kubernetes/helm/istio-init --name istio-init --namespace istio-system | kubectl apply -f -

configmap/istio-crd-10 created
configmap/istio-crd-11 created
configmap/istio-crd-12 created
serviceaccount/istio-init-service-account created
clusterrole.rbac.authorization.k8s.io/istio-init-istio-system unchanged
clusterrolebinding.rbac.authorization.k8s.io/istio-init-admin-role-binding-istio-system unchanged
job.batch/istio-init-crd-10 created
job.batch/istio-init-crd-11 created
job.batch/istio-init-crd-12 created
avinashsingh$ kubectl get crds | grep 'istio.io\|certmanager.k8s.io' | wc -l
23
avinashsingh$ helm template install/kubernetes/helm/istio --name istio --namespace istio-system \
|>     --values install/kubernetes/helm/istio/values-istio-demo.yaml | kubectl apply -f -
```

Figure 3-13. *Installing Istio using Helm*

Demo Installation Without Helm

This installation is quicker and easier and allows use of most of the
istio features. This can be done without installing any other third-party
software. Make sure you are inside the istio folder.

1. All Istio custom resource definitions are present
   ' inside the Istio `init` folder.

   ```
   for i in install/kubernetes/helm/istio-init/
   files/crd*yaml; do kubectl apply -f $i; done
   ```

2. We allow Istio to use both mutual TLS and non-TLS
   mode. `Istio-demo.yaml` inside the `istio` folder
   allows this setup.

   ```
   kubectl apply -f install/kubernetes/istio-demo.yaml
   ```

Refer to Figure 3-14 for this installation and the expected result.

```
avinashsingh$ for i in install/kubernetes/helm/istio-init/files/crd*yaml; do kubectl apply -f $i; done
customresourcedefinition.apiextensions.k8s.io/virtualservices.networking.istio.io configured
customresourcedefinition.apiextensions.k8s.io/destinationrules.networking.istio.io configured
customresourcedefinition.apiextensions.k8s.io/serviceentries.networking.istio.io configured
customresourcedefinition.apiextensions.k8s.io/gateways.networking.istio.io configured
customresourcedefinition.apiextensions.k8s.io/envoyfilters.networking.istio.io configured
customresourcedefinition.apiextensions.k8s.io/clusterrbacconfigs.rbac.istio.io configured
customresourcedefinition.apiextensions.k8s.io/policies.authentication.istio.io configured
customresourcedefinition.apiextensions.k8s.io/meshpolicies.authentication.istio.io configured
customresourcedefinition.apiextensions.k8s.io/httpapispecbindings.config.istio.io configured
customresourcedefinition.apiextensions.k8s.io/httpapispecs.config.istio.io configured
customresourcedefinition.apiextensions.k8s.io/quotaspecbindings.config.istio.io configured
customresourcedefinition.apiextensions.k8s.io/quotaspecs.config.istio.io configured
customresourcedefinition.apiextensions.k8s.io/rules.config.istio.io configured
customresourcedefinition.apiextensions.k8s.io/attributemanifests.config.istio.io configured
customresourcedefinition.apiextensions.k8s.io/rbacconfigs.rbac.istio.io configured
customresourcedefinition.apiextensions.k8s.io/serviceroles.rbac.istio.io configured
customresourcedefinition.apiextensions.k8s.io/servicerolebindings.rbac.istio.io configured
customresourcedefinition.apiextensions.k8s.io/adapters.config.istio.io configured
customresourcedefinition.apiextensions.k8s.io/instances.config.istio.io configured
customresourcedefinition.apiextensions.k8s.io/templates.config.istio.io configured
customresourcedefinition.apiextensions.k8s.io/handlers.config.istio.io configured
customresourcedefinition.apiextensions.k8s.io/sidecars.networking.istio.io configured
customresourcedefinition.apiextensions.k8s.io/authorizationpolicies.rbac.istio.io configured
customresourcedefinition.apiextensions.k8s.io/clusterissuers.certmanager.k8s.io created
customresourcedefinition.apiextensions.k8s.io/issuers.certmanager.k8s.io created
customresourcedefinition.apiextensions.k8s.io/certificates.certmanager.k8s.io created
customresourcedefinition.apiextensions.k8s.io/orders.certmanager.k8s.io created
customresourcedefinition.apiextensions.k8s.io/challenges.certmanager.k8s.io created
avinashsingh$ kubectl apply -f install/kubernetes/istio-demo.yaml
namespace/istio-system created
customresourcedefinition.apiextensions.k8s.io/virtualservices.networking.istio.io unchanged
```

Figure 3-14. *Setting up Istio without Helm using demo.yaml*

GKE Installation

Installing Istio on GKE is similar to the other two installation methods with an additional tool installation. It is assumed that Kubernetes is enabled for the GKE project. Follow these steps:

1. Install gcloud on the local machine. This tool helps manage the resources on GKE. The installation steps are in the Google cloud documentation at https:// cloud.google.com/sdk/docs/#deb.

2. Kubectl can be installed using gcloud.

   ```
   kubectl get svc -n istio-system
   ```

3. Set the project ID and region on which Kubernetes is enabled and Istio is supposed to be installed.

   ```
   gcloud config set project [PROJECT_ID]
   gcloud config set compute/zone [COMPUTE_ENGINE_ZONE]
   ```

4. Create a new cluster.

   ```
   gcloud container clusters create istio-installation
   --machine-type=n1-standard-2 --num-nodes=2
   ```

5. A Kubernetes cluster is now available to install Istio. Use any of these two methods to set up Istio.

Verifying the Installation

After installation, let's verify that the installation was done properly, meaning all the services are running and their pods are live.

1. Find all the running services in the Istio namespace.

   ```
   kubectl get svc -n istio-system
   ```

Figure 3-15 shows the running services.

```
avinashsingh$ kubectl get svc -n istio-system
NAME                    TYPE           CLUSTER-IP       EXTERNAL-IP   PORT(S)
                                                                     AGE
grafana                 ClusterIP      10.108.90.87     <none>       3000/TCP
                                                                     13m
istio-citadel           ClusterIP      10.110.237.222   <none>       8060/TCP,15014/TCP
                                                                     13m
istio-egressgateway     ClusterIP      10.100.112.123   <none>       80/TCP,443/TCP,15443/TCP
                                                                     13m
istio-galley            ClusterIP      10.105.87.235    <none>       443/TCP,15014/TCP,9901/TCP
                                                                     13m
istio-ingressgateway    LoadBalancer   10.101.241.28    <pending>    15020:30238/TCP,80:31380/TCP,443:31390/TCP,31400:31400/TCP,15029:3059
0/TCP,15030:30629/TCP,15031:30718/TCP,15032:31967/TCP,15443:30678/TCP  13m
istio-pilot             ClusterIP      10.97.137.137    <none>       15010/TCP,15011/TCP,8080/TCP,15014/TCP
                                                                     13m
istio-policy            ClusterIP      10.107.122.14    <none>       9091/TCP,15004/TCP,15014/TCP
                                                                     13m
istio-sidecar-injector  ClusterIP      10.99.251.145    <none>       443/TCP
                                                                     13m
istio-telemetry         ClusterIP      10.102.138.130   <none>       9091/TCP,15004/TCP,15014/TCP,42422/TCP
                                                                     13m
jaeger-agent            ClusterIP      None             <none>       5775/UDP,6831/UDP,6832/UDP
                                                                     13m
jaeger-collector        ClusterIP      10.105.219.228   <none>       14267/TCP,14268/TCP
                                                                     13m
jaeger-query            ClusterIP      10.98.88.11      <none>       16686/TCP
                                                                     13m
kiali                   ClusterIP      10.97.205.242    <none>       20001/TCP
                                                                     13m
prometheus              ClusterIP      10.104.132.181   <none>       9090/TCP
                                                                     13m
tracing                 ClusterIP      10.100.91.15     <none>       80/TCP
                                                                     13m
zipkin                  ClusterIP      10.103.25.112    <none>       9411/TCP
                                                                     13m
```

Figure 3-15. *Running services in Istio*

2. Ensure all the pods are up and running in the Istio system.

```
kubectl get pods -n istio-system
```

Figure 3-16 shows the expected output.

```
avinashsingh$ kubectl get pods -n istio-system
NAME                                        READY   STATUS      RESTARTS   AGE
grafana-97fb6966d-596zj                     1/1     Running     0          13m
istio-citadel-7c7c5f5c99-7bpsd              1/1     Running     0          13m
istio-cleanup-secrets-1.2.2-4671f           0/1     Completed   0          13m
istio-egressgateway-f7b8cc667-69st5         1/1     Running     0          13m
istio-galley-585fc86678-h4z5c               1/1     Running     0          13m
istio-grafana-post-install-1.2.2-hnl2s      0/1     Completed   0          13m
istio-ingressgateway-cfbf989b7-dc8pw        1/1     Running     0          13m
istio-pilot-68f587df5d-fd6x9                2/2     Running     0          13m
istio-pilot-68f587df5d-wwjlw                2/2     Running     0          4m41s
istio-policy-76cbcc4774-247cr               2/2     Running     0          4m42s
istio-policy-76cbcc4774-66kw7               2/2     Running     5          13m
istio-security-post-install-1.2.2-kfm9w     0/1     Completed   0          13m
istio-sidecar-injector-97f9878bc-65g2b      1/1     Running     0          13m
istio-telemetry-5f4575974c-xwgdl            2/2     Running     6          13m
istio-tracing-595796cf54-rwjp9              1/1     Running     0          13m
kiali-55fcfc86cc-c8fwg                      1/1     Running     0          13m
prometheus-5679cb4dcd-pbzqg                 1/1     Running     1          13m
```

Figure 3-16. *Running pods in Istio*

Now we have an Istio environment ready to deploy an application. Let's take a look at the services.

Istio Services

Most of the services are straightforward and can be associated with the components discussed earlier in this chapter. Citadel, Galley, Pilot, Policy, and Telemetry are a few of them. The demo installation provides the following additional services:

- **Grafana**: This presents the data collected from different services in a dashboard for analytics and monitoring. It is an excellent tool to monitor what's going on in the cluster.

- **Kiali**: This tracks the services that are part of the service mesh, how they are connected with each other, the flow of data, and their respective performance. This is an excellent tool to check when a microservice is down or is affecting the overall performance of the mesh.

- **Jaeger**: This monitors and troubleshoots transactions in a distributed system. It helps to do performance and latency optimizations.

- **Prometheus**: This is a popular open source metrics-based systems monitoring and alerting toolkit. It has a powerful data model and query language that allows the analysis of applications and infrastructure.

- **Tracing and Zipkin**: These tools track requests across the distributed system.

Now we have an Istio environment ready to deploy an application, but before we go ahead and create a deployment, let's go through a few important Istio commands and CRDs.

Working with Istio

During the installation, we installed a lot of custom resource definitions on top of our Kubernetes cluster, which we will be using in later chapters to see Istio in action. Let's visit a few of them and get an understanding of what they are.

- **Virtualservices**: This defines a set of traffic rules to be used when a service makes a call to another host. The rules define what criteria to match before applying the rules on the call.

- **DestinationRules**: This comes into play when the routing is done. It covers the basic configurations like load balancing, connection pool size, and so on.

- **ServiceEntries**: This adds additional entries to the Istio service registry such that the autodiscovered services can have access to the manually defined ones. It configures the basic details of a service like its address, protocol, ports, and so on. It is helpful when there are services external to the service mesh.

- **Gateways**: This can be seen as a load balancer sitting at the entry of the service mesh and listening to the external connection at a specific port and then distributing traffic inside the mesh.

- **EnvoyFilters**: Using this tool, one can define Envoy proxy-specific filters on top of what Pilot already generates. In other words, it can modify the mesh traffic without Istio being able to autocorrect the faults; hence, it needs to be used with care.

- **Policies**: This tool enforces rules such as rate-limiting traffic to a service, header rewrites, blacklisting, and whitelisting access to services.

There are many other CRDs defined in the installation step, but these are the most common and frequently used ones. We will be using them in later chapters of the book.

Using the Istio CLI

We have now used Kubectl to deploy services and have set up Istio to do all the tasks related to a service mesh. Istio comes with its own CLI, which provide flexibility to configure Istio settings. The first approach to debug an application is to go through logs, but to dive in further, `istioctl` allows us to debug and diagnose each deployment in the mesh. Let's go through some `istioctl` commands that help in application debugging and setup.

authn

This is a command-line argument used to interact with the Istio authentication policies. For example, let's check the `tls-authentication` setting on one of the Istio pods. We will cover more about authentication in Chapter 10.

```
istioctl authn tls-check <pod-name>
```

deregister

This is a command-line argument to deregister an existing IP address from the service it was registered to. This is required when one forcefully wants to remove a pod from a service.

```
istioctl deregister <service-name> <ip-to-be-removed>
```

register

This is a command-line argument to register a pod to a service.

```
istioctl register <service-name> <ip-to-be-added> <port>
```

experimental

This allows playing around with `istioctl` and generating experimental commands that can be modified or deprecated. It allows experimenting across four areas.

experimental auth

This allows interaction with the authentication and authorization policies in the mesh.

```
istioctl experimental auth check <pod-name>
```

experimental convert-ingress

This converts the Kubernetes ingress into a `VirtualService` configuration on a best-effort basis. The result is the beginning of the Istio configuration. A few scenarios will generate warnings where the conversion might have failed, which may require manual intervention. Consider the example ingress in Listing 3-1. We will try to convert it to `VirtualService`.

Listing 3-1. Sample Ingress Config ingress-smaple.yaml

```
apiVersion: extensions/v1beta1
kind: Ingress
metadata:
  name: gateway
spec:
  rules:
```

```
- http:
    paths:
    - path: /
      backend:
        serviceName: frontendservice
        servicePort: 80
```

Figure 3-17 shows the output generated by converting the ingress to an Istio VirtualService.

```
avinashsingh$ cat ingress-smaple.yaml
apiVersion: extensions/v1beta1
kind: Ingress
metadata:
  name: gateway
spec:
  rules:
  - http:
      paths:
      - path: /
        backend:
          serviceName: frontendservice
          servicePort: 80
avinashsingh$ istioctl experimental convert-ingress -f ingress-smaple.yaml
apiVersion: networking.istio.io/v1alpha3
kind: VirtualService
metadata:
  creationTimestamp: null
  name: wild-gateway-istio-autogenerated-k8s-ingress
  namespace: default
spec:
  gateways:
  - istio-system/istio-autogenerated-k8s-ingress
  hosts:
  - '*'
  http:
  - match:
    - uri:
        exact: /
    route:
    - destination:
        host: frontendservice.default.svc.cluster.local
        port:
          number: 80
      weight: 100
```

Figure 3-17. *Converting an ingress config to an Istio VirtualService*

experimental dashboard grafana

Viewing the Grafana dashboard is easy using `istioctl`.

istioctl experimental dashboard grafana

This sets up a proxy to the Grafana service and makes it accessible in a web browser through a random port. Figure 3-18 and Figure 3-19 show the command and dashboard.

```
[^CAvinashs-MacBook-Pro-2:istio-1.2.2 avinashsingh$ istioctl experimental dashboard  grafana


http://localhost:53869
```

Figure 3-18.   *Request to show Grafana dashboard*

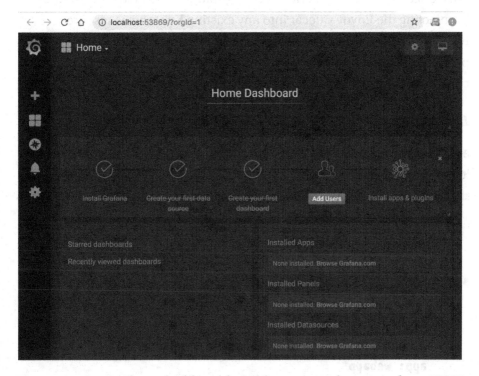

Figure 3-19.   *Grafana dashboard visible on a random port, here 53869*

Similar dashboards are available for Envoy, Jaegar, Kiali, Promethus, and Zipkin in our current setup.

experimental metrics

This prints the metrics of the stated service in Kubernetes. This is dependent on Prometheus. When a service metric is requested, this command fires a series of requests to Prometheus about metrics and prints them.

```
istioctl experimental metrics <service-name>
```

kube-inject

This tool converts the Kubernetes configuration to an Istio configuration by injecting the Envoy sidecar into any existing Kubernetes resource. For unsupported resources, the configurations are left as is. Let's pick a deployment from Chapter 1 and try to convert the Kubernetes configuration to the Istio config (see Listing 3-2).

Listing 3-2. Sample Ingress Config ingress-smaple.yaml

```
apiVersion: apps/v1
kind: Deployment
metadata:
  name: webapp-deployment
  labels:
    app: webapp
spec:
  replicas: 1
  selector:
    matchLabels:
      app: webapp
```

```
template:
  metadata:
    labels:
      app: webapp
  spec:
    containers:
    - name: webapp
      image: web-app:4.0
      imagePullPolicy: Never
      ports:
      - containerPort: 5000
      readinessProbe:
        httpGet:
          path: /health
          port: 5000
        initialDelaySeconds: 40
      livenessProbe:
        httpGet:
          path: /health
          port: 5000
        initialDelaySeconds: 120
```

Listing 3-3 shows the transformed configuration.

Listing 3-3. Sidecar Injected into Kubenetes Deployment

```
apiVersion: apps/v1
kind: Deployment
metadata:
  creationTimestamp: null
  labels:
    app: webapp
  name: webapp-deployment
```

```
spec:
  replicas: 1
  selector:
    matchLabels:
      app: webapp
  strategy: {}
  template:
    metadata:
      annotations:
        sidecar.istio.io/status: '{"version":"761ebc5a6397675
        4715f22fcf548f05270fb4b8db07324894aebdb31fa81d960","
        initContainers":["istio-init"],"containers":["istio-
        proxy"],"volumes":["istio-envoy","istio-certs"],"imageP
        ullSecrets":null}'
      creationTimestamp: null
      labels:
        app: webapp
    spec:
      containers:
      - image: web-app:4.0
        imagePullPolicy: Never
        livenessProbe:
          httpGet:
            path: /health
            port: 5000
          initialDelaySeconds: 120
        name: webapp
        ports:
        - containerPort: 5000
        readinessProbe:
          httpGet:
```

```
      path: /health
      port: 5000
    initialDelaySeconds: 40
  resources: {}
- args:
  - proxy
  - sidecar
  - --domain
  - $(POD_NAMESPACE).svc.cluster.local
  - --configPath
  - /etc/istio/proxy
  - --binaryPath
  - /usr/local/bin/envoy
  - --serviceCluster
  - webapp.$(POD_NAMESPACE)
  - --drainDuration
  - 45s
  - --parentShutdownDuration
  - 1m0s
  - --discoveryAddress
  - istio-pilot.istio-system:15010
  - --zipkinAddress
  - zipkin.istio-system:9411
  - --dnsRefreshRate
  - 300s
  - --connectTimeout
  - 10s
  - --proxyAdminPort
  - "15000"
  - --concurrency
  - "2"
```

```yaml
        - --controlPlaneAuthPolicy
        - NONE
        - --statusPort
        - "15020"
        - --applicationPorts
        - "5000"
        env:
        - name: POD_NAME
          valueFrom:
            fieldRef:
              fieldPath: metadata.name
        - name: POD_NAMESPACE
          valueFrom:
            fieldRef:
              fieldPath: metadata.namespace
        - name: INSTANCE_IP
          valueFrom:
            fieldRef:
              fieldPath: status.podIP
        - name: ISTIO_META_POD_NAME
          valueFrom:
            fieldRef:
              fieldPath: metadata.name
        - name: ISTIO_META_CONFIG_NAMESPACE
          valueFrom:
            fieldRef:
              fieldPath: metadata.namespace
        - name: ISTIO_META_INTERCEPTION_MODE
          value: REDIRECT
        - name: ISTIO_META_INCLUDE_INBOUND_PORTS
          value: "5000"
        - name: ISTIO_METAJSON_LABELS
```

```
value: |
  {"app":"webapp"}
image: docker.io/istio/proxyv2:1.2.2
imagePullPolicy: IfNotPresent
name: istio-proxy
ports:
- containerPort: 15090
  name: http-envoy-prom
  protocol: TCP
readinessProbe:
  failureThreshold: 30
  httpGet:
    path: /healthz/ready
    port: 15020
  initialDelaySeconds: 1
  periodSeconds: 2
resources:
  limits:
    cpu: "2"
    memory: 1Gi
  requests:
    cpu: 10m
    memory: 40Mi
securityContext:
  readOnlyRootFilesystem: true
  runAsUser: 1337
volumeMounts:
- mountPath: /etc/istio/proxy
  name: istio-envoy
- mountPath: /etc/certs/
  name: istio-certs
  readOnly: true
```

```
initContainers:
- args:
  - -p
  - "15001"
  - -u
  - "1337"
  - -m
  - REDIRECT
  - -i
  - '*'
  - -x
  - ""
  - -b
  - "5000"
  - -d
  - "15020"
  image: docker.io/istio/proxy_init:1.2.2
  imagePullPolicy: IfNotPresent
  name: istio-init
  resources:
    limits:
      cpu: 100m
      memory: 50Mi
    requests:
      cpu: 10m
      memory: 10Mi
  securityContext:
    capabilities:
      add:
      - NET_ADMIN
    runAsNonRoot: false
    runAsUser: 0
```

```
volumes:
- emptyDir:
    medium: Memory
  name: istio-envoy
- name: istio-certs
  secret:
    optional: true
    secretName: istio.default
status: {}
---
```

proxy-config bootstrap|cluster|endpoint|listener| route

This tool retrieves information about Bootstrap, a cluster, an endpoint, a listener, or a route-specific configuration of an Envoy instance in a pod.

validate

This validates an Istio configuration before it can be applied to a mesh. Let's validate the output in Listing 3-3. Figure 3-20 shows a warning generated from the file because we haven't added a version to the deployment.

```
Avinashs-MacBook-Pro-2:code avinashsingh$ istioctl validate -f webapp-deployment-istio.yaml
2019-07-28T16:01:13.128067Z     warn    deployment "webapp-deployment/:" may not provide Istio metrics and telemetry
without label "version". See https://istio.io/docs/setup/kubernetes/prepare/requirements/

"webapp-deployment-istio.yaml" is valid
```

Figure 3-20. *Validation of generated Istio configuration*

These commands help in creating, modifying, injecting into, and playing around with an Istio configuration in the service mesh.

Summary

In this chapter, we went through the Istio architecture, and you learned how decoupling the control plane and data plane helps to organize the configuration and data flow. We went through the control plane components Mixer, Pilot, Citadel, and Galley, which take care of configuration, and we showed how they organize the flow of data and convert a number of pods into a distributed system. We also went through how to set up Istio on a local machine and on GKE via a Helm chart and without any third-party software. We briefly went through a few important CRDs of Istio. We also had a small overview of the Istio CLI tool, which will be extensively used in later chapters. In the next chapter, we will be diving into the Istio CRD `VirtualService` and provide some examples of how to create an Istio mesh.

CHAPTER 4

Istio VirtualService

In previous chapter, we discussed the Istio architecture in detail.
We worked with the control plane to configure the data plane. The
decoupling between the two components allows both of them to operate
independently, which leads to improved failure handling. The architecture
enables a centralized operations team to configure the infrastructure with
generic rules. Istio has different types of rules for different purposes. In
this chapter, we will show how to work with the traffic management rules
of Istio. Specifically, we will take an existing Kubernetes service and route
traffic through it.

Request Routing

In this chapter, we will incrementally develop our application from
Chapter 1, so let's recap what has been done so far. In Chapter 1, we
developed a polyglot application and deployed it to a Kubernetes
cluster. The application had a Java-based front end and a Python-
based back end. Both these applications were deployed in the same
Kubernetes namespace. The webapp was deployed by using the following
configuration:

```
apiVersion: apps/v1
kind: Deployment
metadata:
```

© Rahul Sharma, Avinash Singh 2020
R. Sharma and A. Singh, *Getting Started with Istio Service Mesh*,
https://doi.org/10.1007/978-1-4842-5458-5_4

```
    name: webapp-deployment
    labels:
      app: webapp
spec:
  replicas: 1
  selector:
    matchLabels:
      app: webapp
  template:
    metadata:
      labels:
        app: webapp
    spec:
      containers:
      - name: webapp
        image: web-app:4.0
        imagePullPolicy: Never
        ports:
        - containerPort: 5000
-------
apiVersion: v1
kind: Service
metadata:
  name: webservice
spec:
  selector:
    app: webapp
  ports:
  - protocol: TCP
    port: 80
    targetPort: 5000
```

This configuration creates a pod and a service in the Kubernetes cluster. A similar configuration was used to deploy the front-end Java application. Both these applications can refer to each other by using DNS names, as they belong to the same namespace. Similarly, services in different namespaces can refer to each other by using a fully qualified service name.

Up to now we have always updated our Kubernetes deployment with a new version. Thus, there has been one version of our application. But this is an edge use case and does not conform to a regular Kubernetes deployment. Practically, a Kubernetes cluster would have many versions of the same application running. This would help us to meet different use cases like application rollout, A/B testing, and so on. But once we have many versions of the deployed application, we run into various request handling issues.

As we extend our example, we need to add a version identifier to the application response. This can be done by either adding version information to the response headers or by adding a version prefix to the response. Let's modify our Python application to prefix its version to the welcome message (as this is easily identifiable).

```
app = Flask(__name__)
@app.route("/")
def main():
    currentDT = datetime.datetime.now()
    return "[{}]Welcome user! current time is {} ".format(os.en
viron['VERSION'],str(currentDT))
## removed for Brevity
```

We now need to set the VERSION environment variable via our Dockerfile.

```
FROM python:3.7-alpine
COPY ./requirement.txt /app/requirement.txt
WORKDIR /app
```

```
RUN pip install -r requirement.txt
COPY . /app
ENTRYPOINT [ "python" ]
ARG ver=NA
ENV VERSION=$ver
CMD [ "app.py" ]
```

To validate the previous behavior, we need to deploy a couple of versions of this application to our cluster. Thus, first build some Docker images for different versions using the following command lines:

```
$docker build . -t web-app:6.0 --build-arg ver=6.0
$docker build . -t web-app:6.1 --build-arg ver=6.1
$docker build . -t web-app:6.2 --build-arg ver=6.2
```

Now deploy all the previous versions to the Kubernetes cluster. This is done by using the previously discussed webapp-deployment command, with different Docker images. Moreover, the webapp Kubernetes service is configured with the selector app: webapp. This will select all pods matching these attributes and route the request to one of them. If we request the webapp service, we get responses from all versions of the service.

Figure 4-1 shows multiple versions of webapp running in Kubernetes. Let's do a lookup for http://10.152.183.146/, which is the front-end service.

```
NAME                                          READY   STATUS    RESTARTS   AGE
pod/frontend-deployment-c9c975b4-vm8f4        2/2     Running   0          5m50s
pod/webapp-deployment-6.0-6f48fcc5-5pdlr      2/2     Running   8          12h
pod/webapp-deployment-6.1-755cc895d6-bhb4n    2/2     Running   9          12h
pod/webapp-deployment-6.2-654c5fd8f9-mrc22    2/2     Running   8          158m


NAME                      TYPE        CLUSTER-IP       EXTERNAL-IP   PORT(S)    AGE
service/frontendservice   ClusterIP   10.152.183.146   <none>        80/TCP     138m
service/kubernetes        ClusterIP   10.152.183.1     <none>        443/TCP    14d
service/webservice        ClusterIP   10.152.183.230   <none>        80/TCP     3d23h
```

Figure 4-1. *Kubernetes deployed services*

Figure 4-2, Figure 4-3, and Figure 4-4 show the responses.

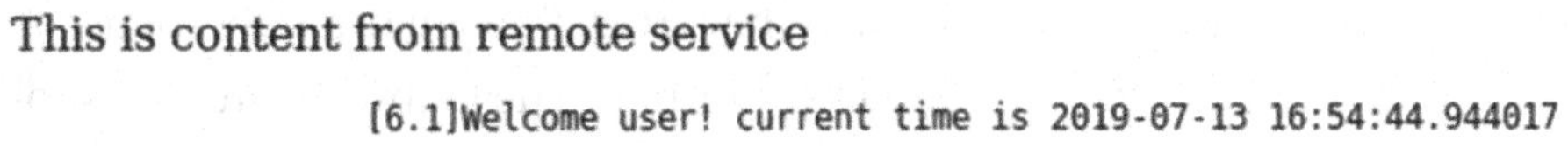

This is content from remote service

```
[6.1]Welcome user! current time is 2019-07-13 16:54:44.944017
```

Figure 4-2. *Response from 6.1*

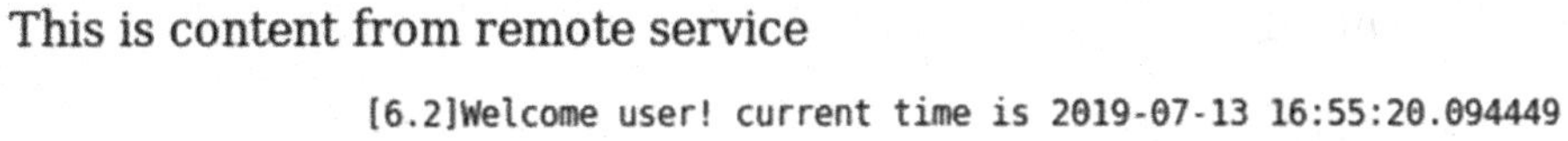

This is content from remote service

```
[6.2]Welcome user! current time is 2019-07-13 16:55:20.094449
```

Figure 4-3. *Response from 6.2*

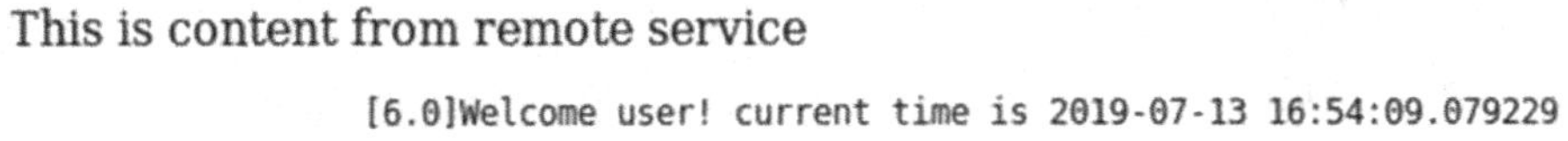

This is content from remote service

```
[6.0]Welcome user! current time is 2019-07-13 16:54:09.079229
```

Figure 4-4. *Response from 6.0*

In the rest of the chapter, we will configure the Istio request routing rules for the required versions. Istio can handle TCP and HTTP services quite well. Istio also provides support for the L4 and L7 attributes lookups for request routing.

Kubernetes Practices

Before we can configure Istio request routing, we need to make sure our Kubernetes cluster adheres to the following listed practices. If there are services that do not meet these requirements, then invocations to such services will not be governed by Istio. Such requests will be resolved by Kubernetes components instead.

Naming Service Ports

Istio routing requires names for ports that are defined in the Kubernetes services in the `<protocol>[<-suffix>]` format. The following are the Istio-supported protocols:

- `http`
- `http2`
- `https`
- `grpc`
- `mysql`
- `mongo`
- `redis`
- `tcp`
- `tls`
- `udp`

In our example, we must name ports for the web service as `http-webapp` or as `http`. Different services can have the same name for their ports, but the same service can't have identical names for different ports. It is important to note that this is a naming convention followed by Istio and does not add any additional protocol values to the Kubernetes specification. So, let's update our web service with the following configuration:

```
apiVersion: v1
kind: Service
metadata:
  name: webservice
```

```
spec:
  selector:
    app: webapp
  ports:
  - name: http-webservice
    protocol: TCP
    port: 80
    targetPort: 5000
```

In the previous configuration, we have added a name attribute with a value of http-webservice. Apply the previous configuration with the following command:

```
$kubectl apply -f ../config/webservice.yaml
```

Pods with Version Labels

Istio will do routing based on application versions. To select nodes of a version, they must be labeled accordingly. Thus, all our deployments and pods must have app and version labels applied. Istio also uses these labels in metrics and telemetry data collection. Let's now label our web service.

```
apiVersion: apps/v1
kind: Deployment
metadata:
  name: webapp-deployment-6.2
  labels:
    app: webapp
    version: v6.2
spec:
  replicas: 1
```

```
selector:
  matchLabels:
    app: webapp
template:
  metadata:
    labels:
      app: webapp
      version: v6.2
  spec:
    containers:

# REMOVED FOR BREVITY
```

In the previous configuration, we have added `version: v6.2` to the deployment and template. Kubernetes tags only support string values; thus, the version of our application is defined as v6.2. Lastly, apply the previous configuration with the following command:

```
$kubectl apply -f ../config/webapp-deployent.yaml
```

Declared Pod Ports

Istio routing can be applied only if the port exposed by the pod is declared in the deployment template. Ports can be declared as a list for the `containerPort` field in the deployment template. According to the Kubernetes documentation, the `containerPort` field is for information purposes. A container can run a service listening on 0.0.0.0 and a port. This port will be accessible from all containers in the cluster. Istio routing will be bypassed if it is applicable to ports that are not part of the deployment template.

```
apiVersion: apps/v1
kind: Deployment
metadata:
  name: webapp-deployment-6.2
```

```
# Removed FOR BREVITY
    containers:
    - name: webapp
      image: web-app:6.0
      imagePullPolicy: Never
      ports:
      - containerPort: 5000
      readinessProbe:
        httpGet:
          path: /health
          port: 5000
        initialDelaySeconds: 40
```

In the previous configuration, we declared 5000 as the port exposed by our container. Apply the previous configuration with the following command:

```
$kubectl apply -f ../config/webapp-deployent.yaml
```

So far we have looked at the prerequisites for Istio routing. Let's now understand how it works before configuring it. Request routing is configured in a service mesh using the `VirtualService` and `DestinationRule` components. Figure 4-5 depicts the interactions between the various involved components.

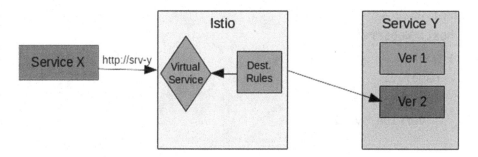

Figure 4-5. *Destination resolution*

The following interactions are involved, as noted in Figure 4-5:

1. Service X tries to connect to service Y using a fully qualified domain name.

2. The service Y FQDN is looked up by a virtual service to determine whether it needs to be handled.

3. If so, then `DestinationRule` is matched to determine the end Kubernetes services.

4. Lastly, the call is forwarded to the required service Y.

Destination Rules

`DestinationRule` resolves a request destination location into a network address in the Kubernetes cluster. In the previous section, you learned that Istio prescribes version numbers to be part of pod labels. These labels can then be matched in `DestinationRule` to define a version-based service subset for request handling. Let's now configure some destination rules for our web service.

```
apiVersion: networking.istio.io/v1alpha3
kind: DestinationRule
metadata:
  name: webapp-destination
spec:
  host: webservice
  subsets:
  - name: v1
    labels:
      version: v6.2
```

The previous defined rule configures a simple destination rule v1. The host: webservice is used to select pods configured with the web service Kubernetes service. It then selects the nodes matching version: v6.2 labels from these sets of nodes to define subset v1. We can create the rule by using this:

```
$kubectl create -f ../config/webapp-destinationrules.yaml
```

After this, validate the created destination rules by using the following, as shown in Figure 4-6:

```
$istioctl get destinationrules:
```

DESTINATION-RULE NAME	HOST	SUBSETS	NAMESPACE	AGE
webapp-destination	webservice	v1	default	4d

Figure 4-6. *Destination rules*

In the previous configuration, the subsets section can be used to define multiple named subsets. Each of these subsets can then be configured with various VirtualService components.

```
apiVersion: networking.istio.io/v1alpha3
kind: DestinationRule
metadata:
  name: webapp-destination
spec:
  host: webservice
  subsets:
  - name: v1
    labels:
      version: v6.2
  - name: v0
    labels:
      version: v6.0
```

Update the rule by using the following command and then validate it using istioctl (see Figure 4-7):

```
$kubectl apply -f ../config/webapp-destinationrules.yaml
```

```
DESTINATION-RULE NAME    HOST          SUBSETS    NAMESPACE    AGE
webapp-destination       webservice    v1,v0      default      4d
```

Figure 4-7. *Multiple destination rules*

The DestinationRule component is supposed to be configured by service owners. The service owners not only can create distinct subsets but also can define connectionPool, load balancing, and outlier detection attributes for each of them. These settings determine how the consumer services connect to each of the respective nodes.

Connection Pool

Needless to say, pooling connections have benefits. In a service mesh where we have enabled a TLS handshake, the cost for every new connection is relatively high. Traditionally, we have added various connection pool drivers to our consumer application. But Istio provides out-of-the-box support for connection pools. The connectionPool configuration determines how a consumer service connects to this provider service. These settings must be fine-tuned by service owners. The connection pool settings are applicable to each host of the consumer service.

Istio connection pooling supports the keepAlive TCP method. Thus, not only can we use a pool but can reuse unused connections. The settings have a separate set of attributes to configure HTTP and TCP connection pools. These attributes enable us to fine-tune the HTTP connection reuse. The following are the most important attributes. We will not cover all of the attributes; refer to the Istio docs to learn more.

- `maxConnections`: This setting defines the upper limit for the number of connections to the service. The default value is set to 1024. This setting is applicable to TCP and HTTPv1.0 services.

- `connectionTimeout`: This setting defines the TCP connection timeout.

- `Http2MaxRequets`: This setting is applicable to HTTPv2.0. In HTTP 2.0 we make a single connection and reuse it for multiple requests. The settings define the upper limit for the number of requests that can be performed over a connection.

- `Http1MaxPendingRequests`: This setting defines the upper limit for the number of HTTP requests pending over a connection. This is also applicable to HTTPv2.0/GRPC services.

We can configure `connectionPool` attributes for each of the defined subsets.

```
apiVersion: networking.istio.io/v1alpha3
kind: DestinationRule
metadata:
  name: webapp-destination
spec:
  host: webservice
  subsets:
  - name: v0
    labels:
      version: v6.0
    trafficPolicy:
      connectionPool:
```

```
tcp:
    maxConnections: 100
    connectTimeout: 30ms
    tcpKeepalive:
        time: 7200s
        interval: 75s
```

In the previous code, we have configured `connectionPool` for v6.0 version of the service. The settings configure the maximum number of pooled resources as well as the connection and keepalive timeouts.

Note   It is important to note that the connection pool is monitored by the Envoy proxy. Envoy initiates the following circuit breakers if the configured limits are breached:

- **upstream_cx_overflow**: This circuit breaker is thrown when a service in the cluster breaches the maximum number of connections. This is often applicable to TCP and HTTP/1 services. Since HTTP/2 reuses the same connection, the limit is not applicable to it.

- **upstream_rq_pending_overflow**: This circuit breaker is thrown when a service in the cluster makes more HTTP requests than the configured limits. This is often applicable to HTTP/2.

- **upstream_rq_retry_overflow**: This circuit breaker is thrown when a service in the cluster makes more HTTP requests than the configured limits.

Load Balancing

Load balancing is the process of distributing requests among the different hosts of the selected destination. There are various mechanisms to achieve this. It can be configured with the `loadBalancer` settings. Istio supports the following types of load balancers:

- **Round robin**: This selects a host at random. This performs better if there is no health checking enabled for the selected pods.

- **Least connection**: The method performs O(1) lookup to determine two healthy hosts. It picks the one that is serving the least number of connections.

- **Random**: The method selects a host randomly. It performs better if there is no health checking enabled for the selected pods.

- **Consistent hash**: This method configures hashing based on request headers or cookies.

Since we are running a single instance of our web service, we will not configure load balancing for it.

Outlier Detection

Outlier detection is the process of determining unhealthy hosts in a load-balanced cluster. The process is then followed by removing the hosts from the load-balanced set. In Istio, Envoy circuit breakers are used to keep track of errors caused by the destination host. These errors can be caused by the service or the respective sidecar. In both cases, the host will be marked as unhealthy.

Istio only records consecutive errors thrown by a service. The default value is set to five consecutive errors. For TCP-based services, connection timeouts are counted as errors. While HTTP-based services, 5xx HTTP responses are also recorded as errors. When recording these errors, Istio, by default, evicts a service for 30 seconds from the load-balanced set. After the elapsed interval, the host is back in the load-balanced set and is re-evaluated at an interval of 10 seconds (by default). These timings can be altered by configuring the various attributes available.

In summary, we have configured subsets in DestinationRule. The subsets select nodes by matching the configured selectors. Istio then applies the connectionPool, load balancing, and outlier detection settings to them. These settings can be configured at the DestinationRule level. The settings will then be applied to each and every subset created under it. But if there is any configuration at the subset level, it will then override the DestinationRule-level configuration.

```
apiVersion: networking.istio.io/v1alpha3
kind: DestinationRule
metadata:
  name: webapp-destination
spec:
  host: webservice 1
  trafficPolicy:
    connectionPool:
      tcp:
        maxConnections: 100
        connectTimeout: 30ms
  subsets:
  - name: v1
    labels:
      version: v6.2
```

```
- name: v0
  labels:
    version: v6.0
```

In the previous code, we have configured connectionPool for all subsets (v0 and v1) defined in the webapp-destination DestinationRule component. The settings configure a maximum number of pooled resources and connection timeouts. As discussed previously, a DestinationRule component is effective only when a virtualService sends a request to it. In the next section, we will cover how we can define a virtualService and work with different configurations of it.

VirtualService

The Istio VirtualService component has a behavior that is similar to the Service component in Kubernetes. Basically a VirtualService is an abstraction that maps a request to a service defined in the service mesh. The service can be either a Kubernetes service or a service defined by Istio. The destination resolution by a VirtualService component is performed using DestinationRule. A VirtualService component can perform destination resolution to handle the following use cases:

- Single version of the service

- Lookup based on HTTP headers to select a service

- Weighted comparison between a set of selected service versions

The VirtualService abstraction decouples request routing from application deployment. Thus, in a cluster, we can deploy many versions of the same service and distribute the load among them in a finely controlled manner.

Forwarding

In our previous example, we defined v0 and v1 subsets. The following configuration sends all requests to the v1 subset:

```
apiVersion: networking.istio.io/v1alpha3
kind: VirtualService
metadata:
  name: webservice-vs
spec:
  hosts:
    - webservice
  http:
  - route:
    - destination:
        host: webservice
        subset: v1
```

The previous configuration is one of the simplest forms of VirtualService. It routes all requests from our virtual service to only a specific version of the destination service. See Figure 4-8.

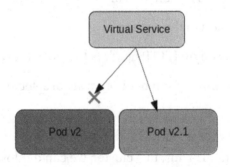

Figure 4-8. *Single service*

The VirtualService behavior is configured using the following attributes:

- The hosts attribute defines the list of hostnames or host and port that must be matched for a request. The host address can be a service name that resolves into an FQDN using DNS (Kubernetes DNS in our example). It can also be a host IP and port.

- After the request is matched, it is then forwarded to the subset v1 of the destination host.

We can create the virtual service as shown in Figure 4-8 by using this:

```
$kubectl create -f ../config/webapp-simple-vs.yaml
```

After this, validate the created virtual service by using this (see Figure 4-9):

```
$istioctl get virtualservices
```

VIRTUAL-SERVICE NAME	GATEWAYS	HOSTS	#HTTP	#TCP	NAMESPACE	AGE
webservice-vs		webservice	1	0	default	11s

Figure 4-9. *v1 virtual service*

The previous configuration sends all requests to v6.2 of the web service. Let's validate this by loading the front-end web service (http://10.152.183.146/) a couple of times. We can see that all our responses are from 6.2 version of webapp (see Figure 4-10).

This is content from remote service

[6.2]Welcome user! current time is 2019-07-21 04:18:55.993673

Figure 4-10. *Request routing to 6.2 versions*

Rewrite

In the previous example, we created request forwarding, but a virtual service is also capable of performing request rewrites. This behavior is configured using the following attributes:

- The match attribute defines which requests will perform the rewrite. The matching can be based on a URI, HTTP headers, query parameters, an HTTP method, scheme, etc. To perform the rewrite, we must specify the URI, along with other selectors (if required).

- The rewrite attribute defines the new URI patch to which the request needs to be sent. Depending on the type of match, the rewrite will replace only the matching URI part. This means if we are matching the URI prefix, then the rewrite will only change the prefix. If the complete URI is matched, then a rewrite will change the complete URI.

- The subset attribute defines the destination host to which the rewritten request is forwarded.

The following configuration matches the /hello request and sends it to the / path of our web service version 6.2:

```
apiVersion: networking.istio.io/v1alpha3
kind: VirtualService
metadata:
  name: webservice-rewrite-vs
spec:
  hosts:
    - webservice
  http:
  - match:
```

```
   - uri:
       prefix: /hello
   rewrite:
     uri: /
   route:
   - destination:
       host: webservice
       subset: v1
```

We can create the virtual service by using this:

```
$kubectl create -f ../config/webapp-rewrite-vs.yaml
```

Now there are two virtual services that are handling the webservice host. This will create issues, so let's first delete the previously created virtual service by using this:

```
$kubectl delete -f ../config/webapp-simple-vs.yaml
```

But how do we validate our changes? We can change our front-end container every time. Alternatively, we can use the exec command provided by Kubernetes. The exec command allows us to execute commands in one of our containers. Thus, we can execute the wget command to validate the request routing.

```
$kubectl exec pod/frontend-deployment-c9c975b4-p8z2t -- wget
-O - http://webservice/hello
Defaulting container name to frontend.
Use 'kubectl describe pod/frontend-deployment-c9c975b4-p8z2t
-n default' to see all of the containers in this pod.
[6.0]Welcome user! current time is 2019-07-21 07:15:59.395367
Connecting to webservice (10.152.183.230:80)
-                  100% |*****************************|  62  0:00:00 ETA
```

HTTP Attributes Lookup

Istio is capable of performing an HTTP attributes lookup. As discussed in the previous section, the match attribute supports URIs, HTTP headers, query parameters, HTTP methods, schemes, etc. We can match any of the previously mentioned attributes and forward the request to a matching host.

```
apiVersion: networking.istio.io/v1alpha3
kind: VirtualService
metadata:
  name: webservice-httplookup-vs
spec:
  hosts:
    - webservice
  http:
  - match:
    - headers:
        x-upgrade:
          exact: "TRUE"
    route:
    - destination:
        host: webservice
        subset: v1
  - route :
    - destination:
        host: webservice
        subset: v0
```

In the previous configuration, we have configured the match attribute to look for an x-upgrade header. If the header is available, then it is forwarded to the newer version of the service. We have also added a default route to which all nonmatching requests are forwarded.

Note   An Istio configuration takes a string for all configuration parts of the `match` attribute. String likes `true`, TRUE, 25, etc., are converted to the appropriate data type and thus can't be directly passed. These values can be converted to strings by enclosing them in double quotes, as we have done in the previous configuration.

Let's apply the configuration.

```
$kubectl create -f code/config/webservice-httplookup-vs.yaml
```

After this, validate the created virtual service by using the following (see Figure 4-11):

```
$istioctl get virtualservices
```

Let's make sure we do not have any of our previously created virtual services.

VIRTUAL-SERVICE NAME	GATEWAYS	HOSTS	#HTTP	#TCP	NAMESPACE	AGE
webservice-httplookup-vs		webservice	2	0	default	3s

Figure 4-11. *HTTP-based virtual service*

Let's first make a request without setting the headers.

```
$kubectl exec pod/frontend-deployment-c9c975b4-p8z2t -- wget
-O - http://webservice/
Defaulting container name to frontend.
Use 'kubectl describe pod/ frontend-deployment-c9c975b4-p8z2 -n
default' to see all of the containers in this pod.
[6.0]Welcome user! current time is 2019-07-21 11:19:35.349452
Connecting to webservice (10.152.183.230:80)
```

Now pass the appropriate header in the wget command line.

```
$kubectl exec frontend-deployment-c9c975b4-p8z2t -- wget -O -
--header='x-upgrade: TRUE' http://webservice/
Defaulting container name to frontend.
Use 'kubectl describe pod/frontend-deployment-c9c975b4-p8z2t -n
default' to see all of the containers in this pod.
[6.2]Welcome user! current time is 2019-07-21 11:19:28.565401
Connecting to webservice (10.152.183.230:80)
```

Weighted Distribution

Istio has the capability to distribute requests among various versions of a service in a configured ratio. The ratio is determined by the weight attribute of a destination. See Figure 4-12.

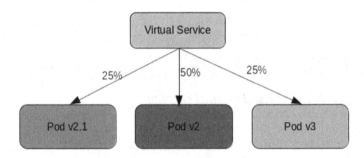

Figure 4-12. *Weight-distributed service*

The following configuration distributes traffic between the v0 and v1 subsets. For every four requests, we want to send three of them to the older versions and one to the new version.

```
apiVersion: networking.istio.io/v1alpha3
kind: VirtualService
metadata:
  name: webservice-wtdist-vs
```

```
spec:
  hosts:
    - webservice
  http:
  - route:
    - destination:
        host: webservice
        subset: v1
      weight: 25
    - destination:
        host: webservice
        subset: v0
      weight: 75
```

Apply the configuration using the following:

```
$kubectl create -f code/config/webservice-wtdist-vs.yaml
```

After this, validate the created virtual service by using the following:

```
$istioctl get virtualservices
```

Let's make sure we do not have any of our previously created virtual services. See Figure 4-13.

VIRTUAL-SERVICE NAME	GATEWAYS	HOSTS	#HTTP	#TCP	NAMESPACE	AGE
webservice-wtdist-vs		webservice	1	0	default	22m

Figure 4-13. *Weighted distribution virtual service*

Now make a wget request a couple of times. We can see that every fourth request is routed to v6.2, while the remaining ones are served from v6.0.

```
$kubectl exec pod/frontend-deployment-c9c975b4-p8z2t
-it -- sh -il
Defaulting container name to frontend.
```

```
Use 'kubectl describe pod/frontend-deployment-c9c975b4-p8z2t -n
default' to see all of the containers in this pod.
frontend-deployment-c9c975b4-p8z2t:/#  wget -qO - http://
webservice
[6.0]Welcome user! current time is 2019-07-22 17:52:24.164478
frontend-deployment-c9c975b4-p8z2t:/#
frontend-deployment-c9c975b4-p8z2t:/#  wget -qO - http://
webservice
[6.0]Welcome user! current time is 2019-07-22 17:52:28.977615
frontend-deployment-c9c975b4-p8z2t:/#
frontend-deployment-c9c975b4-p8z2t:/#  wget -qO - http://
webservice
[6.0]Welcome user! current time is 2019-07-22 17:52:33.068721
frontend-deployment-c9c975b4-p8z2t:/#
frontend-deployment-c9c975b4-p8z2t:/#  wget -qO - http://
webservice
[6.2]Welcome user! current time is 2019-07-22 17:52:41.291074
frontend-deployment-c9c975b4-p8z2t:/#
frontend-deployment-c9c975b4-p8z2t:/#
```

In this example, we have an interactive session unlike the previous examples where we were executing a command in the container. The interactive session allows us to execute multiple commands one after another.

Note   Up to now we have configured the destination as a Kubernetes service and version-based subsets. But we can also distribute requests among different Kubernetes services, without the subset definition. In our example, the host attribute can refer to the Kubernetes services prod.webservice and test.webservice.

Canary Releases

A canary release is the process of releasing software to a subset of users. The process allows developers to validate the new version with a subset of users before rolling it out to the entire user base. If there are issues found with the new version, the release can be rolled back to a smaller set of servers. This helps in mitigating the impact and improving service uptime. Kubernetes also supports canary testing by managing the instance/replication counts of the application. But this process of managing a pod instance quickly becomes complicated and difficult to support. Istio, on the other hand, has rich support for selecting requests and thus can do the job quite easily.

A canary release is supplementary to the blue-green deployment discussed in the first chapter. As a general process, the following steps are undertaken:

1. Using a blue-green deployment process, we deploy the new version on a small number of containers.

2. When the services are marked as healthy, instead of routing all requests, we start with a percentage of requests.

3. We continue testing the newer version until we are satisfied with the results.

4. Lastly, this change is deployed on the entire fleet serving all users.

In the previous sections, we discussed simple request matching. The match method validates a simple attribute and does request forwarding. But this is not good enough for a fairly advanced use case like a canary release. The matching needs to handle multiple clauses joined together with operations like AND/OR. The Istio match attribute supports both these operations in the following manner:

- The AND operation is performed by nesting multiple conditions under a single match attribute.

- The OR operation is performed by having separate conditions under a single match attribute.

Note   In YAML syntax, the values for a list are created by placing a hyphen (-) before each value. This means a condition with a prefixed hyphen is a different value.

```
apiVersion: networking.istio.io/v1alpha3
kind: VirtualService
metadata:
  name: webservice-and-or-vs
spec:
  hosts:
    - webservice
  http:
  - match:
    - headers:
        x-upgrade:
          exact: "TRUE"
    - queryParams:
        ver:
          exact: v1
        method:
          exact: GET
```

```
  route:
  - destination:
      host: webservice
      subset: v1
  - route :
    - destination:
        host: webservice
        subset: v0
```

The previous configuration would try to match either (OR operation) of the following two conditions:

- The HTTP header has the correct value for x-upgrade.

- queryString has ver=v1 *and* the HTTP method is GET.

Deploy and validate the previous configuration.

```
$kubectl exec frontend-deployment-c9c975b4-p8z2t -- wget -O -
--header='x-upgrade: TRUE' http://webservice/
Defaulting container name to frontend.
Use 'kubectl describe pod/frontend-deployment-c9c975b4-p8z2t -n
default' to see all of the containers in this pod.
[6.2]Welcome user! current time is 2019-07-21 18:09:25.296747
Connecting to webservice (10.152.183.230:80)

$kubectl exec frontend-deployment-c9c975b4-p8z2t -- wget -O -
http://webservice/?ver=v1
Defaulting container name to frontend.
Use 'kubectl describe pod/frontend-deployment-c9c975b4-p8z2t -n
default' to see all of the containers in this pod.
[6.2]Welcome user! current time is 2019-07-21 18:10:03.728678
Connecting to webservice (10.152.183.230:80)
```

Since we are making new multiple rules, it is important to understand how Istio evaluates them. Istio evaluates all matching rules based on the order of their declaration. The first declared matching condition is evaluated first. If the condition fails, Istio evaluates the next condition. In the following configuration, we have added the default route in the first position:

```
apiVersion: networking.istio.io/v1alpha3
kind: VirtualService
metadata:
  name: webservice-httplookup-vs
spec:
  hosts:
    - webservice
  http:
  - route :
    - destination:
        host: webservice
        subset: v0
  - match:
    - headers:
        x-upgrade:
          exact: "TRUE"
    route:
    - destination:
        host: webservice
        subset: v1
```

Let's deploy and validate the previous configuration.

```
$ kubectl exec frontend-deployment-c9c975b4-p8z2t -- wget -O -
--header='x-upgrade: TRUE' http://webservice/
Defaulting container name to frontend.
```

```
Use 'kubectl describe pod/frontend-deployment-c9c975b4-p8z2t -n
default' to see all of the containers in this pod.
[6.0]Welcome user! current time is 2019-07-21 18:19:55.581391
Connecting to webservice (10.152.183.230:80)
```

This means that service owners must always make sure that the most specific rule is declared first. All rules for matching should be declared from the most specific to the generic.

A production-ready Istio configuration would have match conditions, rule precedence, and weighted distribution of requests. Thus, for our sample web service, the following configuration includes all these aspects:

```
apiVersion: networking.istio.io/v1alpha3
kind: VirtualService
metadata:
  name: webservice-canary-vs
spec:
  hosts:
    - webservice
  http:
  - match:
    - headers:
        host:
          exact: "user1.com"
    route:
    - destination:
        host: webservice
        subset: v1
      weight: 10
    - destination:
        host: webservice
        subset: v0
      weight: 90
```

```
- route :
  - destination:
      host: webservice
      subset: v0
```

As per the previous configuration, all requests are served by the v0 service except the ones that originate from `user1.com`. Also, 10 percent of the requests originating from `user1.com` are served by the v1 web service; all the remaining ones are routed to the v0 version.

Summary

In this chapter, we worked with `VirtualService` and `DestinationRule` to perform request routing. We started the discussion by deploying multiple versions of our webapp to the Kubernetes cluster. Next, we made sure that we followed Istio's prescribed naming conventions for ports and pods. After this, we defined version subsets using destination rules. The defined destination rules are evaluated when connected by a virtual service. Thus, we built different virtual service configurations for single service routing, HTTP attributes routing, and weighted routing. Lastly, we looked at canary deployment. We found out how the process can help to mitigate application downtime and improve application stability. We built canary deployment examples using multiple match conditions, destination precedence, and weighted request distribution. In this chapter, the focus was on service request routing. In the next chapter, we will look at configuring the `Ingress`, `Egress`, and `ServiceEntry` components for interacting with the world outside of the Kubernetes cluster.

CHAPTER 5

Istio Gateway

In the previous chapter, we discussed Istio request routing. We showed how to configure a virtual service and deployment rules to interact with different versions of our application. Up to now, all our services have been deployed in the Kubernetes cluster. But in real-world scenarios, we need to interact with components outside the Kubernetes cluster. There are many applicable use cases. For example, applications running inside the cluster may interact with a database deployed outside the cluster. Similarly, there can be user applications deployed in the cluster. These applications will need to be accessed from the Internet. In this chapter, we will show how to configure the Istio gateway and service entry, which will enable us to fulfill the discussed behaviors.

Ingress

The term *ingress* is defined as an entry facade. It is a location that provides service access to all externally originated requests. The ingress is configured using an Istio gateway. It is an edge component that is used to expose services outside the cluster. It can be used to expose HTTP as well as TCP services. The gateway provides capabilities such as TLS termination and request forwarding.

In most production clusters, a gateway is configured in conjunction with a Kubernetes load balancer service. In such scenarios, the Kubernetes service creates a cloud-based L4 load balancer. The load balancer has a

© Rahul Sharma, Avinash Singh 2020
R. Sharma and A. Singh, *Getting Started with Istio Service Mesh*,
https://doi.org/10.1007/978-1-4842-5458-5_5

public IP address that can be accessed by the world outside the Kubernetes
cluster. When the load balancer receives a request, then it delegates the
request to the matching Istio gateway. The gateway then uses Istio traffic
routing and dispatches the request to the appropriate service version.
Istio also applies the necessary telemetry and security to the gateway. See
Figure 5-1.

The Istio gateway can be compared to the Kubernetes ingress
resource, but unlike the ingress resource, the gateway does not
have any traffic routing rules configured with it. The gateway
delegates all inbound traffic to a virtual service and applies the
relevant routing configuration. In summary, the gateway works at
L4, L5, and L6 only.

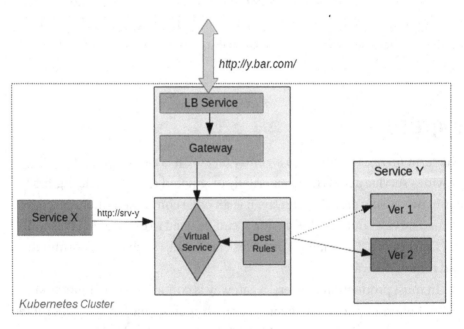

Figure 5-1. *Istio ingress*

Let's now extend the web service example from Chapter 4. Previously, in Chapter 1, we developed a polyglot application and deployed it to a Kubernetes cluster. The application had a Java-based front end and a Python-based back end. Both these applications were deployed in the same Kubernetes namespace. In Chapter 4, we extended the web service application. We deployed two versions of our web service to the Kubernetes cluster. Lastly, we routed the requests to both versions using the following virtual service and the associated distinationRules:

```
apiVersion: networking.istio.io/v1alpha3
kind: VirtualService
metadata:
 name: webservice-wtdist-vs
spec:
 hosts:
 - webservice
 http:
 - route:
 - destination:
 host: webservice
 subset: v1
 weight: 25
 - destination:
 host: webservice
 subset: v0
 weight: 75
```

The previous configuration sends one out of four requests to v1 versions and the remaining three to the v0 version. But this is applicable only to the services inside the Istio mesh. If we want to send requests from the external world, we need to create the following `ingress` gateway:

```
apiVersion: networking.istio.io/v1alpha3
kind: Gateway
metadata:
 name: webapp-gateway
spec:
 selector:
 istio: ingressgateway
 servers:
 - port:
 number: 80
 name: http
 protocol: HTTP
 hosts:
              - "*.greetings.com"
```

The previous gateway configures a load balancer to allow external HTTP traffic for `*.greetings.com` into the mesh. Next, we must configure the associated virtual service for handling the requests from the configured gateway.

```
apiVersion: networking.istio.io/v1alpha3
kind: VirtualService
metadata:
 name: webservice-wtdist-vs
spec:
 hosts:
 - webservice
 - webservice.greetings.com
```

```
gateways :
- webapp-gateway
http:
```

##*REST REMOVED FOR BREVITY*

In the previous configuration, we have modified the webservice-wtdist-vs virtual service to handle webapp-gateway. This is done by adding the gateway name to the gateways field. Additionally, the virtual service must match the host gateway it is configured for. It can be an exact match or a subset of the wildcard supported by the gateway. Thus, we have added webservice.greetings.com to the hosts list.

Now we need to test the configuration. To do so, we need the address of the load balancer. Execute the following command to determine the address (see Figure 5-2):

```
$kubectl get svc istio-ingressgateway -n istio-system
```

NAME	TYPE AGE	CLUSTER-IP	EXTERNAL-IP	PORT(S)
istio-ingressgateway /TCP,15031:30167/TCP	LoadBalancer 20d	10.152.183.243	185.199.183.153	80:31380/TCP,443:31390/TCP,31400:31400/TCP,15011:30838/TCP

Figure 5-2. *Ingress gateway address*

The EXTERNAL-IP value shows the IP address of the load balancer. This works in cloud-based environments like AWS, Azure, and so on. In our case, since we have deployed our application to Minikube, the EXTERNAL-IP column says <PENDING>. In such scenarios, we can skip the load balancer and use the nodePort address of istio-ingressgateway. In our case, the node IP address is the address of the Minikube server, and the port is 31380. We can determine the IP address using this:

```
$ minikube ip
192.168.1.27
```

Since we have exposed the service to the outside world, we can validate it by executing `curl` commands on a host outside the cluster. Since we do not own `greetings.com`, we will be unable to handle any of its subdomains. But this is not required. The gateways checks for the `Host` header field. We can set the header field by using the appropriate `curl` options.

```
$curl -v -HHost:webservice.greetings.com
http://192.168.1.27:31380/
* Trying 192.168.1.27...
* TCP_NODELAY set
* Connected to 192.168.1.27 port 31380 (#0)
> GET / HTTP/1.1
> Host:webservice.greetings.com
> User-Agent: curl/7.58.0
> Accept: */*
>
< HTTP/1.1 200 OK
< content-type: text/html; charset=utf-8
< content-length: 62
< server: istio-envoy
< date: Sun, 04 Aug 2019 08:04:22 GMT
< x-envoy-upstream-service-time: 8
<
* Connection #0 to host 192.168.1.27 left intact
[6.0]Welcome user! current time is 2019-08-04 08:04:22.383137
```

In the previous output, we can see that the gateway matches the header field and routes the request appropriately. We can try executing `curl` a couple of times. We can see that every fourth request is served from the new version of the web service.

```
[6.0]Welcome user! current time is 2019-08-04 14:18:13.330905
[6.0]Welcome user! current time is 2019-08-04 14:18:13.359514
```

```
[6.0]Welcome user! current time is 2019-08-04 14:18:13.381638
[6.2]Welcome user! current time is 2019-08-04 14:18:13.402238
```

In the previous chapter, we configured a virtual service for sidecar proxies in the mesh. But once a virtual service is configured using gateways, the virtual service is removed from each of the Istio service proxies. We can validate this by using our tests from Chapter 4, as shown here:

```
$kubectl exec pod/frontend-deployment-c9c975b4-p8z2t -it -- sh -il
Defaulting container name to frontend.
Use 'kubectl describe pod/frontend-deployment-c9c975b4-p8z2t -n
default' to see all of the containers in this pod.
frontend-deployment-c9c975b4-p8z2t:/# wget -qO - http://
webservice/
[6.2]Welcome user! current time is 2019-08-04 16:55:03.230895
frontend-deployment-c9c975b4-p8z2t:/# wget -qO - http://
webservice/
[6.0]Welcome user! current time is 2019-08-04 16:55:07.876481
frontend-deployment-c9c975b4-p8z2t:/# wget -qO - http://
webservice/
[6.0]Welcome user! current time is 2019-08-04 16:55:12.130989
frontend-deployment-c9c975b4-p8z2t:/# wget -qO - http://
webservice/
[6.2]Welcome user! current time is 2019-08-04 16:55:14.911224
```

In the previous output, we executed wget commands from our front-end pod. We can see that the requests are handled in a round-robin manner across the two versions of our web service. If we want to apply the same routing to all service proxies inside the mesh, we need to add the mesh keyword to the gateways field.

```
apiVersion: networking.istio.io/v1alpha3
kind: VirtualService
```

```
metadata:
 name: webservice-wtdist-vs
spec:
 hosts:
 - webservice
 - webservice.example.com
 gateways :
 - webapp-gateway
 - mesh
 http:
# REMOVED for BREVITY
```

We can validate the previous configuration using the previously executed commands. Our requests should be handled in terms of the configured weights.

---

mesh is the default behavior when the gateways attribute is omitted.

Secure Sockets Layer

Istio gateways provide complete support for SSL exchange. We can set up an SSL certificate exchange in the gateway. Alternatively, the gateway can act as a pass-through medium. This way, SSL termination can be handled by HAProxy or Nginx running in the Kubernetes cluster.

Before we can enable SSL, we need a certificate and a private key. In this section, we will use a self-signed certificate. Self-signed certificates can be generated using openssl. We will cover a few essential steps, but certification generation is beyond the scope of the book. You can proceed to the next section if you already have the certificate.

We will generate a self-signed certificate using the following `openssl` command. It will be followed by prompts asking for a few more details.

```
$openssl req -x509 -newkey rsa:4096 -keyout key.pem -out cert.
pem -days 365
Generating a RSA private key
.................................................++++
...................................................++++
writing new private key to 'key.pem'
Enter PEM pass phrase:
Verifying - Enter PEM pass phrase:
-----
You are about to be asked to enter information that will be
incorporated
into your certificate request.
What you are about to enter is what is called a Distinguished
Name or a DN.
There are quite a few fields but you can leave some blank
For some fields there will be a default value,
If you enter '.', the field will be left blank.
-----
Country Name (2 letter code) [AU]: US
State or Province Name (full name) [Some-State]:
Locality Name (eg, city) []:
Organization Name (eg, company) [Internet Widgits Pty
Ltd]:packt
Organizational Unit Name (eg, section) []:istio-book
Common Name (e.g. server FQDN or YOUR name) []:*.greetings.com
Email Address []:email@greetings .com
```

Let's make sure that the common name has the ∗.greetings. com wildcard, which will allow us to use the certificate for our different services. One more thing to note is that Kubernetes will be unable to read the generated key as it is protected by a passphrase. We can remove the passphrase by using the following command:

```
$ openssl rsa -in key.pem -out key2.pem
Enter pass phrase for key.pem:
writing RSA key
```

Now we have the required cert.pem and key2.pem files. We can use them to configure SSL in different ways.

Configure istio-ingressgateway-certs

Kubernetes provides good support for secret management. We can create a named secret in the cluster. A pod can then be configured with the .spec. volumes[].secret.secretName attribute. Kubernetes will mount the named secret on the specified file location of the pod.

```
apiVersion: v1
kind: Pod
metadata:
 name: mypod
spec:
 containers:
 - name: mypod
 image: redis
 volumeMounts:
 - name: foo
 mountPath: "/etc/foo"
 readOnly: true
 volumes:
 - name: foo
```

```
secret:
secretName: mysecret
```

In our case, we are not going to configure `istio-ingressgateway`. Alternatively, the Istio gateway has been configured with the `istio-ingressgateway-certs` named `secret`. Thus, all we need is to create a Kubernetes secret with that name.

```
$ kubectl create -n istio-system secret tls istio-
ingressgateway-certs --key key2.pem --cert cert.pem
secret "istio-ingressgateway-certs" created
```

We can validate the secret using the following (see Figure 5-3):

```
$kubectl describe secret istio-ingressgateway-certs -n istio-
system
```

```
Name:           istio-ingressgateway-certs
Namespace:      istio-system
Labels:         <none>
Annotations:    <none>

Type:  kubernetes.io/tls

Data
====
tls.crt:   2094 bytes
tls.key:   3247 bytes
```

Figure 5-3. *Istio secret*

The `istio-ingressgateway-certs` secret has been configured for the `/etc/istio/ingressgateway-certs` file path. This means that Kubernetes mounts the key and certificate files at the previous specified path. Now we can configure the certificate in the following manner:

```
apiVersion: networking.istio.io/v1alpha3
kind: Gateway
```

```
metadata:
 name: webapp-gateway
spec:
 selector:
 istio: ingressgateway
 servers:
 - port:
 number: 443
 name: https
 protocol: HTTPS
 tls:
 mode: SIMPLE
 serverCertificate: /etc/istio/ingressgateway-certs/tls.crt
 privateKey: /etc/istio/ingressgateway-certs/tls.key
 hosts:
 - "*.greetings.com"
```

In the previous configuration we have configured the HTTPS protocol on port 443. We have also provided the certificate with the key. The key and the certificate are named tls.key and tls.crt, respectively. We have enabled tls.mode as SIMPLE. This is the standard SSL configuration, where the gateway is not validating the identity of the client. This is all that is required; we can now validate the gateway using curl.

```
$for i in 1 2 3 4; do curl -HHost:webservice.greetings.com
--resolve webservice.greetings.com:31390:127.0.0.1 -k https://
webservice.greetings.com:31390/; echo "; done
[6.0]Welcome user! current time is 2019-08-10 18:16:05.814646
[6.0]Welcome user! current time is 2019-08-10 18:16:05.843160
[6.0]Welcome user! current time is 2019-08-10 18:16:05.872700
[6.2]Welcome user! current time is 2019-08-10 18:16:05.901381
```

In the previous `curl` command, we have used a couple of options besides the -HHost header.

- `--resolve webservice.greetings.com:31390:127.0.0.1`: This will set `webservice.greetings.com:31390:` to `localhost` as we are using NodePort.

- `-k`: Since we have added a self-signed certificate, the `curl` will fail unless we enable insecure access.

Configure istio-ingressgateway-ca-certs

Up to now we have configured server-side TLS. This is good for end-user applications. But often there is a need for mutual TLS authentication. The Istio gateway can be configured for mutual TLS using client-side SSL certificates. Here as well the certificate chain can be loaded into the `istio-ingressgateway-ca-certs` named Kubernetes `secret`.

```
$ kubectl create -n istio-system secret tls istio-
ingressgateway-ca-certs --cert cert.pem
secret "istio-ingressgateway-ca-certs" created
```

The `istio-ingressgateway-ca-certs` secret has been configured for the `/etc/istio/ingressgateway-ca-certs` file path. Now we can configure the client's certificate chain in the following manner:

```
apiVersion: networking.istio.io/v1alpha3
kind: Gateway
metadata:
 name: webapp-gateway

# REMOVED FOR BREVITY

tls:
mode: MUTUAL
```

```
serverCertificate: /etc/istio/ingressgateway-certs/tls.crt
privateKey: /etc/istio/ingressgateway-certs/tls.key
caCertificates: /etc/istio/ingressgateway-ca-certs/ca-chain.
cert.pem
hosts:
        - "*.greetings.com"
```

In the previous configuration, we enabled MUTUAL TLS authentication. The client certificate chain is named `ca-chain.cert.pem`. We can now validate the gateway using `curl`. We will pass a client certificate and key by using the `cacerts` and `key` options, respectively.

```
$for i in 1 2 3 4; do curl -HHost:webservice.greetings.com
--resolve webservice.greetings.com:31390:127.0.0.1 --cacerts
client.certs.pem --key client.key.pem https://webservice.
greetings.com:31390/; echo "; done
[6.0]Welcome user! current time is 2019-08-10 19:16:05.814646
[6.0]Welcome user! current time is 2019-08-10 19:16:05.843160
[6.0]Welcome user! current time is 2019-08-10 19:16:05.872700
[6.2]Welcome user! current time is 2019-08-10 19:16:05.901381
```

Up to now we have configured TLS termination in our gateway. But the gateway also has a PASSTHROUGH mode in which it does not perform any termination. The responsibility of the termination is delegated to the virtual service. We will leave it to you to try to configure TLS termination with Nginx or HAProxy.

External Service Access

So far, we have exposed our services to the external world. But how about consuming services running outside the cluster? Services running inside an Istio mesh can access services outside the cluster. The default Istio configuration does not apply any restrictions to external service access.

This looks like it's a simple default setup, but it may not be what we want. Often businesses have requirements to monitor and control traffic going outside the organization. Previously we saw all traffic flowing through the sidecar proxy. Thus, depending on how the mesh is configured, the following things can be accomplished:

- Allow/deny all external access

- Allow access to limited services

- Control permissions to allow access

By default Istio is configured in ALLOW_ANY mode. This configuration will bypass the proxy for all services unknown to the mesh. In this mode, the requests are not routed to sidecars. Instead, they are directly handled by the application pod network. See Figure 5-4.

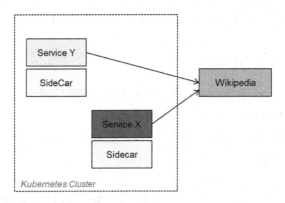

Figure 5-4. *Sidecar bypass*

We can validate Istio mode by using the following command:

```
$kubectl get configmap istio -n istio-system -o yaml |grep -o
"mode: .*"
mode: ALLOW_ANY\n\nlocalityLbSetting:\n {}\n \n\n# The
namespace to treat
```

We can now try to access Wikipedia from one of our mesh nodes. We can execute wget commands to determine the behavior.

```
$ kubectl exec pod/frontend-deployment-c9c975b4-p8z2t -it -- sh -il
frontend-deployment-c9c975b4-p8z2t:/# wget -qSO - http://
en.wikipedia.org/ >/dev/null
 HTTP/1.1 301 Moved Permanently
 Date: Sun, 11 Aug 2019 14:36:07 GMT
 Content-Type: text/html; charset=utf-8
```

We can see that we are able to get to en.wikipedia.org with a 301 response code. Now let's change the mode to REGISTRY_ONLY. Istio configuration is stored in istio named configmap. Let's update it and check the behavior.

```
$ kubectl get configmap istio -n istio-system -o yaml | sed
's/mode: ALLOW_ANY/mode: REGISTRY_ONLY/g' | kubectl replace -n
istio-system -f -
configmap/istio replaced
```

```
$ kubectl exec pod/frontend-deployment-c9c975b4-p8z2t -it -- sh -il
Defaulting container name to frontend.
frontend-deployment-c9c975b4-p8z2t:/# wget -qSO - http://
en.wikipedia.org/
 HTTP/1.1 502 Bad Gateway
wget: server returned error: HTTP/1.1 502 Bad Gateway
```

We can see that the location is no longer accessible. It returns a 502 response, signaling that the proxy configuration needs to be looked at. We need to have controlled access to a limited set of locations. We can configure this using the following components.

Service Entry

A ServiceEntry is a manner by which services external to the mesh can be configured in the Istio service registry. Often it is helpful to configure externally running business components. Once a service entry is configured, all traffic to the service is monitored by Istio. See Figure 5-5.

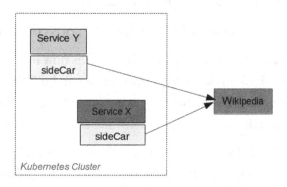

Figure 5-5. *Service entry*

Let's continue our previous example and enable access for en. wikipedia.org. We can configure its service entry endpoint with the following configuration:

```
---
apiVersion: networking.istio.io/v1alpha3
kind: ServiceEntry
metadata:
 name: wikipedia
spec:
 hosts:
 - en.wikipedia.org
 ports:
 - number: 443
 name: https
```

```
protocol: HTTPS
resolution: DNS
location: MESH_EXTERNAL
```

The previous configuration has the following attributes:

- spec.hosts: This attribute defines the list of hosts that are configured using this service entry.

- spec.ports: This attribute defines the ports configured.

- spec.resolution: This attribute defines how the address lookup needs to performed. It can be DNS based or static if the host IP address is defined in the configuration.

- spec.location: This attribute defines where the service is located. The service location can be defined as INTERNAL or EXTERNAL. In the case of an EXTERNAL service, Istio disables the mutual TLS behavior.

Now apply the configuration to the Kubernetes cluster. We should be allowed to access Wikipedia.

```
$ kubectl create -f config/service-entry.yaml
serviceentry.networking.istio.io/wikipedia configured
virtualservice.networking.istio.io/wikipedia configured
$ kubectl exec pod/frontend-deployment-c9c975b4-p8z2t -it --
sh -il
Defaulting container name to frontend.
frontend-deployment-c9c975b4-p8z2t:/# wget -qSO - https://
en.wikipedia.org/
HTTP/1.1 302 Found
Date: Sun, 11 Aug 2019 16:44:19 GMT
Content-Type: text/html; charset=utf-8
```

```
Content-Length: 0
Connection: close
........

frontend-deployment-c9c975b4-p8z2t:/# wget -qSO - http://
en.wikipedia.org/
  HTTP/1.1 502 Bad Gateway
wget: server returned error: HTTP/1.1 502 Bad Gateway
```

We can see that only access to the HTTPS service is allowed. Access to the HTTP service fails with error. We can have the following configuration, which would allow access to both protocols:

```
---
apiVersion: networking.istio.io/v1alpha3
kind: ServiceEntry
metadata:
 name: wikipedia
spec:
 hosts:
 - en.wikipedia.org
 ports:
 - number: 80
 name: http
 protocol: HTTP
 - number: 443
 name: https
 protocol: HTTPS
 resolution: DNS
 location: MESH_EXTERNAL
```

Egress

In the previous section, we have restricted access to a limited set of external services. But still all services running in the mesh can connect to the available external services. Sometimes businesses have requirements that all external traffic must be evaluated to ensure that it follows the authorization rules. Every request must be inspected to restrict access to only authorized ones. Moreover, all traffic flowing outside the mesh must pass from a single location that is monitored. Istio defines an egress gateway for this purpose. This is a component that can intercept traffic exiting the service mesh. See Figure 5-6.

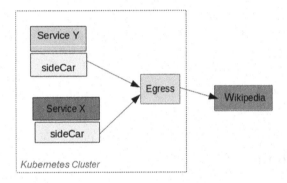

Figure 5-6. *Egress*

In our previous example, we configured direct access to en. wikipedia.org. Now in the following configuration, we have defined the egress host and intercepted all requests in it:

```
---
apiVersion: networking.istio.io/v1alpha3
kind: Gateway
metadata:
 name: wikipedia-egressgateway
spec:
```

```
selector:
istio: egressgateway
servers:
- port:
number: 80
name: http
protocol: HTTP
hosts:
- en.wikipedia.org
---
apiVersion: networking.istio.io/v1alpha3
kind: VirtualService
metadata:
 name: wiki-egress-gateway
spec:
 hosts:
 - en.wikipedia.org
 gateways:
 - wikipedia-egressgateway
 - mesh
 http:
 - match:
 - gateways:
 - mesh
port: 80
route:
- destination:
host: istio-egressgateway.istio-system.svc.cluster.local
port:
number: 80
weight: 100
```

```
- match:
- gateways:
- wikipedia-egressgateway
port: 80
route:
- destination:
host: en.wikipedia.org
port:
number: 80
weight: 100
---
apiVersion: networking.istio.io/v1alpha3
kind: ServiceEntry
metadata:
 name: wikipedia
spec:
 hosts:
 - en.wikipedia.org
 ports:
 - number: 80
 name: http
 protocol: HTTP
 resolution: DNS
 location: MESH_EXTERNAL
```

The previous configuration makes full use of the Istio routing capabilities. We have defined the following behavior in it:

- The service entry for en.wikipedia.org is configured so that it can be accessed by services inside the mesh.

- We defined wikipedia-egressgateway, which can handle the requests matching the specified host and port.

- We defined a `wiki-egress-gateway` virtual service. The service is the glue between the two components. It was configured for the following things:

  - The virtual service handles all requests for `en.wikipedia.org`. It is applicable to the gateway and all sidecar proxies.

  - Requests originating from sidecars are routed to `istio-egressgateway`. The gateway is deployed in the `istio-system` namespace.

  - The gateway matches these incoming requests for `wikipedia-egressgateway`. The virtual service then routes requests made by the gateway to the service entry host.

This way, all traffic leaving for `en.wikipedia.org` gets captured in the `istio-egress` gateway. Let's apply the configuration and test it using the `wget` command, as shown here:

```
$ kubectl create -f config/egress-gateway.yaml
gateway.networking.istio.io/wikipedia-egressgateway created
virtualservice.networking.istio.io/wiki-egress-gateway created
serviceentry.networking.istio.io/wikipedia created
```

```
$kubectl exec pod/frontend-deployment-c9c975b4-p8z2t -it -- sh
-il
frontend-deployment-c9c975b4-p8z2t:/# wget -qSO - http://
en.wikipedia.org/
HTTP/1.1 301 Moved Permanently
date: Sun, 11 Aug 2019 17:53:52 GMT
server: envoy

......
```

We can check the logs in the egressgateway. It should have captured the request.

```
$microk8s.kubectl logs -l istio=egressgateway -c istio-proxy -n
istio-system
......
[2019-08-11T17:53:52.214Z] "GET / HTTP/2" 301 - "-" "-" 0 0 395
355 "10.1.1.8" "Wget" "e2766b89-6b38-9744-9b02-fe9a32c6deea"
"en.wikipedia.org" "103.102.166.224:80" outbound|80||en.
wikipedia.org - 10.1.1.7:80 10.1.1.8:49880 -
```

Summary

In this chapter, we exposed our Kubernetes cluster to the external world. At the beginning, we defined the ingress gateway to allow external clients to connect to services running in the cluster. We also configured SSL termination on the edge gateway. Next we tried to control access to services running outside the cluster. We modified the default ALLOW_ANY policy to RESTRICTED_ONLY. Next, we configured the access to Istio services using the service entry. The service entry helped to monitor the external connection. Istio has provided egress gateways to have logging and access control for services defined by the service entry. Lastly, we worked with egress gateways to control service entry access.

CHAPTER 6

Service Resiliency

In the previous chapter, we went through how to configure the `Ingress`, `Egress`, and `ServiceEntry` components for interacting with the world outside of the Kubernetes cluster. We also went through how to encrypt requests between the microservices. So now we can deploy a secure application on Kubernetes with the ability and control to interact with the external network. In an ideal scenario, this setup should be sufficient to run a production application, but developers tend to forget the fallacies of distributed computing, as rightly pointed out by Peter Deutsch and the people at Sun Microsystems.

One must look at the fallacies in a distributed system and work on these while developing an application.

- The network is assumed to be reliable. This assumption leads to the development of little to no error handling on network errors. The results of this are network issues, application stalls, and long response times. When the network is restored, the stalled applications may not resume their regular functions and may require a restart.

- When using the network as a channel of communication, all responses are spontaneous; in other words, no latency is introduced in an operation.

© Rahul Sharma, Avinash Singh 2020
R. Sharma and A. Singh, *Getting Started with Istio Service Mesh*,
https://doi.org/10.1007/978-1-4842-5458-5_6

- There is no cap on bandwidth available for
  communication. In a real-world scenario, if a
  bandwidth threshold is crossed, the service is unable to
  communicate.

Figure 6-1 shows the challenges in a distributed system.

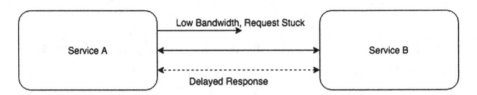

Figure 6-1. *Challenges in a distributed system*

In addition, there are failures if one of the service nodes is down or
not responding, even if the other ones are working fine. This leads to the
failure of a few of the requests and impacts end users. To resolve these
scenarios, one must do the following:

- Make an application handle network failures in the
  service to such an extent that it should recover with a
  network restore.

- The applications should adapt if latency increases and
  ultimately should not affect the end customer.

- In the case of a bandwidth block or other node failure,
  the service should retry or have a handler similar to a
  network outage scenario.

Earlier, developers used popular frameworks like CORBA, EJB, RMI, and
so on, to make network calls appear like a local method call, but this made
the system susceptible to cascading failure where one service failure was
propagated to all the calling services. Istio offers resilience implementations
via sidecars, helping developers to focus on the business logic.

Application Setup

Let's continue with the example from Chapters 4 and 5. See Figure 6-2.

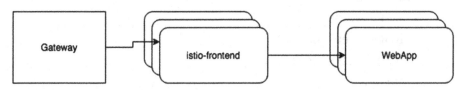

Figure 6-2. *Istio example application*

Let's do a quick walk-through of the config describing the istio-frontent deployment and service, webapp deployment, and service. See Listing 6-1, Listing 6-2, Listing 6-3, and Listing 6-4.

Listing 6-1. WebApp-deployment-v7.yaml

```
apiVersion: apps/v1
kind: Deployment
metadata:
  name: webapp-deployment-7.0
  labels:
    app: webapp
    version: v7.0
spec:
  replicas: 2
  selector:
    matchLabels:
      app: webapp
      version: v7.0
  template:
    metadata:
      labels:
```

```
      app: webapp
      version: v7.0
    spec:
      containers:
      - name: webapp
        image: web-app:7.0
        imagePullPolicy: Never
        ports:
        - containerPort: 5000
```

Listing 6-2. frontend-deployment.yaml

```
apiVersion: apps/v1   '
kind: Deployment
metadata:
  name: frontend-deployment
  labels:
    app: frontend
spec:
  replicas: 1
  selector:
    matchLabels:
      app: frontend
  template:
    metadata:
      labels:
        app: frontend
    spec:
      containers:
      - name: frontend
        image: frontend-app:1.0
```

```
      imagePullPolicy: Never
      ports:
      - containerPort: 8080
```

Listing 6-3. webapp-service.yaml to Expose Web App Deployment

```
apiVersion: v1
kind: Service
metadata:
  name: webservice
spec:
  selector:
    app: webapp
  ports:
  - name: http-webservice
    protocol: TCP
    port: 80
    targetPort: 5000
```

Listing 6-4. frontend-service.yaml to Expose Front-End
Deployment

```
apiVersion: v1
kind: Service
metadata:
  name: frontendservice
spec:
  selector:
    app: frontend
  ports:
  - protocol: TCP
    port: 80
    targetPort: 8080
```

Now a destination rule as an intermediate layer to interact with webapp-service. It has policies to allow the distribution of traffic across pods. See Listing 6-5.

Listing 6-5. Destination-rule.yaml

```
apiVersion: networking.istio.io/v1alpha3
kind: DestinationRule
metadata:
  name: webapp-destination
spec:
  host: webservice
  subsets:
  - name: v0
    labels:
      version: v7.0
```

Now define a gateway to make a front-end service accessible outside the Kubernetes cluster in Minikube. Without this, the pods and services are accessible only inside the private network via private IPs or domain names. See Listing 6-6.

Listing 6-6. gateway.yaml

```
apiVersion: networking.istio.io/v1alpha3
kind: Gateway
metadata:
  name: webapp-gateway
spec:
  selector:
    istio: ingressgateway # use istio default controller
  servers:
  - port:
```

```
      number: 80
      name: http
      protocol: HTTP
    hosts:
    - "*"
---
apiVersion: networking.istio.io/v1alpha3
kind: VirtualService
metadata:
  name: frontendservice
spec:
  hosts:
  - "*"
  gateways:
  - webapp-gateway
  http:
  - match:
    - uri:
        prefix: /
    route:
    - destination:
        host: frontendservice
```

With the services deployed, the output when we hit the gateway using an Minikube IP is shown in Figure 6-3.

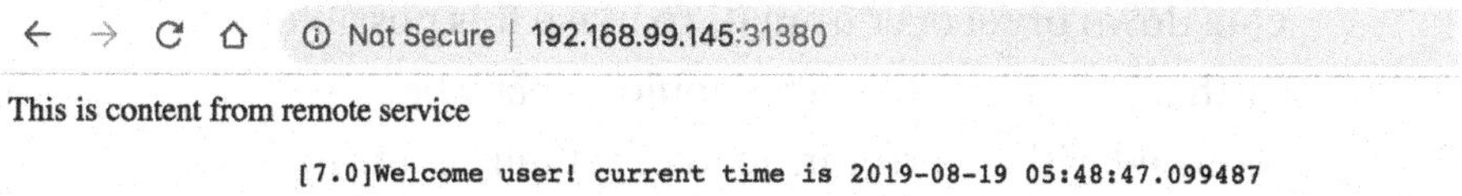

← → C ⌂   ⓘ Not Secure | 192.168.99.145:31380

This is content from remote service

[7.0]Welcome user! current time is 2019-08-19 05:48:47.099487

Figure 6-3. *Output of application*

We have a running application now; let's see what all could go wrong as per the fallacies explained earlier.

- One of the nodes of the webapp service goes down. The front-end service makes calls to the webapp service and sees UNKNOWN ERROR in response.

- A webapp node has a longer response time than expected. This could be because of a slow network or the node itself has issues. The front-end service waits for the time that the response is not received.

- A webapp node is now overloaded with more requests than expected, and new requests keep coming, which further complicates the issue.

How do we solve these issues in an environment?

1. If the front-end service gets an error stating the service is down, retry the request and check if some other node can serve the same request.

2. The front-end service should add a timeout to the request to avoid users waiting for a long time. After that, it can either retry the request or show an error to the user, based on the product flow, without wasting their time.

3. If a node or service is overloaded and repeatedly returning an error, it should be given some time to cool down or recover from it. To make this possible, further incoming requests should directly be returned with an error instead of actually going to the service. The process is called *circuit breaking*, similar to how we have in households to prevent permanent damage to appliances.

Let's go through these scenarios and figure out how Istio can help solve these challenges.

Load Balancing

Load balancing is a common concept meaning to distribute load among several nodes to increase throughput and efficiency. A load balancer is the node to which all the requests come in, and it forwards/proxies the load to distributed nodes. Though this seems like a good approach, it creates a single point of failure that we are trying to avoid in the first place. It also creates a bottleneck since all the requests are routed through this single entry point.

Istio comes with the concept of client-side load balancing. The requesting service can decide where to send the request based on load balancing criteria. This means no single point of failure and higher throughput. Istio supports the following load balancing techniques:

- **Round-robin**: Requests are evenly distributed across all the nodes one after the other.

- **Random**: A random node is picked to serve the request. It eventually becomes similar to round-robin but without any order.

- **Weighted**: Weightage can be added to instances, and requests can be forwarded based on the percentage.

- **Least requests**: This seems to be an effective technique but depends on the use case. It forwards the request to the node that has received the least number of requests up to that time.

Istio uses the service discovery feature of the platform to get details of new nodes and distribute its presence to the rest of the nodes. The rest of the nodes include the new service in their load balancing. Let's use webapp 4.0 to see the load balancer in action. Refer to Listing 6-7 for the configuration.

Listing 6-7. Deployment Configuration and Load Balancing Config

```
apiVersion: apps/v1
kind: Deployment
metadata:
  name: webapp-deployment-4
  labels:
    app: webservice
    version: v4
spec:
  replicas: 1
  selector:
    matchLabels:
      app: webservice
      version: v4
  template:
    metadata:
      labels:
        app: webservice
        version: v4
    spec:
      containers:
      - name: webapp
        image: web-app:4.0
        imagePullPolicy: Never
        ports:
        - containerPort: 5000
---
```

```
apiVersion: networking.istio.io/v1alpha3
kind: DestinationRule
metadata:
  name: webservice
spec:
  host: webservice
  subsets:
  - name: v0
    labels:
      version: v7.0
  - name: v1
    labels:
      version: v4
  trafficPolicy:
    loadBalancer:
      simple: ROUND_ROBIN
---
apiVersion: v1
kind: Service
metadata:
  name: webservice
spec:
  selector:
    app: webservice
  ports:
  - name: http-webservice
    protocol: TCP
    port: 80
    targetPort: 5000
---
apiVersion: networking.istio.io/v1alpha3
kind: VirtualService
```

```
metadata:
  name: webservice
spec:
  hosts:
    - "*"
  gateways:
    - webapp-gateway
  http:
  - route:
    - destination:
        host: webservice
    match:
    - uri:
        prefix: /
```

Figure 6-4 shows the output of request distribution on the service.

```
avinashsingh$ for i in {1..20}; do curl "http://192.168.99.153:31380";echo "";done
[7.0]Welcome user! current time is 2019-08-27 03:45:24.288212
[4.0]Welcome user! current time is 2019-08-27 03:45:24.330264
[7.0]Welcome user! current time is 2019-08-27 03:45:24.352380
[4.0]Welcome user! current time is 2019-08-27 03:45:24.383013
[4.0]Welcome user! current time is 2019-08-27 03:45:24.424206
[7.0]Welcome user! current time is 2019-08-27 03:45:24.449253
[7.0]Welcome user! current time is 2019-08-27 03:45:24.474622
[4.0]Welcome user! current time is 2019-08-27 03:45:24.515953
[7.0]Welcome user! current time is 2019-08-27 03:45:24.537651
[4.0]Welcome user! current time is 2019-08-27 03:45:24.581533
[7.0]Welcome user! current time is 2019-08-27 03:45:24.604193
[7.0]Welcome user! current time is 2019-08-27 03:45:24.627046
[4.0]Welcome user! current time is 2019-08-27 03:45:24.659631
[4.0]Welcome user! current time is 2019-08-27 03:45:24.692002
[7.0]Welcome user! current time is 2019-08-27 03:45:24.713843
[4.0]Welcome user! current time is 2019-08-27 03:45:24.753464
[7.0]Welcome user! current time is 2019-08-27 03:45:24.776220
[4.0]Welcome user! current time is 2019-08-27 03:45:24.832172
[7.0]Welcome user! current time is 2019-08-27 03:45:24.855265
[4.0]Welcome user! current time is 2019-08-27 03:45:24.888551
```

Figure 6-4. *Round-robin load balancing*

Since round-robin balancing is done, alternate requests are sent to each of the versions for most of the cases.

Retry Requests

When a service call fails because of latency or a temporary glitch in a service, the end user sees an error, for which we assume that the user may retry the request. In a microservice architecture, this retrial is multiplied at each layer of network call. With users retrying the requests, the combination of request failures at each layer increases. In Figure 6-2, assume calls fail between the gateway and front-end service, with a second chance of failure between the front-end service and the webapp service. Relying on the user to not to give up until nothing fails is an unrealistic expectation. The solution is to build automatic retries at each network call.

In a microservice architecture, one can either incorporate retries and time out in every network call, which increases the development effort and coding time and has nothing to do with business logic, or it can be left to the network layer to handle the failures.

Let's make a small change in our webapp service to randomly return the 503 error code, which states the service is down. This happens if a service is overloaded and unable to accept new requests and fails for a few existing ones. Refer to Listing 6-8 for the change.

Listing 6-8. Change in Web App Service to Return Error in About 50 Percent of Cases

```
from flask import Flask
import datetime
import time
import os
import random
```

```python
app = Flask(__name__)

@app.route("/")
def main():
    currentDT = datetime.datetime.now()
    status = 200
    if random.random() > 0.5:
        status = 503
    return "[{}]Welcome user! current time is {} ".format(os.en
    viron['VERSION'],str(currentDT)), status

@app.route("/health")
def health():
    return "OK"

if __name__ == "__main__":
    app.run(host='0.0.0.0')
```

Now let's send some traffic on the gateway and see the result.
We will be using siege to make continuous requests on the application.
See Figure 6-5.

```
avinashsingh$ siege -c1 -r20 "http://192.168.99.147:31380/"
** SIEGE 4.0.4
** Preparing 1 concurrent users for battle.
The server is now under siege...
HTTP/1.1 200      0.02 secs:      161 bytes ==> GET  /
HTTP/1.1 503      0.01 secs:      113 bytes ==> GET  /
HTTP/1.1 503      0.02 secs:      113 bytes ==> GET  /
HTTP/1.1 503      0.00 secs:      113 bytes ==> GET  /
HTTP/1.1 503      0.01 secs:      113 bytes ==> GET  /
HTTP/1.1 200      0.01 secs:      161 bytes ==> GET  /
HTTP/1.1 200      0.01 secs:      161 bytes ==> GET  /
HTTP/1.1 200      0.01 secs:      161 bytes ==> GET  /
HTTP/1.1 503      0.02 secs:      113 bytes ==> GET  /
HTTP/1.1 503      0.01 secs:      113 bytes ==> GET  /
HTTP/1.1 200      0.01 secs:      161 bytes ==> GET  /
HTTP/1.1 503      0.01 secs:      113 bytes ==> GET  /
HTTP/1.1 200      0.01 secs:      161 bytes ==> GET  /
HTTP/1.1 503      0.01 secs:      113 bytes ==> GET  /
HTTP/1.1 200      0.01 secs:      161 bytes ==> GET  /
HTTP/1.1 503      0.01 secs:      113 bytes ==> GET  /
HTTP/1.1 503      0.01 secs:      113 bytes ==> GET  /
HTTP/1.1 503      0.01 secs:      113 bytes ==> GET  /
HTTP/1.1 200      0.00 secs:      161 bytes ==> GET  /
HTTP/1.1 503      0.01 secs:      113 bytes ==> GET  /

Transactions:                  8 hits
Availability:              40.00 %
Elapsed time:               0.21 secs
Data transferred:           0.00 MB
Response time:              0.03 secs
Transaction rate:          38.10 trans/sec
Throughput:                 0.01 MB/sec
Concurrency:                1.00
Successful transactions:       8
Failed transactions:          12
Longest transaction:        0.02
Shortest transaction:       0.00
```

Figure 6-5. *Request output if service node returns an error*

The downtime or failure of a service is propagated to the user. The availability can be increased by simply retrying the failed request one more time. Instead of changing the code, let's achieve this via the Istio VirtualService component. VirtualService allows us to retry a request in the case of failure. By default, Envoy retries one time in the case of a request failure. Let's add this configuration as per Listing 6-9.

Listing 6-9. Changing webapp-virtualservice to Allow One Retry

```
apiVersion: networking.istio.io/v1alpha3
kind: VirtualService
metadata:
  name: webservice
spec:
  hosts:
  - webservice
  http:
  - route :
    - destination:
        host: webservice
    retries:
      attempts: 1
```

Simply apply the configuration using `istioctl`, and let's send the same traffic again and look at the failed requests to users.

As visible in Figure 6-6, the availability has improved from 40 percent to 80 percent. We can further increase the retries, resulting in even fewer failures, but this comes at the cost of response time. Every failed request takes time, and that time is added to the total response time of the calling service. See Figure 6-7.

```
avinashsingh$ siege -c1 -r20 "http://192.168.99.147:31380/"
** SIEGE 4.0.4
** Preparing 1 concurrent users for battle.
The server is now under siege...
HTTP/1.1 200     0.02 secs:     161 bytes ==> GET  /
HTTP/1.1 200     0.01 secs:     161 bytes ==> GET  /
HTTP/1.1 200     0.03 secs:     161 bytes ==> GET  /
HTTP/1.1 200     0.04 secs:     161 bytes ==> GET  /
HTTP/1.1 200     0.02 secs:     161 bytes ==> GET  /
HTTP/1.1 200     0.01 secs:     161 bytes ==> GET  /
HTTP/1.1 200     0.02 secs:     161 bytes ==> GET  /
HTTP/1.1 200     0.01 secs:     161 bytes ==> GET  /
HTTP/1.1 200     0.02 secs:     161 bytes ==> GET  /
HTTP/1.1 200     0.01 secs:     161 bytes ==> GET  /
HTTP/1.1 200     0.01 secs:     161 bytes ==> GET  /
HTTP/1.1 200     0.03 secs:     161 bytes ==> GET  /
HTTP/1.1 503     0.03 secs:     113 bytes ==> GET  /
HTTP/1.1 200     0.02 secs:     161 bytes ==> GET  /
HTTP/1.1 200     0.03 secs:     161 bytes ==> GET  /
HTTP/1.1 503     0.04 secs:     113 bytes ==> GET  /
HTTP/1.1 503     0.02 secs:     113 bytes ==> GET  /
HTTP/1.1 503     0.03 secs:     113 bytes ==> GET  /
HTTP/1.1 200     0.01 secs:     161 bytes ==> GET  /
HTTP/1.1 200     0.02 secs:     161 bytes ==> GET  /

Transactions:                     16 hits
Availability:                  80.00 %
Elapsed time:                   0.43 secs
Data transferred:               0.00 MB
Response time:                  0.03 secs
Transaction rate:              37.21 trans/sec
Throughput:                     0.01 MB/sec
Concurrency:                    1.00
Successful transactions:          16
Failed transactions:               4
Longest transaction:            0.04
Shortest transaction:           0.01
```

Figure 6-6. *With retries, the end user gets better availability*

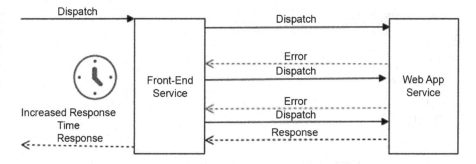

Figure 6-7. *The response time of the calling service increases with each retry*

Though retrying seems to be a good way to improve the availability, there are obvious scenarios where retries should be avoided.

- Retries should be idempotent. Retry request should be avoided where the response would change based on the request count.

- If a request is known to take a lot of time, in other words, is an expensive request, then retries should be avoided. This can cause failures of the next requests as well and may lead to a consumption of extra resources.

We made changes to the code to test the durability of the application to withstand errors in one microservice. There is a simpler way of doing this via fault injection. We can configure the virtual service such that a fault is intentionally inserted to test the durability. Let's revert our webapp code to the previous version and inject a fault in the service using VirtualService. Listing 6-10 shows the abort injection forcing 50 percent of the requests to fail.

Listing 6-10. Modified VirtualService Component to Forcefully Inject Fault

```
apiVersion: networking.istio.io/v1alpha3
kind: VirtualService
metadata:
  name: webservice
spec:
  hosts:
  - webservice
  http:
  - fault:
      abort:
        httpStatus: 503
        percent: 50
```

```
route :
- destination:
    host: webservice
retries:
  attempts: 0
```

The retries are intentionally made zero to demonstrate the failed requests using siege. Figure 6-8 shows the output of failed requests.

```
avinashsingh$ siege -c1 -r20 "http://192.168.99.147:31380/"
** SIEGE 4.0.4
** Preparing 1 concurrent users for battle.
The server is now under siege...
HTTP/1.1 503     0.01 secs:     113 bytes ==> GET  /
HTTP/1.1 503     0.01 secs:     113 bytes ==> GET  /
HTTP/1.1 503     0.01 secs:     113 bytes ==> GET  /
HTTP/1.1 503     0.00 secs:     113 bytes ==> GET  /
HTTP/1.1 503     0.02 secs:     113 bytes ==> GET  /
HTTP/1.1 200     0.01 secs:     161 bytes ==> GET  /
HTTP/1.1 503     0.01 secs:     113 bytes ==> GET  /
HTTP/1.1 503     0.02 secs:     113 bytes ==> GET  /
HTTP/1.1 200     0.02 secs:     161 bytes ==> GET  /
HTTP/1.1 200     0.02 secs:     161 bytes ==> GET  /
HTTP/1.1 503     0.00 secs:     113 bytes ==> GET  /
HTTP/1.1 503     0.01 secs:     113 bytes ==> GET  /
HTTP/1.1 503     0.01 secs:     113 bytes ==> GET  /
HTTP/1.1 503     0.01 secs:     113 bytes ==> GET  /
HTTP/1.1 503     0.01 secs:     113 bytes ==> GET  /
HTTP/1.1 200     0.01 secs:     161 bytes ==> GET  /
HTTP/1.1 200     0.01 secs:     161 bytes ==> GET  /
HTTP/1.1 200     0.02 secs:     161 bytes ==> GET  /
HTTP/1.1 503     0.01 secs:     113 bytes ==> GET  /
HTTP/1.1 503     0.00 secs:     113 bytes ==> GET  /

Transactions:                    6 hits
Availability:                30.00 %
Elapsed time:                 0.22 secs
Data transferred:             0.00 MB
Response time:                0.04 secs
Transaction rate:            27.27 trans/sec
Throughput:                   0.01 MB/sec
Concurrency:                  1.00
Successful transactions:         6
Failed transactions:            14
Longest transaction:          0.02
Shortest transaction:         0.00
```

Figure 6-8. *Siege response with Istio fault injection*

Here the number of failures is more than 50 percent since the requests to webapp are also failing from inside the code. Changing the retries to 1 results in better availability of the application.

Though retries resolve the issue when a few pods of a service are not responding or are down, it tries to serve the request using the available pod, but what happens if a pod is overloaded and has put a request in the queue? The result could be that a response is served after a long time or that the calling service receives an error after a long time. In both cases, the end user is affected with the delay in response. Timeouts become an important factor here before the user gives up.

Timeout Requests

Timeout is an important component to make systems available. During a network call to a service, if a call is taking a lot of time, it is difficult to determine whether the service is down or is simply slow or overloaded. In such scenarios, the calling service cannot sit idle waiting for the request to complete since the end user is affected by this latency. An alternative to this is to fail fast instead of keeping the user waiting. Istio provides a feature to time out a request if the response time crosses a threshold.

Let's inject a fault in the webapp service to increase the response time beyond five seconds for 50 percent of the requests. Listing 6-11 shows the modified VirtualService configuration.

Listing 6-11. Modified Virtual Service to Forcefully Inject a Delay
for Some Requests

```
apiVersion: networking.istio.io/v1alpha3
kind: VirtualService
metadata:
  name: webservice
spec:
  hosts:
  - webservice
  http:
  - fault:
      delay:
        fexedDelay: 5s
        percent: 50
    route :
    - destination:
        host: webservice
    retries:
      attempts: 0
```

The average response time of the request has increased to 2.5 seconds,
making 50 percent of the users wait for five seconds for a response.
Figure 6-9 shows the performance using siege. This is a common scenario
if the service keeps waiting for the response.

```
avinashsingh$ siege -c1 -r10 "http://192.168.99.147:31380/"
** SIEGE 4.0.4
** Preparing 1 concurrent users for battle.
The server is now under siege...
HTTP/1.1 200     5.01 secs:     161 bytes ==> GET  /
HTTP/1.1 200     0.01 secs:     161 bytes ==> GET  /
HTTP/1.1 200     0.01 secs:     161 bytes ==> GET  /
HTTP/1.1 200     5.01 secs:     161 bytes ==> GET  /
HTTP/1.1 200     0.01 secs:     161 bytes ==> GET  /
HTTP/1.1 200     5.01 secs:     161 bytes ==> GET  /
HTTP/1.1 200     5.02 secs:     161 bytes ==> GET  /
HTTP/1.1 200     0.01 secs:     161 bytes ==> GET  /
HTTP/1.1 200     5.01 secs:     161 bytes ==> GET  /
HTTP/1.1 200     0.01 secs:     161 bytes ==> GET  /

Transactions:                    10 hits
Availability:                100.00 %
Elapsed time:                 25.11 secs
Data transferred:             0.00 MB
Response time:                2.51 secs
Transaction rate:             0.40 trans/sec
Throughput:                   0.00 MB/sec
Concurrency:                  1.00
Successful transactions:        10
Failed transactions:             0
Longest transaction:          5.02
Shortest transaction:         0.01
```

Figure 6-9. *Siege response with delay injection*

Now one way is to time out the request if no response is received within one second. Since we have injected a fault in webapp service, we will add a timeout to the front-end service. The modified VirtualService config looks like Listing 6-12.

Listing 6-12. Modified Front-End Virtual Service to Set Timeout to 1 Second

```
apiVersion: networking.istio.io/v1alpha3
kind: VirtualService
metadata:
  name: frontendservice
```

```
spec:
  hosts:
  - "*"
  gateways:
  - webapp-gateway
  http:
  - match:
    - uri:
        prefix: /
    route:
    - destination:
        host: frontendservice
    timeout: 1s
    retries:
      attempts: 0
```

The siege output for the application shows some errors, but the upper cap on the response time is one second. See Figure 6-10.

```
avinashsingh$ siege —c1 —r20 "http://192.168.99.147:31380/"
** SIEGE 4.0.4
** Preparing 1 concurrent users for battle.
The server is now under siege...
HTTP/1.1 504     1.00 secs:     24 bytes ==> GET  /
HTTP/1.1 200     0.01 secs:    161 bytes ==> GET  /
HTTP/1.1 200     0.01 secs:    161 bytes ==> GET  /
HTTP/1.1 200     0.01 secs:    161 bytes ==> GET  /
HTTP/1.1 200     0.01 secs:    161 bytes ==> GET  /
HTTP/1.1 200     0.02 secs:    161 bytes ==> GET  /
HTTP/1.1 200     0.01 secs:    161 bytes ==> GET  /
HTTP/1.1 504     1.00 secs:     24 bytes ==> GET  /
HTTP/1.1 504     1.00 secs:     24 bytes ==> GET  /
HTTP/1.1 200     0.01 secs:    161 bytes ==> GET  /
HTTP/1.1 200     0.01 secs:    161 bytes ==> GET  /
HTTP/1.1 200     0.01 secs:    161 bytes ==> GET  /
HTTP/1.1 504     1.01 secs:     24 bytes ==> GET  /
HTTP/1.1 504     1.00 secs:     24 bytes ==> GET. /
HTTP/1.1 504     1.00 secs:     24 bytes ==> GET  /
HTTP/1.1 504     1.01 secs:     24 bytes ==> GET  /
HTTP/1.1 200     0.01 secs:    161 bytes ==> GET  /
HTTP/1.1 200     0.01 secs:    161 bytes ==> GET  /
HTTP/1.1 200     0.00 secs:    161 bytes ==> GET  /
HTTP/1.1 504     1.01 secs:     24 bytes ==> GET  /

Transactions:                  12 hits
Availability:               60.00 %
Elapsed time:                8.15 secs
Data transferred:            0.00 MB
Response time:               0.68 secs
Transaction rate:            1.47 trans/sec
Throughput:                  0.00 MB/sec
Concurrency:                 1.00
Successful transactions:       12
Failed transactions:            8
Longest transaction:         1.01
Shortest transaction:        0.00
```

Figure 6-10. *Siege response with timeout of one second*

We have successfully fulfilled one criterion that the user will not have to wait for response. Let's try to work on the criteria that the user receives an OK response. For this, simply retry the failed request one more time. Please note this means the error response time now will increase to 1.5 seconds, or 0.5 seconds for each try. The change in configuration is shown in Listing 6-13.

Listing 6-13. Modified Web App Virtual Service to Set Timeout to 1
Second and Add Retries to 1

```
apiVersion: networking.istio.io/v1alpha3
kind: VirtualService
metadata:
  name: frontendservice
spec:
  hosts:
  - "*"
  gateways:
  - webapp-gateway
  http:
  - match:
    - uri:
        prefix: /
    route:
    - destination:
        host: frontendservice
        port:
          number: 80
    retries:
        attempts: 1
        perTryTimeout: 0.5s
```

Figure 6-11 shows the siege result of all requests being successful,
but this comes at the cost of three hits in a few cases. From the figure, it
is easily identifiable that any request with a response time close to 1.5
seconds has been hit three times.

```
avinashsingh$ siege -c1 -r20 "http://192.168.99.153:31380"
** SIEGE 4.0.4
** Preparing 1 concurrent users for battle.
The server is now under siege...
HTTP/1.1 200      1.52 secs:        161 bytes ==> GET  /
HTTP/1.1 200      0.02 secs:        161 bytes ==> GET  /
HTTP/1.1 200      0.00 secs:        161 bytes ==> GET  /
HTTP/1.1 200      0.02 secs:        161 bytes ==> GET  /
HTTP/1.1 200      1.51 secs:        161 bytes ==> GET  /
HTTP/1.1 200      1.51 secs:        161 bytes ==> GET  /
HTTP/1.1 200      0.01 secs:        161 bytes ==> GET  /
HTTP/1.1 200      1.51 secs:        161 bytes ==> GET  /
HTTP/1.1 200      1.51 secs:        161 bytes ==> GET  /
HTTP/1.1 200      0.01 secs:        161 bytes ==> GET  /
HTTP/1.1 200      1.51 secs:        161 bytes ==> GET  /
HTTP/1.1 200      1.51 secs:        161 bytes ==> GET  /
HTTP/1.1 200      1.51 secs:        161 bytes ==> GET  /
HTTP/1.1 200      1.51 secs:        161 bytes ==> GET  /
HTTP/1.1 200      0.01 secs:        161 bytes ==> GET  /
HTTP/1.1 200      1.51 secs:        161 bytes ==> GET  /
HTTP/1.1 200      0.01 secs:        161 bytes ==> GET  /
HTTP/1.1 200      1.51 secs:        161 bytes ==> GET  /
HTTP/1.1 200      1.51 secs:        161 bytes ==> GET  /
HTTP/1.1 200      1.51 secs:        161 bytes ==> GET  /

Transactions:                        20 hits
Availability:                    100.00 %
Elapsed time:                     19.72 secs
Data transferred:                  0.00 MB
Response time:                     0.99 secs
Transaction rate:                  1.01 trans/sec
Throughput:                        0.00 MB/sec
Concurrency:                       1.00
Successful transactions:             20
Failed transactions:                  0
Longest transaction:               1.52
Shortest transaction:              0.00
```

Figure 6-11. *Siege response with three retries and 0.5 seconds of timeout for each try*

With the increasing number of hits, we ensure that the user gets a response but at the supply end; in other words, the service providing the response may have to serve way more requests than expected. There are scenarios when the service becomes overloaded with requests and may start failing for consecutive requests. Even though the timeout saves the end user from facing the issue, even with timeout the service continues to process the requests that lead to the further consumption of resources. Under such circumstances, the service will always be overloaded with requests and may never be able to recover if the application is consumed throughout the day.

To solve this, the service needs a cooldown time to finish all the pending requests, even though timed out, and start serving new requests. This is done using a circuit breaker.

Circuit Breaker

Circuit breakers are quite common in electrical appliances. It ensures that any one device does not overdraw the electric current. Overdrawing the current could result in heating up the circuit and can result in fire and overall breakdown. To avoid this scenario, the circuit breaker kills the power supply of the current-overdrawing appliance.

In a microservice architecture, the most common problem is the cascading of service failures. If a service is not responding for any reason, repeatedly sending requests to the service increases latency and puts unnecessary load on the service. Circuit breakers allow the overloaded service to get some cooldown time before it can start reserving new requests. Figure 6-12 shows the request behavior before and after the circuit breaker in action.

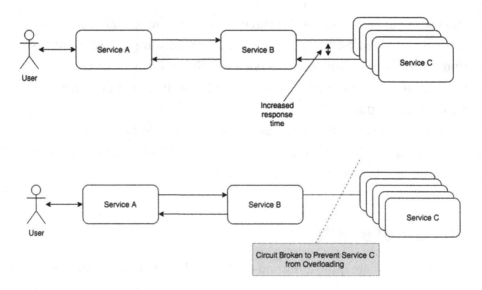

Figure 6-12. *Circuit breaker in action*

When the number of consecutive failures crosses a threshold in Service C, the circuit breaker trips, and for some period of time, all the calls to Service C fail immediately. After a period of time, a few requests are allowed to go through the circuit to test whether Service C has recovered. If the requests are successful, Service C is restored or the service remains in a circuit-broken state for another period of time. Figure 6-13 shows the recovery of the service after the circuit breaker.

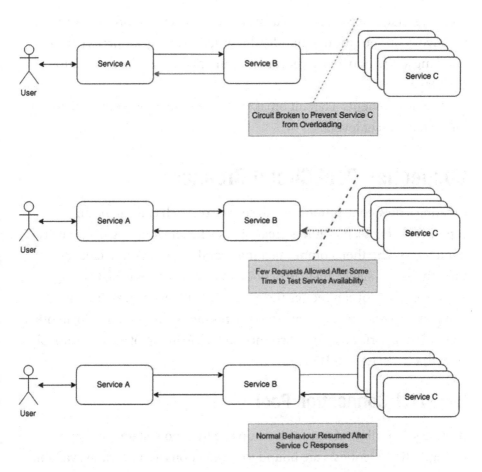

Figure 6-13. *Circuit breaker released after service recovery*

Circuit breakers in software can be implemented using the popular client-side circuit breaker libraries. If Java is the development language, one example of a client-side circuit breaker is the Netflix library Hysterix, but again, this requires developers to take care of circuit breaking within the application, which doesn't have much to do with the application logic. At the same time, it needs to be implemented in multiple languages

221

for polyglot applications. Istio abstracts out the circuit breaker and uses an Envoy configuration to handle the process. Envoy enforces circuit breaking at the network layer rather than having it at the application code layer.

Istio implements a circuit breaker at the connection pool level and at the load balancer level.

Connection Pool Circuit Breaker

Creating a new connection to each service on each call can be an expensive process. It requires creating a socket, negotiating the security parameters, and then communicating over the network and closing the connection safely. Instead of doing this for each request, keeping a connection pool can reduce the expensive process of creating a new connection each time. Envoy provides this out of the box for Istio; in other words, it supports an abstract connection pool on top of a wire protocol such as HTTP/1.1 and HTTP/2.

HTTP/1.1 Connection Pool

It creates a number of connections up to a threshold stated in the configuration. Requests are bound to connections as and when available. The availability of a connection can be based on the existing connection becoming free or the spawning of a new connection since the number of connections is still below the configured threshold. If a connection is broken, a new connection is established to replace it.

HTTP/2 Connection Pool

It creates a single connection to an upstream host and requires that all requests be multiplexed over it. If the host resets the connection or the connection reaches its maximum stream limit, the pool creates a new connection and releases the earlier one.

Istio abstracts the above pools at the Envoy layer and optimizes the connections. Now let's look at an example to see a circuit breaker in action.

We will create a new version of the webapp service and create a new deployment of it in the mesh. To differentiate it from the old version, we are adding a delay of 0.5 seconds to the code. Listing 6-14 introduces the new method to the service, which will add a fault to the service.

Listing 6-14. Addition of a Fault to the Webapp Application

```
from flask import Flask
import datetime
import time
import os
import random

app = Flask(__name__)

global status
status = 200

@app.route("/")
def main():
    currentDT = datetime.datetime.now()
    if (status == 200):
        time.sleep(0.5)
    return "[{}]Welcome user! current time is {} ".format
    (os.environ['VERSION'],str(currentDT)), status

@app.route("/health")
def health():
    return "OK"

@app.route("/addfault")
def addfault():
    global status
```

223

```python
    if (status == 200):
        status = 503
    else:
        status = 200
    return "OK"

if __name__ == "__main__":
    app.run(host='0.0.0.0')
```

Listing 6-15 shows the new deployment.

Listing 6-15. Webapp-deployment-v7.1.yaml

```yaml
apiVersion: networking.istio.io/v1alpha3
kind: VirtualService
metadata:
  name: frontendservice
spec:
  hosts:
  - "*"
  gateways:
  - webapp-gateway
  http:
  - match:
    - uri:
        prefix: /
    route:
    - destination:
        host: frontendservice
        port:
          number: 80
```

```
retries:
    attempts: 1
    perTryTimeout: 0.5s
```

Let's change the destination rule to accommodate both v7.0 and v7.1 (see Listing 6-16).

Listing 6-16. Destination rule modified to add v7.1

```
apiVersion: networking.istio.io/v1alpha3
kind: DestinationRule
metadata:
  name: webservice
spec:
  host: webservice
  subsets:
  - name: v0
    labels:
      version: v7.0
  - name: v1
    labels:
      version: v7.1
```

With these changes, let's check the performance of the application using siege. Refer to Figure 6-14.

```
avinashsingh$ siege —c1 —r20 "http://192.168.99.153:31380"
** SIEGE 4.0.4
** Preparing 1 concurrent users for battle.
The server is now under siege...
HTTP/1.1 200      0.52 secs:       161 bytes ==> GET   /
HTTP/1.1 200      0.02 secs:       161 bytes ==> GET   /
HTTP/1.1 200      0.51 secs:       161 bytes ==> GET   /
HTTP/1.1 200      0.01 secs:       161 bytes ==> GET   /
HTTP/1.1 200      0.52 secs:       161 bytes ==> GET   /
HTTP/1.1 200      0.01 secs:       161 bytes ==> GET   /
HTTP/1.1 200      0.51 secs:       161 bytes ==> GET   /
HTTP/1.1 200      0.01 secs:       161 bytes ==> GET   /
HTTP/1.1 200      0.51 secs:       161 bytes ==> GET   /
HTTP/1.1 200      0.01 secs:       161 bytes ==> GET   /
HTTP/1.1 200      0.51 secs:       161 bytes ==> GET   /
HTTP/1.1 200      0.01 secs:       161 bytes ==> GET   /
HTTP/1.1 200      0.51 secs:       161 bytes ==> GET   /
HTTP/1.1 200      0.01 secs:       161 bytes ==> GET   /
HTTP/1.1 200      0.52 secs:       161 bytes ==> GET   /
HTTP/1.1 200      0.01 secs:       161 bytes ==> GET   /
HTTP/1.1 200      0.51 secs:       161 bytes ==> GET   /
HTTP/1.1 200      0.01 secs:       161 bytes ==> GET   /
HTTP/1.1 200      0.51 secs:       161 bytes ==> GET   /
HTTP/1.1 200      0.00 secs:       161 bytes ==> GET   /

Transactions:                  20 hits
Availability:              100.00 %
Elapsed time:                5.24 secs
Data transferred:            0.00 MB
Response time:               0.26 secs
Transaction rate:            3.82 trans/sec
Throughput:                  0.00 MB/sec
Concurrency:                 1.00
Successful transactions:       20
Failed transactions:            0
Longest transaction:         0.52
Shortest transaction:        0.00
```

Figure 6-14. *Application performance with v7.0 and v7.1 webapp*

We can easily differentiate that v7.1 is the one responding in 0.5+
seconds. All the calls seem to be successful in the experiment, but in a
live environment, the 0.5-second delays may keep piling up, keeping the
calling service (front-end service) in the queue if the concurrent users
increase. This will increase the response time of the service, leading to
the timeouts that we configured in earlier steps, but at the same time
still making the service process the request. So assuming after a certain

number of response failures, the service will fail, we can configure a circuit breaker to prevent the service from being bombarded with further requests that it cannot handle. Let's create a rule to demonstrate the failure of requests and see the circuit breaker in action.

Listing 6-17 shows a destination rule restricting the number of connections and max requests per connection to v7.1.

Listing 6-17. Destination Rule for v7.1 Restricting Number of Connections

```
apiVersion: networking.istio.io/v1alpha3
kind: DestinationRule
metadata:
  name: webservice-circuitbreaker
spec:
  host: webservice
  subsets:
  - name: v1
    labels:
      version: v7.1
  trafficPolicy:
    connectionPool:
      tcp:
        maxConnections: 1
      http:
        http1MaxPendingRequests: 1
        maxRequestsPerConnection: 1
```

With this configuration, we will bombard the service with concurrent requests. The result of this restriction is shown in Figure 6-15.

```
avinashsingh$ siege -v -c4 -r5 "http://192.168.99.153:31380"
** SIEGE 4.0.4
** Preparing 4 concurrent users for battle.
The server is now under siege...
HTTP/1.1 503      0.04 secs:      113 bytes ==> GET  /
HTTP/1.1 200      0.04 secs:      161 bytes ==> GET  /
HTTP/1.1 200      0.05 secs:      161 bytes ==> GET  /
HTTP/1.1 200      0.02 secs:      161 bytes ==> GET  /
HTTP/1.1 200      0.01 secs:      161 bytes ==> GET  /
HTTP/1.1 503      0.01 secs:      113 bytes ==> GET  /
HTTP/1.1 503      0.03 secs:      113 bytes ==> GET  /
HTTP/1.1 200      0.54 secs:      161 bytes ==> GET  /
HTTP/1.1 200      0.01 secs:      161 bytes ==> GET  /
HTTP/1.1 200      0.99 secs:      161 bytes ==> GET  /
HTTP/1.1 503      0.02 secs:      113 bytes ==> GET  /
HTTP/1.1 503      1.03 secs:      113 bytes ==> GET  /
HTTP/1.1 503      0.02 secs:      113 bytes ==> GET  /
HTTP/1.1 503      0.02 secs:      113 bytes ==> GET  /
HTTP/1.1 200      0.99 secs:      161 bytes ==> GET  /
HTTP/1.1 200      0.02 secs:      161 bytes ==> GET  /
HTTP/1.1 200      2.03 secs:      161 bytes ==> GET  /
HTTP/1.1 200      0.02 secs:      161 bytes ==> GET  /
HTTP/1.1 200      1.00 secs:      161 bytes ==> GET  /
HTTP/1.1 200      0.99 secs:      161 bytes ==> GET  /

Transactions:                    13 hits
Availability:                 65.00 %
Elapsed time:                  3.59 secs
Data transferred:              0.00 MB
Response time:                 0.61 secs
Transaction rate:              3.62 trans/sec
Throughput:                    0.00 MB/sec
Concurrency:                   2.19
Successful transactions:         13
Failed transactions:              7
Longest transaction:           2.03
Shortest transaction:          0.01
```

Figure 6-15. *Bombarding service with four concurrent requests*

As compared to the previous result, most of our requests are
completed in 0.1 seconds. From a user's perspective, there is an increase
in the number of errors, but the service gets a cooldown period to settle
below the threshold. In our case, since we have set the max connection
limit to 1, we are easily able to demonstrate this in the example.

Load Balancer Circuit Breaker

So far we have seen how a service is saved from traffic bombardment in the case of low performance, but this increases the number of errors that users get. This can be fine as long as it's a temporary glitch, but if the glitches go on for a long time, the end users will keep receiving these errors. In such a scenario, the way out should be to remove the service node from the cluster until it recovers. Istio tries to detect the outperforming node or outlier and removes that from the load balancer.

Let's reconfigure our destination rule to add a check for the outlier and remove that from the load balancer if required. Listing 6-18 shows the modified configuration.

Listing 6-18. Destination Rule for v7.1 Adding Configuration to Remove Outliers

```
apiVersion: networking.istio.io/v1alpha3
kind: DestinationRule
metadata:
  name: webservice-circuitbreaker
spec:
  host: webservice
  subsets:
  - name: v1
    labels:
      version: v7.1
  trafficPolicy:
    connectionPool:
      tcp:
        maxConnections: 1
      http:
        http1MaxPendingRequests: 1
        maxRequestsPerConnection: 1
```

```
outlierDetection:
  baseEjectionTime: 10s
  consecutiveErrors: 1
  interval: 1s
  maxEjectionPercent: 100
```

In this configuration, a faulty node is ejected if more than one consecutive error occurs. It keeps checking if the node is back or not at an *interval* frequency. We are also allowing the ejection of all the replicas of the service if required. Refer to Figure 6-16 for fault addition to the service and the complete result. Now the outlier has been popped out, and every request's maximum response time is less than 0.15 seconds.

```
avinashsingh$ kubectl exec -it webapp-deployment-8-757d78c9c4-7hf8t -- /bin/sh
Defaulting container name to webapp.
Use 'kubectl describe pod/webapp-deployment-8-757d78c9c4-7hf8t -n default' to see all of the containers in this pod.
!/app # wget localhost:5000/addfault
Connecting to localhost:5000 (127.0.0.1:5000)
addfault            100% |*********************************************************************************|
avinashsiege -v -c10 -r4 "http://192.168.99.153:31380"
** SIEGE 4.0.4
** Preparing 10 concurrent users for battle.
The server is now under siege...
HTTP/1.1 200     0.04 secs:      161 bytes ==> GET /
HTTP/1.1 200     0.04 secs:      161 bytes ==> GET /
HTTP/1.1 200     0.05 secs:      161 bytes ==> GET /
HTTP/1.1 200     0.05 secs:      161 bytes ==> GET /
HTTP/1.1 200     0.05 secs:      161 bytes ==> GET /
HTTP/1.1 200     0.06 secs:      161 bytes ==> GET /
HTTP/1.1 200     0.06 secs:      161 bytes ==> GET /
HTTP/1.1 200     0.07 secs:      161 bytes ==> GET /
HTTP/1.1 200     0.10 secs:      161 bytes ==> GET /
HTTP/1.1 200     0.06 secs:      161 bytes ==> GET /
HTTP/1.1 200     0.11 secs:      161 bytes ==> GET /
HTTP/1.1 200     0.09 secs:      161 bytes ==> GET /
HTTP/1.1 200     0.09 secs:      161 bytes ==> GET /
HTTP/1.1 200     0.09 secs:      161 bytes ==> GET /
HTTP/1.1 200     0.08 secs:      161 bytes ==> GET /
HTTP/1.1 200     0.08 secs:      161 bytes ==> GET /
HTTP/1.1 200     0.09 secs:      161 bytes ==> GET /
HTTP/1.1 200     0.08 secs:      161 bytes ==> GET /
HTTP/1.1 200     0.05 secs:      161 bytes ==> GET /
HTTP/1.1 200     0.05 secs:      161 bytes ==> GET /
HTTP/1.1 200     0.03 secs:      161 bytes ==> GET /
HTTP/1.1 200     0.05 secs:      161 bytes ==> GET /
HTTP/1.1 200     0.06 secs:      161 bytes ==> GET /
HTTP/1.1 200     0.05 secs:      161 bytes ==> GET /
HTTP/1.1 200     0.04 secs:      161 bytes ==> GET /
HTTP/1.1 200     0.07 secs:      161 bytes ==> GET /
HTTP/1.1 200     0.08 secs:      161 bytes ==> GET /
HTTP/1.1 200     0.05 secs:      161 bytes ==> GET /
HTTP/1.1 200     0.12 secs:      161 bytes ==> GET /
HTTP/1.1 200     0.11 secs:      161 bytes ==> GET /
HTTP/1.1 200     0.09 secs:      161 bytes ==> GET /
HTTP/1.1 200     0.05 secs:      161 bytes ==> GET /
HTTP/1.1 200     0.06 secs:      161 bytes ==> GET /
HTTP/1.1 200     0.03 secs:      161 bytes ==> GET /
HTTP/1.1 200     0.11 secs:      161 bytes ==> GET /
HTTP/1.1 200     0.07 secs:      161 bytes ==> GET /
HTTP/1.1 200     0.06 secs:      161 bytes ==> GET /
HTTP/1.1 200     0.05 secs:      161 bytes ==> GET /
HTTP/1.1 200     0.09 secs:      161 bytes ==> GET /
HTTP/1.1 200     0.05 secs:      161 bytes ==> GET /

Transactions:                40 hits
```

Figure 6-16. Outlier removed from the load balancer and all requests going to v7.0 of the webapp service

The circuit breaker in itself is sufficient to save a disaster but not solve the complete problem of a distributed system.

Resiliency

The overall architecture of the system should be not only to serve an end user's request but also to keep the application up and running for future requests. Combining all these Istio features should give you a stable system, as follows:

1. The end user requests a service to respond. If the response takes a lot of time, the request times out.

2. Once the request is timed out, instead of making the end user retry the request, retry it at each network hop. This time, the request should go to a different pod, assuming the earlier one might have had a temporary glitch.

3. Distribute further requests to different pods of the service via load balancing, making sure no single pod is overloaded.

4. There's no overload of the load balancer since a client-side load balancer is used. If the client goes down, its replica can take over in the meantime until a replacement is spawned.

5. If one of the nodes is not responding, give it a cool-off period using a circuit breaker, while the calling service can try the request to a different node.

6. If the cool-off period is not sufficient, eject the node from the service pool to avoid any future requests until the service recovers.

Summary

In this chapter, we went through Istio resiliency. We saw how retries and timeouts can hide the errors and latency in the application from the end user. Load balancing can be important since retries may re-fail for the same instance. Client-side load balancing with the concept of no single point of failure prevents throttling of requests directed to a single node for balancing. Circuit breakers and connection pools try to keep the application services in a healthy state, saving them from overloading and from the overhead of network connections. In the next chapter, we will look into application metrics and monitoring using tools like Grafana and Prometheus.

CHAPTER 7

Application Metrics

In the previous chapter, we went through the resiliency offered by Istio to improve service availability and durability by abstracting the complexity out from the code to the Envoy proxy. In a production environment, there is always a time when it might fail. This can be determined by the data collected from the system, which can then be prepared accordingly. Metrics collection is an important part of any system, but in a distributed system, it is difficult to simply read the data and make sense out of it quickly. There are open source tools that help in the collection and visualization of data. We will go through a couple of them in this chapter.

Application Monitoring

Monitoring is subjective for the different use cases of an application. For a static web site, a mere check of whether the web site is running or not is sufficient. This can be done with popular service providers like Pingdom since a web site is exposed publicly. Whereas for a web application running using a microservices architecture, a lot of services including the database may not be public. For such scenarios, the external check may say that the web application is not running but will not be able to determine the point of failure. An internal check on which service is failing could be a little more helpful in this scenario. This is why we need monitoring tools inside the private network on which application is running. K8s, which we

© Rahul Sharma, Avinash Singh 2020
R. Sharma and A. Singh, *Getting Started with Istio Service Mesh*,
https://doi.org/10.1007/978-1-4842-5458-5_7

have been using in this book, provides the automatic recovery of failing services. Figure 7-1 shows the monitoring mechanisms in different types of applications.

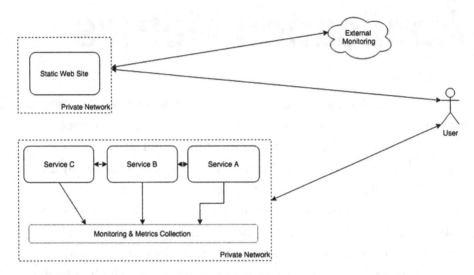

Figure 7-1. *Monitoring of static web site and monitoring of a distributed system*

Identifying and fixing failing components is fine, but this process creates some downtime. These days, all applications are targeting 99.9 percent availability, which can be possible by following precautions rather than curing a failed system after the fact. Before any application reaches production, one works on the load capacity and identifies the threshold at which the system might fail. Still, there are scenarios where a system may fail because of unknown circumstances. Keeping this in mind, developers capture basic metrics of a service such as the number of requests, response time, response status, etc., and the basic metrics of the node on which the services are running such as CPU utilization and memory consumption. The load capacity helps to determine the request- and response-related thresholds, and there are standards around when a node gets overloaded or runs out of memory. Once we have these metrics and threshold details, we can monitor the application by collecting and analysing these metrics. Based on analysis, we can determine when an application is about to fail.

When an application is about to fail, a message to the developer or DevOps or respective stakeholder might help to prepare them or rescue the system before the application crashes. This is where alerting comes into the picture. Alerting can use different channels from simple e-mail to phone calls depending upon the severity of the alert and use case of the application.

Figure 7-2 demonstrates the threshold of a couple of parameters and the action when the threshold is crossed.

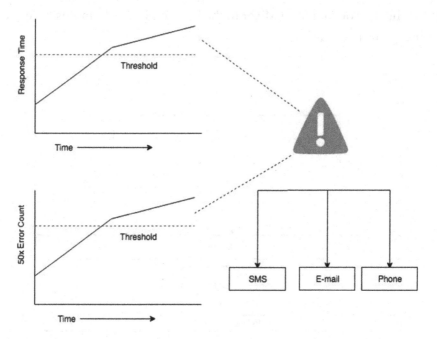

Figure 7-2. *Alerts sent to stakeholders after threshold has been reached*

As shown in Figure 7-2, the whole monitoring process can be divided into three major steps.

1. Application metrics collection

2. Analysis of metrics

3. Alerting stakeholders when required

Let's see how Istio can help in the three-step process.

Istio Mixer

We saw in previous chapters how Mixer gets telemetry data from the Istio data plane. The data collected is about how the services interact with each other and the CPU and memory consumption of instances. Figure 7-3 shows the flow of data from Mixer to the back-end service; in this case, we are using Prometheus.

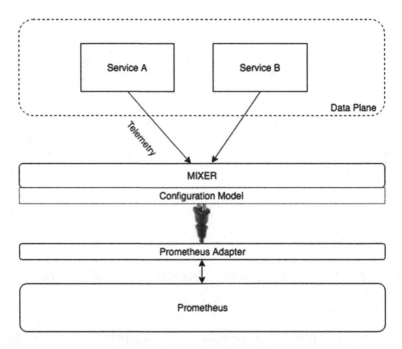

Figure 7-3. *Metrics flowing from the data plane to Prometheus*

The metrics flow from the data plane to Mixer, which extracts the *attributes* and passes them through the configuration model, which determines what needs to go through and in what form to the adapter. The adapter communicates the data to the back-end service, in this case Prometheus. Before we get into this further, let's take a look at how Prometheus works.

Prometheus

Prometheus is an open source monitoring and alerting tool. It fundamentally stores all data as a time series grouped together on the basis of metric name and key-value pairs called labels. Prometheus offers the following:

- Time-series data of different metrics

- A query language to analyze the data

- An alerting system to send notifications based on analysis done in the second step

Prometheus collects metrics via a pull model over HTTP. In other words, endpoints need to be provided to a Prometheus configuration to scrape the metrics data. It stores all data locally and runs rules over the data either to conclude new time-series data or to generate alerts. Figure 7-4 shows the flow of data across all the stakeholders.

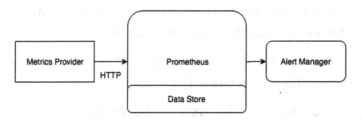

Figure 7-4. Prometheus metrics flow

Let's start by setting up Prometheus on the K8s cluster.

Installation

Prometheus comes preconfigured with Istio. Mixer has a built-in Prometheus adapter exposing endpoints serving the generated metric values. A Prometheus server is present as an add-on in the Istio cluster that is installed. It can also be installed using a Helm chart in a single step.

```
helm install --name prometheus stable/prometheus
```

This can be further configured to provide different storage, ingress rules, and so on, but we are not covering those here. Please refer to the Prometheus documentation for more configuration information.

The Prometheus add-on for Istio is preconfigured to scrape Mixer endpoints to collect exposed metrics. The available endpoints are as follows:

- `istio-telemetry.istio-system:42422/metrics`: This returns all Mixer-generated metrics.

- `istio-telemetry.istio-system:15014/metrics`: This returns all Mixer-specific metrics. This returns the metrics from Mixer.

- `istio-proxy:15090/metrics`: This returns raw stats generated by Envoy. Prometheus is configured to look for pods with the `envoy-prom` endpoint exposed. The add-on configuration filters out a large number of Envoy metrics during collection in an attempt to limit the scale of data by the add-on processes.

- `istio-pilot.istio-system:15014/metrics`: This returns the Pilot-generated metrics.

- `istio-galley.istio-system:15014/metrics` This returns the Galley-generated metrics.

- `istio-policy.istio-system:15014/metrics`: This returns all policy-related metrics.

- `istio-citadel.istio-system:15014/metrics`: This returns all Citadel-generated metrics.

The add-on saves the time-series data in its file system. This works well for us. For a production environment, it may be better to set up Prometheus separately or define a different data store for it.

As shown in Figure 7-3, the metrics reach Prometheus via the configuration model that has instances and handlers connected by rules. The predefined instances provided by the Istio Prometheus configuration are as follows:

- `accesslog`: Captures the log entry for request source and destination details

- `attributes`: Captures source and destination pod, workload, and namespace details

- `requestcount`: Captures the number of source to destination requests

- `requestduration`: Captures the response time of all the calls in the mesh

- `requestsize`: Captures the request size of the payload sent from the source to the destination

- `responsesize`: Captures the response size of the payload sent from the source to the destination

- `tcpaccesslog`: Captures metrics of the TCP request

- `tcpbytereceived`: Captures bytes received by the destination in the TCP request

- `tcpbytesent`: Captures bytes sent by the source in the TCP request

- `tcpconnectionsclosed`: Captures the number of times the TCP connection is closed

- `tcpconnectionsopened`: Captures the number of times TCP connection is opened

Each instance data is pushed into Prometheus via its handlers. Let's access the Prometheus node in the mesh and look at the dashboard before moving further.

Prometheus Dashboard

The Prometheus node resides inside the `istio-system` namespace and as stated earlier saves time-series data on the local file system. Getting access to the pod is simple by port forwarding the requests, as shown in Figure 7-5 and Figure 7-6. One may configure a gateway and rules to access it, but we are not describing those steps here.

```
avinashsingh$ kubectl -n istio-system get pods
NAME                                         READY   STATUS      RESTARTS   AGE
grafana-97fb6966d-lcmzt                      1/1     Running     4          7d21h
istio-citadel-7c7c5f5c99-xh989               1/1     Running     8          7d21h
istio-cleanup-secrets-1.2.2-pt6xf            0/1     Completed   0          7d21h
istio-egressgateway-f7b8cc667-sj5ss          1/1     Running     4          7d21h
istio-galley-585fc86678-12xpd                1/1     Running     7          7d21h
istio-grafana-post-install-1.2.2-v2bc2       0/1     Completed   0          7d21h
istio-ingressgateway-cfbf989b7-btp8q         1/1     Running     4          7d21h
istio-pilot-68f587df5d-6hkbj                 2/2     Running     8          7d21h
istio-policy-76cbcc4774-qr46p                2/2     Running     17         3d1h
istio-security-post-install-1.2.2-rk5z4      0/1     Completed   0          7d21h
istio-sidecar-injector-97f9878bc-xgzx4       1/1     Running     15         7d21h
istio-telemetry-5f4575974c-6xjjk             2/2     Running     22         7d21h
istio-tracing-595796cf54-jxqd2               1/1     Running     8          7d21h
kiali-55fcfc86cc-2q4mc                       1/1     Running     4          7d21h
prometheus-5679cb4dcd-szfcx                  1/1     Running     0          4s
avinashsingh$ kubectl -n istio-system port-forward prometheus-5679cb4dcd-szfcx 9090:9090
Forwarding from 127.0.0.1:9090 -> 9090
Forwarding from [::1]:9090 -> 9090
```

Figure 7-5. *Port forwarding to Prometheus instance in Istio mesh*

Figure 7-6 shows how to access the dashboard on localhost:9090.

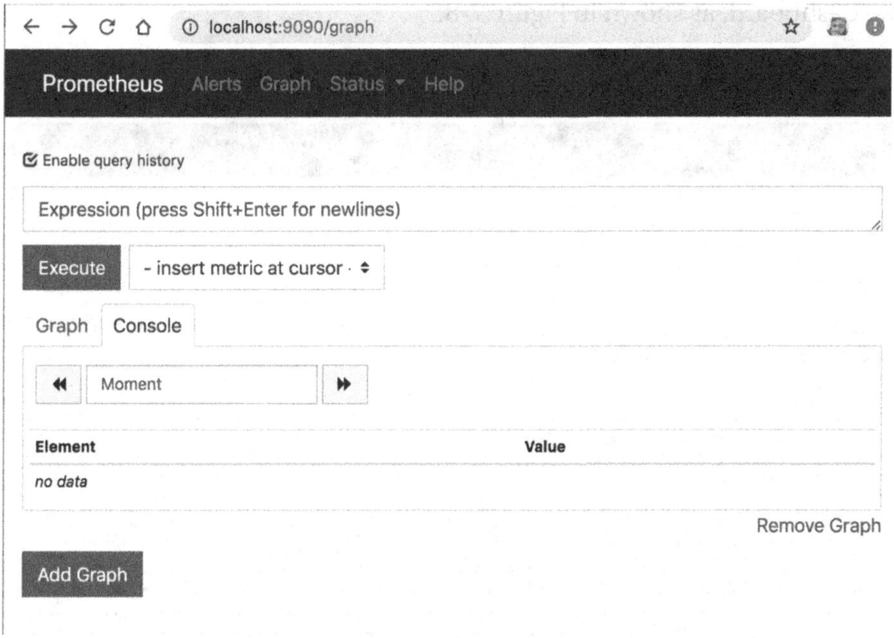

Figure 7-6. *Prometheus dashboard running inside the Istio mesh*

The dashboard allows us to query through different metrics collected from the mesh. Let's see a simple example of request count metrics. For that, let's put some requests into our service, as shown in Figure 7-7.

```
avinashsingh$ siege -v -c1 -r4 "http://192.168.99.159:31380"
** SIEGE 4.0.4
** Preparing 1 concurrent users for battle.
The server is now under siege...
HTTP/1.1 200     0.02 secs:     161 bytes ==> GET  /
HTTP/1.1 200     0.03 secs:     161 bytes ==> GET  /
HTTP/1.1 200     0.53 secs:     161 bytes ==> GET  /
HTTP/1.1 200     0.02 secs:     161 bytes ==> GET  /
```

Figure 7-7. *siege request to front-end service*

The metrics of these requests are collected by Mixer and passed on to the Prometheus back-end service. The metrics collected are now visible in the dashboard, as shown in Figure 7-8.

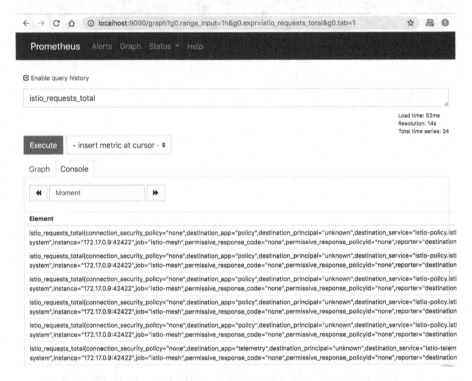

Figure 7-8. *All requests metrics recorded by Prometheus*

We made only four requests, but a lot of request metrics are available in the console. This is because Prometheus has tracked all the requests including the request sent to `istio-system` to record telemetry. Let's try to limit the requests to our namespace using the Prometheus query language, also known as PromQL. Figure 7-9 shows the filtered result.

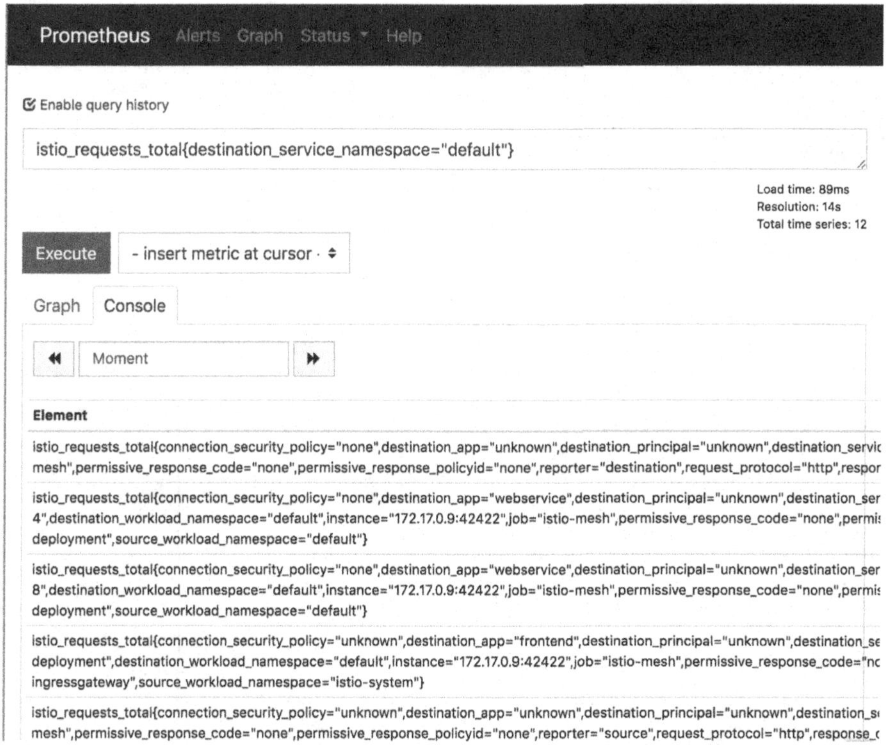

Figure 7-9. *Limiting the metrics to the default namespace*

This may not look readable, but the graph section gives a fair estimate that the number of requests to the mesh is increasing. We are bombarding the service with more requests to make the changes visible on the graph, as shown in Figure 7-10.

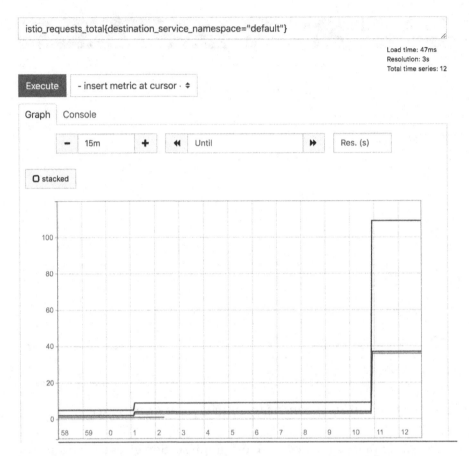

Figure 7-10. *Graph view of the number of requests to the mesh*

The request to individual services can be filtered using queries as follows:

```
istio_requests_total{destination_service_namespace="default",
destination_service_name="webservice"}
```

These all are predefined metrics that should be sufficient for most monitoring cases, but Istio allows the addition of custom metrics as well.

Custom Metrics

Istio Mixer collects all the attributes and injects them into Prometheus, but there are scenarios when the metrics need to be recalculated to make sense. Mixer allows the addition of configuration to do this. As stated earlier in the chapter, one can configure the instance and handler and add rules to add metrics to Prometheus.

Let's create a scenario to double all the requests to the webapp service. The instance configuration can be found in Listing 7-1.

Listing 7-1. Requestdouble-instance.yaml Configuration

```
apiVersion: config.istio.io/v1alpha2
kind: instance
metadata:
  name: requestdouble
  namespace: istio-system
spec:
  compiledTemplate: metric
  params:
    value: "2"
    dimensions:
      source: source.workload.name | "unknown"
      destination: destination.workload.name | "unknown"
```

This configuration simply gets metrics from the mesh and reports each metric value times, in this case 2. Two new dimensions specific to this instance have been introduced that are further handled in the handler in Listing 7-2.

Listing 7-2. Requestdouble-handler.yaml Configuration

```
apiVersion: config.istio.io/v1alpha2
kind: handler
metadata:
  name: doublehandler
  namespace: istio-system
spec:
  compiledAdapter: prometheus
  params:
    metrics:
    - name: doublerequest_count # Prometheus metric name
      instance_name: requestdouble.instance.istio-system
      kind: COUNTER
      label_names:
      - source
      - destination
```

The previous configuration simply pushes the metrics to Prometheus from the stated `instance_name`. It also accommodates the two new dimensions and propagates them as labels in Prometheus. Connecting the handler with an instance is defined by the rule shown in Listing 7-3.

Listing 7-3. Requestdouble-rule.yaml Configuration

```
apiVersion: config.istio.io/v1alpha2
kind: rule
metadata:
  name: requestdouble-prometheus
  namespace: istio-system
spec:
  actions:
  - handler: doublehandler
    instances: [ requestdouble ]
```

This records all requests two times in Prometheus. The output of the metric in Prometheus is in Figure 7-11.

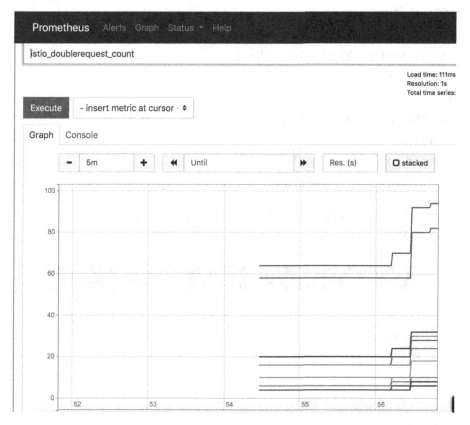

Figure 7-11. *All requests counted twice in istio_doublerequest_count metric*

Let's tweak the rule to connect an instance and handler only for the web service. Listing 7-4 shows the addition of match.

Listing 7-4. Requestdouble-rule.yaml Configuration

```
apiVersion: config.istio.io/v1alpha2
kind: rule
metadata:
  name: requestdouble-prometheus
  namespace: istio-system
spec:
  match: match(destination.service.name, "webservice")
  actions:
  - handler: doublehandler
    instances: [ requestdouble ]
```

Now the request count increases for only one service, as shown in Figure 7-12.

Figure 7-12. *Request count increasing twice for only the web service*

Now we have the metrics collected on our end. Though we are able to see the metrics, it becomes difficult to visualize different metrics at the same time. Prometheus supports Grafana to allow the visualization part. Let's see Grafana in action.

Grafana

Grafana is an open source platform to visualize, analyze, and monitor metrics. It supports data import from multiple sources and allows analysis on a single platform. In our case, we will limit ourselves to data captured from Prometheus.

Grafana can be seen as a UI visualization tool that uses data from Prometheus and sends alerts as and when required. Figure 7-13 shows the metrics flowing from Istio to Grafana. Let's start by setting up Grafana to use our Prometheus server.

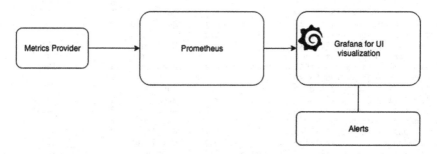

Figure 7-13.   *Data flowing from Istio to Grafana*

Installation

Similar to Prometheus, Grafana comes preconfigured with Istio set up already. We saw in Chapter 3 that Grafana comes with a demo setup, and we also viewed the Grafana dashboard. Here we will put Grafana to use by setting up new dashboards and alerts.

Istio Grafana is preconfigured to fetch data from the Prometheus service running in the mesh. The data store of Grafana can be configured to switch from SQLite to MySQL, Redis, or Postgres by making changes in the configuration.

Grafana can be installed using a Helm chart with a custom configuration. Let's set up a separate Grafana configuration with a Helm chart.

```
helm install --name grafana --tiller-namespace kube-system
stable/grafana
```

Custom configurations can be done here, providing a separate database connection, credentials, alert management, etc. Once Grafana is set up, we can set up a data source in Grafana.

Let's try to access the default Grafana dashboard available in the mesh, as shown in Figure 7-14.

```
avinashsingh$ kubectl -n istio-system get pods
NAME                                          READY   STATUS      RESTARTS   AGE
grafana-97fb6966d-lcmzt                       1/1     Running     6          10d
istio-citadel-7c7c5f5c99-xh989                1/1     Running     12         10d
istio-cleanup-secrets-1.2.2-pt6xf             0/1     Completed   0          10d
istio-egressgateway-f7b8cc667-gz2bk           1/1     Running     1          39h
istio-galley-585fc86678-12xpd                 1/1     Running     11         10d
istio-grafana-post-install-1.2.2-v2bc2        0/1     Completed   0          10d
istio-ingressgateway-cfbf989b7-btp8q          1/1     Running     6          10d
istio-pilot-68f587df5d-5nxk8                  2/2     Running     2          42h
istio-policy-76cbcc4774-8sxgj                 2/2     Running     6          41h
istio-policy-76cbcc4774-br2sg                 2/2     Running     0          4h46m
istio-policy-76cbcc4774-qr46p                 2/2     Running     28         5d21h
istio-policy-76cbcc4774-rzw2d                 2/2     Running     0          4h25m
istio-policy-76cbcc4774-x2qxl                 2/2     Running     7          41h
istio-security-post-install-1.2.2-rk5z4       0/1     Completed   0          10d
istio-sidecar-injector-97f9878bc-xgzx4        1/1     Running     23         10d
istio-telemetry-5f4575974c-6xjjk              2/2     Running     35         10d
istio-tracing-595796cf54-jxqd2                1/1     Running     13         10d
kiali-55fcfc86cc-2q4mc                        1/1     Running     6          10d
prometheus-5679cb4dcd-7z7qb                   1/1     Running     0          4h8m
avinashsingh$ kubectl -n istio-system port-forward grafana-97fb6966d-lcmzt 3000:3000
Forwarding from 127.0.0.1:3000 -> 3000
Forwarding from [::1]:3000 -> 3000
```

Figure 7-14. *Accessing the Grafana dashboard in the mesh*

Grafana is accessible to us and ready to use. Let's take a look at the dashboard.

Grafana Dashboard

Grafana has a set of preconfigured dashboards available that can be used out of the box. Accessing the Istio preconfigured dashboard directly to view the performance of the Istio mesh is shown in Figure 7-15.

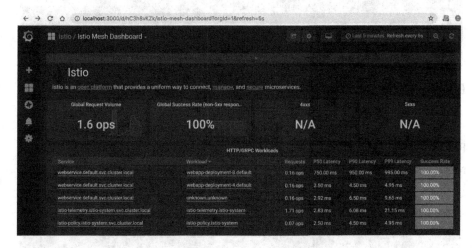

Figure 7-15. *Preconfigured Istio mesh dashboard*

As stated, this Grafana configuration is preconfigured to read metrics from the preconfigured Prometheus data source, which is shown in Figure 7-16. Additional data sources can also be added in Grafana to create new dashboards.

Figure 7-16. *Grafana preconfigured Prometheus data source*

Let's create a new dashboard to monitor the recently configured RequestDouble metrics. We will create a visual showing the rate of requests to `webapp-deployment-8`, as shown in Figure 7-17.

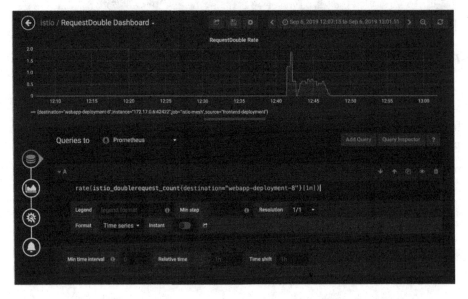

Figure 7-17. *New dashboard with graph to monitor the request rate*

Saving the dashboard creates a view of the request rate on this specific destination. Let's assume this service may be impacted if it crosses the three-request threshold. To prepare the infrastructure and the team, we'll set up Alert to go out before the threshold is reached.

Grafana Alert

Grafana provides a simple mechanism to alert stakeholders when the metrics crosses a specific threshold. Let's set up an alert when the requests rate to `webapp-deployment-v8` crosses the threshold 2.5. Before we start, let's set up the channel for alerting. Grafana allows a fair set of channels to send notifications. They include the following:

- HipChat

- OpsGenie

- Sensu

- Threema Gateway

- Prometheus Alertmanager

- Discord, Email

- VictorOps

- Google Hangouts Chat

- Kafka REST Proxy

- LINE

- Pushover

- Webhook

- DingDing

- PagerDuty

- Slack

- Microsoft Teams

- Telegram

Let's set up a webhook as an example. We will push an alert to this link:

`https://jsonblob.com/api/jsonBlob/0d0ef717-d0a0-11e9-8538-43dbd386b327`

Refer to Figure 7-18 to see how to add a webhook on Grafana.

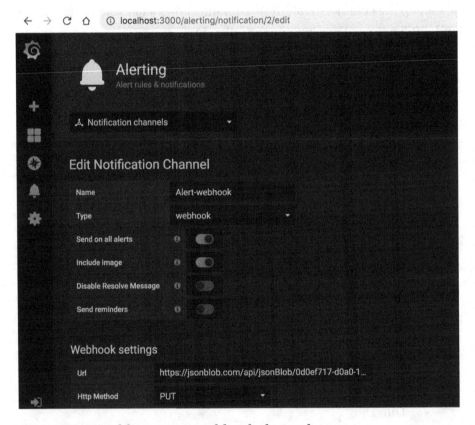

Figure 7-18. *Adding a new webhook channel*

Any notification sent is visible via the link shared earlier. Now let's set up an alert. Edit the panel we created in the previous step, as in Figure 7-19.

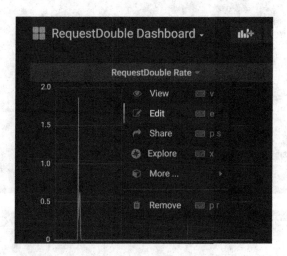

Figure 7-19. *Editing the RequestDouble rate panel*

Visit the Alert tab and set up an alert to go out when the request threshold crosses 2.5 requests, as shown in Figure 7-20.

Figure 7-20. *Creating the alert based on a condition with a custom message*

Let's use siege to make multiple requests to the front-end service.

```
siege -c40 -r10 "http://192.168.99.160:31380"
```

Within seconds Grafana starts showing an alert, as shown in Figure 7-21.

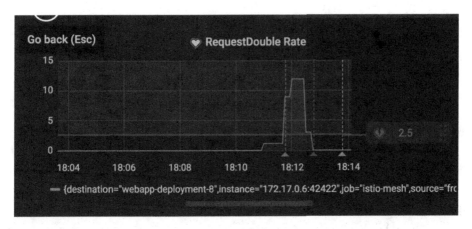

Figure 7-21. *RequestDouble dashboard showing the threshold being crossed*

The webhook receives data with details, as shown in Listing 7-5.

Listing 7-5. Response Received on the Webhook

```
{
    "evalMatches": [{
        "value": 107.19741952834556,
        "metric": "{destination=\"webapp-deployment-8\",
        instance=\"172.17.0.6:42422\", job=\"istio-mesh\",
        source=\"frontend-deployment\"}",
        "tags": {
            "destination": "webapp-deployment-8",
            "instance": "172.17.0.6:42422",
            "job": "istio-mesh",
            "source": "frontend-deployment"
        }
    }],
```

```
    "message": "Requests threshold of web-deployment-8 reaching
    threshold, action required",
    "ruleId": 1,
    "ruleName": "RequestDouble Rate alert",
    "ruleUrl": "http://localhost:3000/d/hpc70ncWk/
    requestdouble-dashboard?fullscreen\u0026edit\
    u0026tab=alert\u0026panelId=2\u0026orgId=1",
    "state": "alerting",
    "title": "[Alerting] RequestDouble Rate alert"
}
```

Summary

In this chapter, we covered monitoring using Prometheus and how to set up custom metrics. We gave you a glimpse into how PromQL can help in data filtering, but still it showed one metric at a time. We integrated Grafana with Prometheus and created a new dashboard visualizing multiple metrics. We worked on configuring alerts in Grafana and integrated a channel to send those alerts. In the next chapter, we will work on collecting logs from distributed services and tracing calls to analyze any challenges in the system.

CHAPTER 8

Logs and Tracing

In the previous chapter, we worked with a few of the observability features offered by Istio. We were able to capture application metrics, but metrics are just one dimension of observability. Observability is about gathering data in all possible dimensions. During application outages, looking at various aspects of observability helps developers understand the application behavior in order to perform incident analysis. There are many tools that can help achieve this objective. However, it is important to know the cost it takes to add a behavior. The operations team should be able to configure tools of their choice without needing developers. In this chapter, we will see how seamlessly we can capture additional behaviors such as request tracing and application logs. We will also work with the Istio plug-and-play model that provides a uniform mechanism for capturing additional application behavior.

Distributed Tracing

In a microservices application, a request is often served, in part, by multiple applications deployed in the cluster. Distributed tracing is the process of tracking a request flow across different applications. Traces often describe application behavior by showing the request and the response and the latencies, at a moment in time. The operations team often used traces to determine which services are causing performance issues for the application. There are many solutions for distributed tracing

© Rahul Sharma, Avinash Singh 2020
R. Sharma and A. Singh, *Getting Started with Istio Service Mesh*,
https://doi.org/10.1007/978-1-4842-5458-5_8

such as Zipkin, Jagger, Skywalking, and so on. The Istio service mesh can work with all of them. Traces are often generated by the Envoy proxy. These traces are then sent to the tracer back end.

Distributed tracing relies on an additional set of HTTP headers. These are widely known as b3 request headers. These headers build a request context that is used to identify the parent request and then propagate from one system to another. The Envoy proxy can generate these headers for every outgoing request. But for every incoming request, the headers must be propagated to the subrequests. If this is not done properly, then Envoy will generate new headers, and thus the spans will not correlate with one another.

In summary, the following set of headers must be propagated from an incoming request to all outgoing subrequests:

- `x-request-id`

- `x-b3-traceid`

- `x-b3-spanid`

- `x-b3-parentspanid`

- `x-b3-sampled`

- `x-b3-flags`

There are language-specific OpenTracing libraries that can help to achieve the required header propagation. Details of OpenTracing are beyond the scope of the book. Refer to one of the previously mentioned libraries to learn more.

Before we proceed, we will need to deploy a tracer application to our Kubernetes cluster. In this chapter, we are going to work with Jagger, an open source distributed tracing application developed at Uber. Jagger is built upon the concepts outlined by Dapper and OpenZipkin. For our

purposes, we will deploy Jagger using the Jagger operator (https://
github.com/jaegertracing/jaeger-operator). Kubernetes has an
operator extension that can be used to package and deploy applications on
a Kubernetes cluster. As a first step, we need to install the Jagger operator
by executing the following commands:

```
$ git clone https://github.com/jaegertracing/jaeger-operator.git
$ kubectl create namespace observability
namespace/observability created
$ kubectl create -f jaeger-operator/deploy/crds/jaegertracing_
v1_jaeger_crd.yaml
serviceaccount/jaeger-operator created
$ kubectl create -f jaeger-operator/deploy/service_account.yaml
serviceaccount/jaeger-operator created
$ kubectl create -f jaeger-operator/deploy/role.yaml
clusterrole.rbac.authorization.k8s.io/jaeger-operator created
$ kubectl create -f jaeger-operator/deploy/role_binding.yaml
clusterrolebinding.rbac.authorization.k8s.io/jaeger-operator
created
$ kubectl create -f jaeger-operator/deploy/operator.yaml
deployment.apps/jaeger-operator created
```

These executed commands deploy the operator in the observability
namespace. Details of the Kubernetes operator are beyond the scope of the
book. Refer to the Kubernetes documentation to learn more.

We can verify the operator as shown here:

```
$ kubectl get all -n observability
NAME                                  READY   STATUS
RESTARTS    AGE
pod/jaeger-operator-5574c4fb9-4vn5q   1/1     Running
0           2m4s
```

```
NAME                                     READY    UP-TO-DATE
AVAILABLE    AGE
deployment.apps/jaeger-operator    1/1      1
1            2m4s

NAME                                          DESIRED    CURRENT
READY     AGE
replicaset.apps/jaeger-operator-5574c4fb9    1          1
1         2m4s
```

The Jagger operator is now available for our Kubernetes cluster. It is used to deploy a Jagger instance. We will deploy the simplest possible configuration, namely, the default AllInOne Jagger package configured with in-memory storage. The "all-in-one" image deploys an agent, collector, query, ingester, and Jaeger UI in a single pod. This can be done by using the following configuration:

```
---
apiVersion: jaegertracing.io/v1
kind: Jaeger
metadata:
  name: simplest
```

Apply this configuration to our Kubernetes cluster using this:

```
$kubectl apply -f jagger.yaml
```

Let's now check if the Jagger installation is working fine. We can first check our cluster for the deployed services, as shown here:

```
$kubectl get all
```

```
NAME                                          READY
STATUS             RESTARTS    AGE
pod/frontend-deployment-c9c975b4-p8z2t        2/2
Running            38          35d
pod/simplest-56c7bd47bf-z7cnx                 0/1
ContainerCreating  0           16s
pod/webapp-deployment-6.2-654c5fd8f9-mrc22    2/2
Running            140         43d

NAME                              TYPE       CLUSTER-IP
EXTERNAL-IP    PORT(S)                               AGE
service/simplest-agent            ClusterIP  None
<none>         5775/TCP,5778/TCP,6831/TCP,6832/TCP   16s
service/simplest-collector        ClusterIP  10.152.183.169
<none>         9411/TCP,14250/TCP,14267/TCP,14268/TCP   16s
service/simplest-collector-headless ClusterIP  None
<none>         9411/TCP,14250/TCP,14267/TCP,14268/TCP   17s
service/simplest-query            ClusterIP  10.152.183.25
<none>         16686/TCP                             16s
```

We can see that all the components that were deployed are running. Let's now open the UI by looking up the NodePort address of the simplest-query service. See Figure 8-1.

Figure 8-1. *Jagger UI*

We have deployed Jagger using in-memory mode only. This is good enough for testing purposes. Jagger provides configuration options to deploy it in production (with a persistent store). Refer to the Jagger documentation to learn more.

Once Jagger is available, the Istio service mesh needs to refer to it. There are a couple of ways to accomplish this.

- If we are installing the service mesh, we can provide the Jagger address in the variable `global.tracer.zipkin.address=jagger-FQDN:16686`.

- In an existing installation, we need to edit the configuration and specify the `trace_zipkin_url` variable. Let's edit our configuration by using the following command:

  ```
  $ kubectl -n istio-system edit deployment istio-
  telemetry
  ```

We now have the correct infrastructure in place. Next, we need to instruct the sidecar to start generating the traces. The Envoy proxy can be configured to sample a subset of all the received requests. This can be done in one of these ways:

- Set the `pilot.traceSampling` variable as part of the Istio installation.

- Set the `PILOT_TRACE_SAMPLING` variable to an existing installation by using the following command:

```
$ kubectl -n istio-system edit deploy istio-pilot
```

After this, Envoy will generate request spans and send them to the Jagger server. We can validate this by executing requests for our front-end Java application.

```
$ for i in {1..500}; do  curl http://10.152.183.230/;echo "; done
```

Let's now look up the Jagger UI and search for the previously executed requests. All requests will have a span for both the front-end and webapp applications. See Figure 8-2.

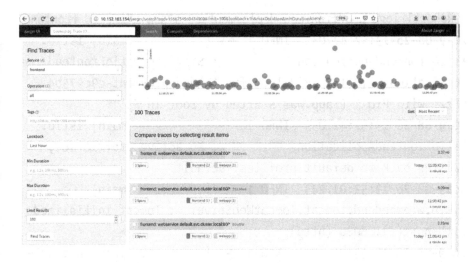

Figure 8-2. *Jagger traces*

265

As shown in Figure 8-2, Jagger provides a histogram of all the executed requests. It shows the time taken as well as the applications invoked when processing the request. We can click individual traces and look at individual application latencies and timelines in detail.

Application Logs

Istio does not provide any support for managing the logs generated by applications running in our Kubernetes cluster. This is a big challenge in large deployments, as logs generated for each of our applications remain on the container running the application. Let's look back at the example we developed in Chapter 3. We created a front-end application in Java and a web service back end in Python. We deployed two instances of the back end and one instance of the front-end application in our cluster. We can execute requests against our front end, which will invoke the back end. To debug the behavior, we need to look at the application logs. This is accomplished by performing log lookup for each container using this command:

```
$ kubectl logs pod/frontend-deployment-c9c975b4-p8z2t -c frontend
2019-08-26 13:52:42.032  INFO 1 --- [        main] istio.
IstioFrontendApplication         : Starting IstioFrontend
Application v0.0.1-SNAPSHOT on frontend-deployment-c9c975b4-
p8z2t with PID 1 (/app.war started by root in /)
2019-08-26 13:52:42.039  INFO 1 --- [        main] istio.
IstioFrontendApplication         : No active profile set,
falling back to default profiles: default
2019-08-26 13:53:01.243  INFO 1 --- [        main]
o.s.b.w.embedded.tomcat.TomcatWebServer  : Tomcat initialized
with port(s): 8080 (http)
2019-08-26 13:53:01.471  INFO 1 --- [        main] o.apache.
catalina.core.StandardService    : Starting service [Tomcat]
```

```
2019-08-26 13:53:01.471  INFO 1 --- [          main] org.
apache.catalina.core.StandardEngine  : Starting Servlet engine:
[Apache Tomcat/9.0.19]
```

This is quite cumbersome and error prone as we need to look up each container. Moreover, as containers get restarted, we lose the information in application logs. Logging contains the most verbose state of the system, and teams must be able to refer to the logs to track, verify, and diagnose the state of an application. Thus, we can say that the handling of application logs is not good enough, and we need a better solution to do so.

Besides the application logs, an application can also create access logs. Traditionally we have seen this in our front-end proxy, where an Apache HTTP server is creating the access.log file. The logging contains the request received by our application and the response for it. This is quite useful information. Now, if we look at the Istio service mesh, all requests are outed via the Envoy sidecar. The sidecar thus keeps track of what request-response it has received. We can configure the Envoy proxy to print these logs or create a log file. But this will not help us, as a container restart will lose all this information.

Kubernetes describes a cluster-level logging approach that leverages a logging back-end application like ELK, Splunk, Stackdriver, and so on. The approach leverages the sidecar pattern used by the service mesh. The complete solution for the application logs looks like the following:

- The application deployed in the cluster needs to write logs to a file. The log file is created at a location created by volume-mount.

- We run a second container mounted with the exported volume. The containers will run a fluentd process that can perform log parsing.

- The sidecar container then reads the logs and sends them to the appropriate back end. See Figure 8-3.

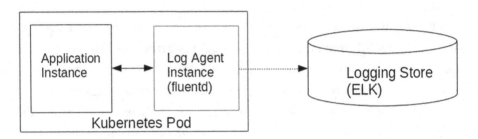

Figure 8-3. *Kubernetes logging*

Looking at the previous solution, the configuration for our front-end application looks as follows:

```
apiVersion: apps/v1
kind: Deployment
metadata:
  name: frontend-deployment
###############   OMITTED FOR BREVITY
    containers:
    - name: frontend
      image: frontend-app:1.0
      imagePullPolicy: Never
      env:
      - name: LOG_PATH
        value: /var/log
      volumeMounts:
      - name: varlog
        mountPath: /var/log
###############   OMITTED FOR BREVITY
    - name: log-agent
      image: k8s.gcr.io/fluentd-gcp:1.30
```

```
      env:
      - name: FLUENTD_ARGS
        value: -c /etc/fluentd-config/fluentd.conf
      volumeMounts:
      - name: varlog
        mountPath: /var/log
      - name: config-volume
        mountPath: /etc/fluentd-config
############### OMITTED FOR BREVITY
```

In the previous code, we have done the following:

- We have added the /var/log volume to our front-end
  Spring Boot container. The path has been exported to
  the LOG_PATH variable. The variable instructs Spring
  Boot to create the spring.log file at the /var/log path.

- Next we have a log-agent container in our pod.
  The container runs the fluentd process with the
  configuration file /etc/fluentd-config/fluentd.conf.

The following fluentd.conf file reads the logs generated by our
application and sends them to the ELK aggregator:

```
<source>
  type tail
  format /^\[[^ ]* (?<time>[^\]]*)\] \[(?<level>[^\]]*)\]
(?<message>.*)$/
  time_format %b %d %H:%M:%S %Y
  path /var/log/spring.log
  pos_file /var/log/agent/spring.log.pos
  tag hostname.system
</source>
```

```
<match *.**>
  type forward
<server>...</server>
<!--removed for Brevity -->
</match>
```

Before we can apply the previous configuration, we need to deploy the fluentd aggregator. This could be done by using the Kubernetes operator. The details of configuring fluentd are beyond the scope of the book. Refer to https://github.com/vmware/kube-fluentd-operator for more details.

Lastly, we need to set up the fluentd aggregator. The fluentd aggregator needs to send data to the ELK stack. It needs to run with the following sample configuration:

```
<match **>
        type elasticsearch
        log_level info
        host elasticsearch
        port 9200
        logstash_format true
        buffer_chunk_limit 2M
        buffer_queue_limit 8
        flush_interval 5s
        num_threads 2
  </match>
```

If the previous configuration works, we will see our application logs in the ELK stack. Now the next step is to send the access logs generated by Istio to the ELK instance. In the next section, we will look at the Mixer extension, which can be used to send the required logs.

Mixer

Istio captures all telemetry using an extensible Mixer subsystem. The subsystem is quite flexible and allows a plug-and-play approach for different monitoring and alerting systems. This abstraction enables the operations team to alter their application monitoring approach without needing any development changes. Istio Mixer is deployed with a number of adapters. Each of these adapters submits the required data to a monitoring system such as Prometheus, StatsD, etc. The Envoy sidecar invokes Mixer for every request and thus captures all data via the adapters. Since Envoy is invoking Mixer for every request it receives, it may sound logical to have the Mixer component embedded in the sidecar. But the approach of having a separate Mixer component has the following benefits:

- Mixer is an Istio-built component; thus, it is more aligned with the Istio design principles. On the other hand, Envoy is a proxy service by Lyft. This inherent difference makes Mixer more extensible to the complete approach.

- The approach makes the system more fault-tolerant. Mixer has many external dependencies and thus is more prone to networking failures. On the other hand, Envoy can't tolerate failures. It must keep operating even if the Mixer dependencies are unavailable.

- The approach of having separate Mixer and Envoy components makes the complete ecosystem more secure. Mixer integrates with various external systems. Thus, it can have many security vulnerabilities. But these issues get boxed at the Mixer level. Each Envoy instance can be configured to have a very narrow scope of interaction, thus limiting the impact of potential attacks.

- Istio deploys a sidecar for each and every instance; thus, the sidecar must be as light as possible. Keeping all third-party adaptations separate from the sidecar makes the sidecar more agile.

Mixer makes the Istio system more flexible, but it also increases the complexity of the system. The Mixer currently supports the following three use cases:

- Precondition checking

- Quota management, such as API limits

- Telemetry reporting such as logs and requests

Istio provides a variety of adapters that can be configured with Mixer. We can try to extend our logging example from the previous section. We were able to send our application logs in an ELK instance. We now need to send the access logs. Let's now try to achieve this with Mixer. Before we proceed, invoke the following command to get a list of available adapters:

```
$ kubectl get crd -listio=mixer-adapter
NAME                            CREATED AT
adapters.config.istio.io        2019-07-14T07:46:10Z
bypasses.config.istio.io        2019-07-14T07:45:59Z
circonuses.config.istio.io      2019-07-14T07:45:59Z
deniers.config.istio.io         2019-07-14T07:46:00Z
fluentds.config.istio.io        2019-07-14T07:46:00Z
Kubernetes envs.config.istio.io 2019-07-14T07:46:00Z
listcheckers.config.istio.io    2019-07-14T07:46:00Z
memquotas.config.istio.io       2019-07-14T07:46:01Z
noops.config.istio.io           2019-07-14T07:46:01Z
opas.config.istio.io            2019-07-14T07:46:02Z
prometheuses.config.istio.io    2019-07-14T07:46:02Z
rbacs.config.istio.io           2019-07-14T07:46:03Z
redisquotas.config.istio.io     2019-07-14T07:46:03Z
```

```
servicecontrols.config.istio.io       2019-07-14T07:46:04Z
signalfxs.config.istio.io             2019-07-14T07:46:04Z
solarwindses.config.istio.io          2019-07-14T07:46:04Z
stackdrivers.config.istio.io          2019-07-14T07:46:05Z
statsds.config.istio.io               2019-07-14T07:46:05Z
stdios.config.istio.io                2019-07-14T07:46:05Z
```

Istio 1.2 comes with a rich set adapters like Zipkin, StatsD, Stackdriver, CloudWatch, etc. The complete list of adapters can be accessed at https://istio.io/docs/reference/config/ policy-and-telemetry/adapters/.

Now that we know there are various adapters available, we will try to configure them for our applications. Each of the available adapters can be configured using the components shown in Figure 8-4.

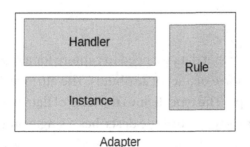

Adapter

Figure 8-4. Adapter components

Handler

A handler describes how the adapter needs to be invoked. It provides the necessary options that can used to configure the behavior of the associated adapter. The list of available handlers depends on the adapters deployed in the service mesh. Also, we need to refer to the adapter documentation

273

to know what configuration options are available. As an example let's look at the fluentds.config.istio.io adapter. The adapter is used to send access logs to the fluentd aggregator demon.

```
---
apiVersion: config.istio.io/v1alpha2
kind: handler
metadata:
  name: fluentdhandler
  namespace: istio-system
spec:
  compiledAdapter: fluentd
  params:
    address: "fluentd-aggregator-host:port"
```

Note that we have not described the log format, which we did for our application logs.

Instance

An instance defines what data we need to capture for a request. The data is represented in the form of a set of attributes. The attribute is represented as a name and a type. The type defines the kind of data that the attribute holds. Thus, we can say an attribute describes a single property of a request. For example, an attribute can be used to specify the HTTP response code or each of the HTTP headers. For every request, the Envoy sidecar sends the associated attributes to the Mixer subsystem. The Envoy sidecar generates these attributes by using the available environment/request/response values.

Istio has a common set of attributes that are available in all requests. The list of these attributes is available at `https://istio.io/docs/reference/config/policy-and-telemetry/attribute-vocabulary/`.

Adapters cannot understand any kind of data. The data understood by an adapter is compiled in four *templates*. Each template has a set of properties that can be captured by the adapter. Each adapter has a list of templates that can be used to send the data. Thus, an instance can be defined as a mapping of attributes, sent by the sidecar, into a template of the associated adapter. The following command shows the list of available templates:

```
$ kubectl get crd -listio=mixer-instance
NAME                                       CREATED AT
apikeys.config.istio.io                    2019-07-14T07:46:06Z
authorizations.config.istio.io             2019-07-14T07:46:06Z
checknothings.config.istio.io              2019-07-14T07:46:06Z
edges.config.istio.io                      2019-07-14T07:46:07Z
instances.config.istio.io                  2019-07-14T07:46:11Z
Kubernetes es.config.istio.io              2019-07-14T07:46:06Z
listentries.config.istio.io                2019-07-14T07:46:07Z
logentries.config.istio.io                 2019-07-14T07:46:07Z
metrics.config.istio.io                    2019-07-14T07:46:08Z
quotas.config.istio.io                     2019-07-14T07:46:08Z
reportnothings.config.istio.io             2019-07-14T07:46:08Z
servicecontrolreports.config.istio.io      2019-07-14T07:46:08Z
tracespans.config.istio.io                 2019-07-14T07:46:09Z
```

We can determine existing instances with the previous templates using the following commands:

```
$ kubectl get logentries.config.istio.io --all-namespaces
NAMESPACE       NAME           AGE
istio-system    accesslog      41d
istio-system    tcpaccesslog   41d
```

We can look at the accesslog definition to know which details are captured by it:

```
$ kubectl get logentries.config.istio.io accesslog -n istio-
system -o yaml
apiVersion: config.istio.io/v1alpha2
kind: logentry
metadata:
  // REMOVED FOR BREVITY
spec:
  monitored_resource_type: '"global"'
  severity: '"Info"'
  timestamp: request.time
  variables:
    apiClaims: request.auth.raw_claims | ""
    apiKey: request.api_key | request.headers["x-api-key"] | ""
    .......
    destinationApp: destination.labels["app"] | ""
    destinationIp: destination.ip | ip("0.0.0.0")
    destinationName: destination.name | ""
    latency: response.duration | "0ms"
    method: request.method | ""
    protocol: request.scheme | context.protocol | "http"
    receivedBytes: request.total_size | 0
    // REMOVED for brevity
```

The previous log entry captures the complete set of request-response attributes. The template also assigns default values for missing attributes. The previous entry is a precompiled instance. But in case it is not available, we can add an instance using the following YAML configuration:

```
apiVersion: config.istio.io/v1alpha2
kind: instance
metadata:
  name: myaccesslog
  namespace: istio-system
spec:
  compiledTemplate: logentry
  params:
    severity: '"info"'
    timestamp: request.time
    variables:
      source: source.labels["app"] | source.workload.name |
      "unknown"
      user: source.user | "unknown"
      destination: destination.labels["app"] | destination.
      workload.name | "unknown"
      responseCode: response.code | 0
      responseSize: response.size | 0
      latency: response.duration | "0ms"
    monitored_resource_type: '"UNSPECIFIED"'
```

Rules

A rule combines the deployed handlers with the deployed instances. It matches a request for the specified condition before invoking the associated instances. A rule must specify fully qualified names of the handlers and the instances. If all of them are deployed in the same namespace, then the rule can use short names. The following rule sends the accesslog and myaccesslog logs to the fluentd handler created earlier:

```
---
apiVersion: config.istio.io/v1alpha2
kind: rule
metadata:
  name: fluentdrule
  namespace: istio-system
spec:
  match: "true"
  actions:
  - handler: fluentdhandler
    instances: [ myaccesslog, accesslog ]
```

Now we can deploy all these components using the following command:

```
$ kubectl apply -f fluentd-adapter.yaml
```

Next, let's access our service using the curl command. This will generate the logs and send them to the ELK instance. Let's validate this by doing a lookup in Kibana.

The previous example was used as a simple stepping-stone. Istio can be extended for other use cases as well.

- Using StatsD to build stats and send them to Icinga/ Nargios

- Validating for quota-like API limits

Summary

In this chapter, we looked at the observability features offered by Istio. We started by capturing request traces to determine application performance. Istio allows us to use the tracing solution of our choice. Next we wanted to capture application-level logs. We realized that Istio does not offer a solution for application logging. Nevertheless, we can extend our Kubernetes cluster to have a logging solution for our deployed applications. The solution needs to work without any additional development effort. To that end, we deployed an ELK instance and routed application logs using the Sidecar pattern. The next aim was to extend the logging solution to include the logs generated by Istio. During the journey, we worked with the Mixer component to enable sidecar logs ingestion. In summary, we worked with Istio's extensibility feature, which can be used interface it with third-party systems.

CHAPTER 9

Policies and Rules

Application security is challenge in a microservice architecture. Developers build business process microservices in various languages. All these applications must be secured with the proper authentication and authorization. Most enterprises have one way of doing authentication and authorization. In this chapter, we will discuss the security features provided in Istio. Previously we saw that every Istio feature is driven by the Envoy proxy. Security is no exception to this. Istio provides security features using the Envoy proxy. It thus offloads the authentication and authorization logic from the business services.

Authentication

Authentication is the process of establishing the user's identity for a received request. But in a distributed architecture, a single user request spans multiple subrequests across different applications. It is easier to validate the original request for user identity, but each of the subrequests must also establish the identity of the user. This is often accomplished by using token-based authentication such as SSO, OAuth, and so on. Furthermore, distributed architectures are prone to network vulnerabilities. In such architectures, applications communicate across a network that none of them controls. The network can have adversaries that can forge, copy, replay, alter, destroy,

© Rahul Sharma, Avinash Singh 2020
R. Sharma and A. Singh, *Getting Started with Istio Service Mesh*,
https://doi.org/10.1007/978-1-4842-5458-5_9

and delay responses. To work effectively, applications must be able to trust the communication exchange. Istio supports all the previous requirements using various authentication mechanisms.

Transport Authentication

In microservices, architecture applications are prone to network attacks. Applications can safeguard against these attacks by implementing the TLS protocol for their communication. The protocol aims to provide privacy and data integrity between two or more communicating applications. But it is expensive and complex for each service to implement TLS communication. The Istio service mesh offloads this cost by supporting the TLS exchange using the Envoy proxy.

The TLS protocol works on the concepts of public key infrastructure (PKI). PKI states that there is a private key that defines an identity. Each private key also has a public key. The public key is specified in the certificate issued to the application. Applications communicate over the network by encrypting requests using their private key and decrypting the response using the other service's public key. To work successfully, the public key/certificate needs to be signed by a trusted party (a certificate authority). Istio implements the PKI logic by using two components: Citadel and Node-Agent. Citadel takes the role of certificate authority. It is responsible for issuing certificates. The process of issuing a certificate is as follows:

1. The Istio node agent generates a private key and a certificate-signing request (CSR).

2. The Istio node agent sends the CSR with its keys to Citadel for signing.

3. Citadel validates the credentials associated with the CSR and signs the CSR to generate the certificate.

4. The node agent sends both the certificate received from Citadel and the private key to the Envoy proxy.

The previous process is repeated at periodic intervals for key and certificate rotation. Now each sidecar has a certificate-key pair, so they can perform TLS communication using the following steps:

1. The client-side Envoy starts a mutual TLS handshake with the server-side Envoy proxy.

2. During the handshake, the client-side Envoy proxy does a secure naming check to verify that the service account presented in the server certificate is authorized to run the target service.

3. The client-side Envoy proxy and the server-side Envoy proxy establish a mutual TLS connection, and Istio forwards the traffic from the client-side Envoy proxy to the server-side Envoy proxy.

After authorization, the server-side Envoy proxy forwards the traffic to the server service through local TCP connections.

This process, as shown in Figure 9-1, mandates TLS communication for all interactions. It is challenging to implement the process for the entire application estate. Inside the cluster, Istio provides a cost-effective solution. It is often regarded as a best practice to have mtls mode enabled in the service mesh. But if the services are communicating with applications deployed outside the service mesh, then implementing the handshake becomes a major roadblock. Thus, Istio provides a permissive mode, which allows services to accept both plain-text traffic and mutual TLS traffic at the same time. This greatly simplifies the service mesh onboarding process.

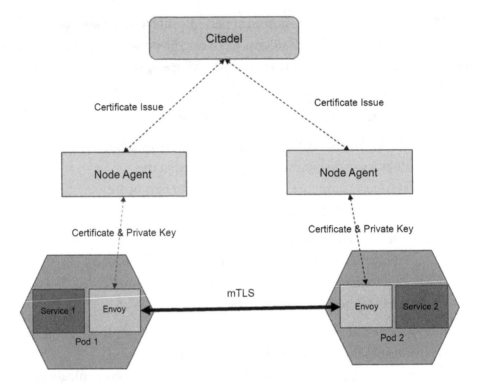

Figure 9-1. Citadel CA

Istio mutual TLS authentication is configured by creating a policy. The policy enforces the type of exchange supported by the application. The policy can be created at various levels. Once created, the policy is applicable to all the services deployed under the specified level. If there are policies at more than one level, then Istio applies the most specific policy.

- **Mesh:** This is a global policy impacting the entire service mesh.

- **Namespace:** This policy impacts services running in a specific namespace.

- **Service:** This policy impacts a specific service only.

The mesh policy is already deployed in Istio. The policy shows the configuration bundled with an Istio installation.

```
$ kubectl get meshpolicies.authentication.istio.io -o yaml
apiVersion: v1
items:
- apiVersion: authentication.istio.io/v1alpha1
  kind: MeshPolicy
  metadata:
  ## REMOVED for BREVITY
    generation: 1
    labels:
      app: security
      chart: security
      heritage: Tiller
      release: istio
    name: default
  spec:
    peers:
    - mtls:
        mode: PERMISSIVE
kind: List
metadata:
  resourceVersion: ""
  selfLink: ""
```

We can see that mtls is set to PERMISSIVE mode. Therefore, we have been able to do curl commands from outside the mesh. We can now configure STRICT mode for our webapp. In the following code, we have configured the web service to accept only mtls-based requests:

```
apiVersion: "authentication.istio.io/v1alpha1"
kind: "Policy"
```

```
metadata:
  name: "strict-policy"
spec:
  targets:
  - name: webservice
  peers:
  - mtls:
      mode: null
```

Let's deploy the policy and execute our curl commands from outside the mesh. We need the IP of the web service. (You can determine this by using kubectl.)

```
$curl  http://10.152.183.230/
curl: (56) Recv failure: Connection reset by peer
```

In the previous curl command, we are trying a plain-text request, which is dropped by the Envoy proxy. After doing the previous steps, we will notice that the pod starts failing. This is because the liveness probe requests from the Kubernetes server start failing, and the pod is marked as failed. See Figure 9-2.

```
NAME                                              READY   STATUS    RESTARTS   AGE
pod/frontend-deployment-78d98b75f4-rwkbm          3/3     Running   25         11d
pod/simplest-56c7bd47bf-m7pxf                     1/1     Running   2          2d5h
pod/webapp-deployment-5.0-5697656959-6qjfr        1/2     Running   28         2d5h
pod/webapp-deployment-6.2-654c5fd8f9-qs6r4        1/2     Running   28         2d5h
```

Figure 9-2. *Failing pod due to mtls*

As a first step, we must fix the requests from the Kubernetes server. This can be done by having checks on ports other than the application port. This will bypass them from the Envoy proxy. Alternatively, we can configure ProbeRewrite for the checks. This will send the check requests to `Pilot-Agent`, which will send them to the application containers. Before we can accomplish this, we need to enable `ProbeRewrite` using the following command:

```
$ kubectl get cm istio-sidecar-injector -n istio-system -o yaml
| sed -e "s/ rewriteAppHTTPProbe: false/ rewriteAppHTTPProbe:
true/" | kubectl apply -f -
configmap/istio-sidecar-injector configured
```

After this, we need to configure the `rewriteAppHTTPProbers` annotation for our deployment.

```
apiVersion: apps/v1
kind: Deployment
metadata:
  name: webapp-deployment-6.0
 ## REMOVED for BREVITY
  template:
    metadata:
      labels:
        app: webapp
        version: v6.0
      annotations:
        sidecar.istio.io/rewriteAppHTTPProbers: "true"
    spec:
      containers:
      - name: webapp
 ## REMOVED for BREVITY
```

Now the pod should not fail any longer. The pods are running fine, but we cannot run the `curl` command from outside the mesh. Services running in the mesh have the key-certificate pair set up, so we can try a `curl` command from our front-end pod.

```
frontend-deployment-78d98b75f4-rwkbm:/# curl  http://
webservice/
curl: (56) Recv failure: Connection reset by peer
```

The request still fails with the same error message as the `mtls` exchange has not happened. Let's understand what is going under the hood. Previously we enabled the application server to enforce `mtls`. Now, we need to instruct the clients to perform the `mtls` handshake. This is done by configuring a destination rule.

```
apiVersion: "networking.istio.io/v1alpha3"
kind: "DestinationRule"
metadata:
  name: "wb-rule"
  namespace: "default"
spec:
  host: webservice
  trafficPolicy:
    tls:
      mode: ISTIO_MUTUAL
```

In Chapter 4, we used a destination rule with a virtual service to define subsets. Here, in the previous configuration, we have instructed the Envoy sidecar to perform an `mtls` handshake for the web service destination. Now execute the request again. We can see that it works as expected.

In the previous example, we have enabled policies at the service level; alternatively, we can enable policies at the mesh or namespace level. This would make it applicable to all services running under the configured scope. Applying such a policy would ask for specific service rules to override it.

User Authentication

Istio provides OAuth token-based authentication. Every request is accompanied with an OAuth token. Before responding to the request, the Envoy proxy validates the token with the configured OpenID provider. Then the token is sent in JSON Web Token (JWT) format. Istio authentication is performed as per the following steps:

1. Make an initial request to the authorization server to exchange credentials and generate a token. The generated JWT is associated with a set of specific user roles and permissions.

2. Each subsequent request must specify the token, allowing the user to access authorized routes, services, and resources that are permitted with that token.

The Envoy proxy validates the token. It also replicates the token on each of the subrequests. See Figure 9-3.

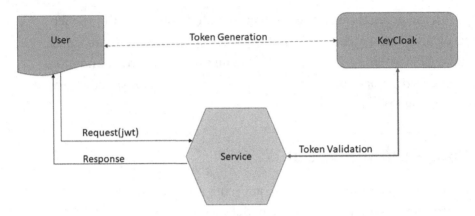

Figure 9-3. *JWT-based authentication*

JWT is an open standard (RFC 7519) that defines a compact and self-contained way to securely transmit information between parties as a JSON object. This information can be verified and trusted as it is digitally signed. The encrypted token can be used to specify user roles and permissions associated with it. Thus, it is most commonly used to specify user authorization.

Before we proceed, we need to have an OpenID provider. Istio allows us to work with many providers such as Auth0, Google Auth, and so on. In this chapter, we are going to work with KeyCloak (http://KeyCloak.org). We have a deployed a KeyCloak instance on one of our workstations. See Figure 9-4.

Figure 9-4. *KeyCloak*

Now, we need to add users in KeyCloak. These users will have access to our Kubernetes application. To do so, we need to first select/add a realm in KeyCloak. A realm, in KeyCloak, can have clients specified by an ID-secret pair. The clients can be equated to different applications in an ecosystem. In turn, each of these applications has users. This is mapped by creating different users for each client. Each of the created users can have different attributes/privileges. The previous description is a 50,000-foot view of the KeyCloak security provider. Details of KeyCloak are beyond the scope of the book. Please refer to the KeyCloak documentation to learn more.

The following are the steps taken to add users to KeyCloak. We can skip the section if we already have users set up in our OpenID provider.

1. Log in to the KeyCloak admin console using the admin account.

2. The Master drop-down menu shows existing realms; click Add Realm and create a K8s-dev realm.

3. Now select the K9s-dev realm and click Users to open the user list page.

4. Open the Add User page. Enter a name for the username and click Save.

5. While on the User page, click the Credentials tab to set a temporary password for the new user. Type a new password and confirm it.

In our current example, we created a K8s-dev realm. The realm contains a client ID for the web service and front-end applications. Both these clients have a user mapped to it. At this point, we haven't added any additional privileges to these users. See Figure 9-5.

Figure 9-5. *KeyCloak configuration*

After performing the previous configuration, we will get back details of the OpenID endpoints. These endpoints are used to perform user authentication and token validation. The following are a few important endpoints that we will use:

```
issuer              "http://172.18.0.1:8181/auth/realms/k8s-dev"
authorization_endpoint   "http://172.18.0.1:8181/auth/realms/
                         k8s-dev/protocol/OpenID -connect/
                         auth"
token_endpoint      "http://172.18.0.1:8181/auth/realms/k8s-
                     dev/protocol/OpenID -connect/token"
jwks_uri     "http://172.18.0.1:8181/auth/realms/k8s-dev/
             protocol/OpenID -connect/certs"
```

Now we will configure Istio user authentication by using the previously provided endpoints. We will create a policy as shown in the previous section.

```
apiVersion: "authentication.istio.io/v1alpha1"
kind: "Policy"
metadata:
  name: "user-auth"
spec:
  targets:
  - name: webservice
  origins:
  - jwt:
      issuer: http://172.18.0.1:8181/auth/realms/k8s-dev
      jwksUri: http://172.18.0.1:8181/auth/realms/k8s-dev/
      protocol/OpenID -connect/certs
      trigger_rules:
      - excluded_paths:
        - exact: /health
  principalBinding: USE_ORIGIN
```

In the previous configuration, we have done the following:

1. We configured the JWT settings to point to our k8s-dev realm.

2. Now, there is a possibility of two security principals in our proxy. One is from the `mtls` configuration, and the other is from the user-identity token. In such cases, we configure the binding principal from the user token.

3. We have excluded the `/heath` URL from the authentication as this is used by Kubernetes for a liveness check. If we block this path, then the pod will start failing, as seen when we enabled `mtls`.

The JWT token authentication can be enabled or disabled for a specific path. Also, we can add multiple JWT blocks to handle different paths. If all JWTs are disabled for a request path, authentication also passes as if there is none defined. Now let's test our configuration by executing these `curl` commands:

```
$curl  -v http://10.152.183.230/
< HTTP/1.1 401 Unauthorized
< content-length: 29
< content-type: text/plain
< date: Thu, 05 Sep 2019 08:50:03 GMT
< server: istio-envoy
< x-envoy-decorator-operation: webservice.default.svc.cluster.
local:80/*
<
Origin authentication failed.
```

The service returned 401 error code. To make it work, we need to add a JWT to the request. Let's first generate one by sending an OAuth request. We will generate it using Postman, but you can use any other suitable method as well. The aim is to have a JWT value that can be passed in the authorization header.

We can use Postman in the following manner:

1. Select the Authorization tab in Postman, and set the type to OAuth 2.0.

2. Click Get New Access Token. This will open a new form where we need to fill in the values from our OpenID configuration.

3. After positioning the correct values, click Request Token. See Figure 9-6.

Figure 9-6. JWT token

It then asks for login credentials. On successful login, it sends back a token. We need to copy the value and send it in the authentication headers.

```
$curl --header "Authorization: Bearer $TOKEN" -v
http://10.152.183.230/
> GET / HTTP/1.1
> Host: 10.152.183.230
> User-Agent: curl/7.58.0
> Accept: */*
> Authorization: Bearer eyJhbGciOiJSUzI1NiIsInR5cCIgOiAiSldUIiw
  ia2lkIiA6ICJpejZyRi1RQUw4STVlNFRDcVdaSE9SLWpLN1A2UjVEUnR2d2Zs
  Zk5MSnZVIn0.eyJqdGkiOiI4NzYyOGQ4Ni04MTg3LTQ1ZGEtOWRiMi1iZGIyN
  ThkYzk5MGMiLCJleHAiOjE1Njc2MTkyMDcsIm5iZiI6MCwiaWF0IjoxNTY3Nj
  E4OTA3LCJpc3MiOiJodHRwOi8vMTcyLjE4LjAuMTo4MTgxL2F1dGgvcmVhbG1
  zL2s4cy1kZXYiLCJhdWQiOiJhY2NvdW50Iiwic3ViIjoiNmY3MTNlMDMtOWYy
  NCOOMmMyLTgzMDktZWI2ZGYONmZiNzU1IiwidHlwIjoiQmVhcmVyIiwiYXpwI
  joid2Vic2VydmljZS11c2VyIiwiYXV0aF90aW1lIjoxNTY3NjE4MDQyLCJzZX
  NzaW9uX3N0YXRlIjoiYzNhOTk1NWMtYTA5YS0ONGFlLWE3NzEtMzM3OTEOOTR
  jZTg1IiwiYWNyIjoiMCIsImFsbG93ZWQtb3JpZ2lucyI6WyIqIl0sInJlYWxt
  X2FjY2VzcyI6eyJyb2xlcyI6WyJvZmZsaW5lX2FjY2VzcyIsInVtYV9hdXRob
  3JpemF0aW9uIl19LCJyZXNvdXJjZV9hY2Nlc3MiOnsid2Vic2VydmljZS11c2
  VyIjp7InJvbGVzIjpbInVzZXIiXX0sImFjY291bnQiOnsicm9sZXMiOlsibWF
  uYWdlLWFjY291bnQiLCJtYW5hZ2UtYWNjb3VudC1saW5rcyIsInZpZXctcHJv
  ZmlsZSJdfX0sInNjb3BlIjoib3BlbmlkIHByb2ZpbGUgZW1haWwiLCJlbWFpb
  F92ZXJpZmllZCI6ZmFsc2UsInByZWZlcnJlZF91c2VybmFtZSI6InJhaHVsIi
  wiZW1haWwiOiJyYWh1bEBrOHMuY29tIn0.aHrwRFT2jGOFFBEhNA-bbaY-NxG
  IGGDBqn9XxqvHUJLIagnjhkTZGioH44kog_A_LT9IeGj2bMeOBebONQn4K1a-
  c66EpQa4bwt9kcsFfcSKb1Z1dtOhp8tg7jjST93220dq9h9SqHdrMbhJ_eLOr
  dOKs5VE8DiOOONaP1OkQj4B5Ya58VMuIEAeajgOsSivRRKZlseXp-kr2rPlS2
  fbPmGFPCfxZl_OEygGaiKWPyQ79DvI_ecEDKxUmg4iLtp86ieVWcu6H_X6ETH
  mdk9QInWTXI4ORHygd9loYOBoDFtVG9K3STPv9Cn6eDwn6jHCuyyEJ9VOk-
  2OXqqopF-ggA
>
```

```
< HTTP/1.1 200 OK
< content-type: text/html; charset=utf-8
< content-length: 62
< server: istio-envoy
< date: Wed, 04 Sep 2019 17:44:50 GMT
< x-envoy-upstream-service-time: 3
< x-envoy-decorator-operation: webservice.default.svc.cluster.
  local:80/*
<
* Connection #0 to host 10.152.183.230 left intact
[6.0]Welcome user! current time is 2019-09-05 17:44:50.140684
```

Authorization

In the previous section, we accomplished authentication. This means that we have established the identity of the user. But all users are not allowed to access all parts of the application. The process of controlling access to the only the allowed parts is known as *authorization*. Roles-based access control (RBAC) is often used to limit the users to the functions that are applicable to them. Users must not be allowed to perform operations beyond their realm. Istio runs an RBAC engine in the Envoy proxy. The proxy gets the applicable RBAC policies from Pilot. It compares the JWT in the request against the configured authorization policies. As a result, it either allows or denies the request.

Istio by default disables the roles-based access control. As a first step, we need to enable RBAC for Istio. This can be done by applying the following configuration:

```
apiVersion: "rbac.istio.io/v1alpha1"
kind: ClusterRbacConfig
metadata:
  name: default
```

```
spec:
  mode: 'ON_WITH_INCLUSION'
  inclusion:
    namespaces: ["default"]
```

The previous configuration enables RBAC control for the "default" namespace. It is important to note that `ClusterRbacConfig` is a singleton cluster-scoped object, named `default`. There are other values for the mode that can be used to fine-tune RBAC:

- **OFF**: Istio authorization is disabled.

- **ON**: Istio authorization is enabled for all services in the mesh.

- **ON_WITH_INCLUSION**: Istio authorization is enabled only for services and namespaces specified in the inclusion field.

- **ON_WITH_EXCLUSION**: Istio authorization is enabled for all services in the mesh except the services and namespaces specified in the exclusion field.

We can try to access the service using the `curl` command, but it fails with a 403 response.

```
$ curl --header "Authorization: Bearer $TOKEN" -v
http://10.152.183.230/
< HTTP/1.1 403 Forbidden
< content-length: 19
< content-type: text/plain
RBAC: access denied
```

Once RBAC is enabled, we need to define roles/permissions.
Permissions can be defined at a service level. They can also be fine-tuned
for a path, an HTTP method, and request headers. These permissions are
defined using the ServiceRole configuration.

```
---
apiVersion: "rbac.istio.io/v1alpha1"
kind: ServiceRole
metadata:
  name: http-viewer
spec:
  rules:
  - services: ["webservice"]
    methods: ["GET"]
```

The previous configuration defined an http-viewer role for
accessing webservice. The defined role needs to be assigned to a user.
The assignment can be done for a user or a user identified by attributes
of its token. Alternatively, it can be left as anonymous access as well. In
applications, we may want to allow a GET request so that users can view
the data. But the POST request needs a role-based authorization. So, let's
define one more role for performing updates.

```
---
apiVersion: "rbac.istio.io/v1alpha1"
kind: ServiceRole
metadata:
  name: http-update-webservice
spec:
  rules:
  - services: ["webservice"]
    methods: ["POST"]
```

We have added the update role for the POST method, but it can be limited using the URL path. Now we need to assign the http-viewer rights to everyone and only assign http-update-webservice to authenticated users. This is done by configuring ServiceRoleBinding.

```
---
apiVersion: "rbac.istio.io/v1alpha1"
kind: ServiceRoleBinding
metadata:
  name: bind-http-viewer
spec:
  subjects:
  - user:  "*"
  roleRef:
    kind: ServiceRole
    name: "http-viewer"
```

The previous binding assigns the http-viewer role to all users. Alternatively, we can validate the user principal and assign a corresponding role to it. This is accomplished in the following configuration:

```
---
apiVersion: "rbac.istio.io/v1alpha1"
kind: ServiceRoleBinding
metadata:
  name: bind-http-update
spec:
  subjects:
  - properties:
      request.auth.claims[scope]: "webservice"
  roleRef:
    kind: ServiceRole
    name: "http-update-webservice"
```

The previous binding assigns the `http-update-webservice` role to requests having jwt with a `webservice` scope. The `request.auth.claims` is used to read different parts of the JWT. Apply the previous `ServiceRole` and `ServiceRoleBinding` configurations. Now we can try the `curl` command. It should work as expected.

Rules

In the previous section, we enforced policies for authentication and authorization. But policies can also be used to enforce application rules. This is quite useful for the operations team, which can create rules to manage resource utilization or control application black/whitelisting, and so on. It is important to note that these requirements are based on runtime behavior and thus are quite diverse. It is a good idea to implement these changing needs using a rule engine instead of developing custom code. Istio supports rule validation using the Mixer component. Previously we configured the Mixer component to work with third-party extensions like Jagger. The Mixer consists of three parts.

- **Handler:** Defines the adapter configuration

- **Instance:** Defines the attributes that need to be captured for a request

- **Rule:** Associates a handler with instances that can send the required data

The Envoy proxy sends requests to the Istio Pilot. The Pilot invokes Mixer, which captures data as defined in the instance configuration and sends it to the handler. Previously, the handler was capturing data in external systems. Alternatively, the handler can perform a Boolean check for the received request. The Envoy proxy can allow or deny a request based on the check response. Like most other features, Istio provides a disablePolicyChecks flag to toggle a rules check. Let's first enable it using the following command:

```
$ kubectl get cm istio -n istio-system -o yaml | sed -e
"s/ disablePolicyChecks: true/ disablePolicyChecks: false/" |
kubectl apply -f - configmap/istio configured
```

In the following example, we will configure a whitelisting rule. Basically we want to allow a webapp to be accessed from our front-end service only. Any other source should not be allowed. To do this, we need to configure a listchecker handler with a listentry template.

```
---
apiVersion: config.istio.io/v1alpha2
kind: handler
metadata:
  name: whitelist
spec:
  compiledAdapter: listchecker
  params:
    overrides: ["frontend"]
    blacklist: true
---
apiVersion: config.istio.io/v1alpha2
kind: instance
metadata:
  name: appsource
spec:
  compiledTemplate: listentry
  params:
    value: source.labels["app"]
---
```

```
apiVersion: config.istio.io/v1alpha2
kind: rule
metadata:
  name: checksrc
spec:
  match: destination.labels["app"] == "webapp"
  actions:
  - handler: whitelist
    instances: [ appsource ]
```

We can now execute our `curl` commands, which will fail with the following error:

```
$curl -v  http://10.152.183.230/
> GET / HTTP/1.1
> Host: 10.152.183.146
> User-Agent: curl/7.58.0
> Accept: */*
>
* Empty reply from server
* Connection #0 to host 10.152.183.
curl: (52) Empty reply from server
```

But if we try to do a `curl` to our front-end service, we will get the expected response. In the previous code, we implemented whitelisting, and it can be toggled to blacklisting by changing the `blacklist` attribute of the handler. So far, we have worked with application whitelisting. Istio bundles a couple of handlers that can be used to perform diverse checks such as quota management, simple denials, and so on.

Summary

In this chapter, we worked with the security features of Istio. We looked at the two kinds of authentication offered by Istio. Transport authentication is implemented using a mutual TLS mode for all service communication. This makes it mandatory for a server and client to have a private key and certificate pair. Istio implements PKI logic, which simplifies the mtls handshake in a service mesh. Istio supports a PERMISSIVE mode to offer plain-text interactions. This simplifies interactions with services deployed outside the service mesh. Istio provides user authentication using an OAuth-based token in JWT format. Next, we discussed authorization using Istio RBAC. The RBAC can be used to build fine-grained permissions for a service, path, HTTP method, and request attributes. Lastly, we discussed the Istio rule engine, which can be used to enforce checks such as blacklisting, request quotas, etc.

CHAPTER 10

Troubleshooting

Troubleshooting issues in an Istio service mesh is quite complex. There are many components that are working together to deliver the required behavior, and each of these systems has its own nuances. It is quite impossible to account for all conditions. Thus, during an incident, the troubleshooting process may feel like looking for a needle in a haystack. In this chapter, we will introduce some tools we can use to troubleshoot service-mesh issues. The commands discussed in this chapter are applicable to a bare-metal Kubernetes installation. It is important to know what configuration we are looking-for. It may require slight variant commands in a cloud based cluster.

Configmaps

Istio has many features driven by corresponding feature flags. We have seen these flags in policy checks, request tracing, and so on. The configuration flags are the first place to determine how a feature is configured. It can answer a broad set of questions such as the following:

- What configuration is used for the envoy proxy?

- How is the gateway working?

- Is Istio's distributed tracing enabled, and which tracing provider is configured?

© Rahul Sharma, Avinash Singh 2020
R. Sharma and A. Singh, *Getting Started with Istio Service Mesh*,
https://doi.org/10.1007/978-1-4842-5458-5_10

The flags are part of the Istio configuration defined using the Kubernetes configmaps. Specifically, Istio is driven by two configmaps.

- istio: This defines the configuration for the Istio pilot, Mixer, Tracing, Prometheus, Grafana, and so on. Configuration options for each of the component are prefixed by the component name.

- istio-sidecar-injector: This defines the configuration for the Istio sidecar, including the location of the Pilot, Kubernetes api-server, etc.

We can get these configmaps using the following commands:

```
$kubectl -n istio-system get cm istio -o jsonpath="{@.data.mesh}"
disablePolicyChecks: false
enableTracing: true
accessLogFile: "/dev/stdout"
#REMOVED for BREVITY
```

```
$kubectl -n istio-system get cm istio-sidecar-injector -o
jsonpath="{@.data.config}"
policy: enabled
alwaysInjectSelector:
  []
template: |-
  rewriteAppHTTPProbe: {{ valueOrDefault .Values.sidecarInjector
  Webhook.rewriteAppHTTPProbe false }}
  {{- if or (not .Values.istio_cni.enabled) .Values.global.
  proxy.enableCoreDump }}
  initContainers:
#REMOVED for BREVITY
```

Next we can determine how the sidecar is injected. Istio supports automatic injection, provided it is configured for a namespace. We can list all the namespaces for the automatic `istion-sidecar` using the following command:

```
$kubectl get namespace -L istio-injection
NAME              STATUS   AGE    ISTIO-INJECTION
default           Active   221d   enabled
istio-system      Active   60d    disabled
kube-node-lease   Active   75d
kube-public       Active   221d
kube-system       Active   221d
```

Proxy

Istio applies most of the features using the Envoy proxy. The Istio proxy connects with the Istio pilot to get the latest configuration. Thus, it is imperative to know whether the Envoy proxy is in sync with the latest policies available in the pilot. `istioctl proxy-status` is a useful command to get the status of all the proxies.

```
$ istioctl proxy-status
PROXY                                                          CDS
LDS     EDS     RDS        PILOT                          VERSION
istio-ingress-6458b8c98f-7ks48.istio-system          SYNCED
SYNCED  SYNCED  NOT SENT  istio-pilot-75bdf98789-n2kqh  1.1.2
istio-ingressgateway-7d6874b48f-qxhn5.istio-system   SYNCED
SYNCED  SYNCED  SYNCED    istio-pilot-75bdf98789-n2kqh  1.1.2
productpage-v1-6c886ff494-hm7zk.default               SYNCED
SYNCED  SYNCED  STALE     istio-pilot-75bdf98789-n2kqh  1.1.2
ratings-v1-5d9ff497bb-gslng.default                   SYNCED
SYNCED  SYNCED  SYNCED    istio-pilot-75bdf98789-n2kqh  1.1.2
```

```
webservice-v1-55d4c455db-zjj2m.default                    SYNCED
SYNCED  SYNCED  SYNCED   istio-pilot-75bdf98789-n2kqh  1.1.2
webservice-v2-686bbb668-99j76.default                     SYNCED
SYNCED  SYNCED  SYNCED   istio-pilot-75bdf98789-tfdvh  1.1.2
webservice-v3-7b9b5fdfd6-4r52s.default                    SYNCED
SYNCED  SYNCED  SYNCED   istio-pilot-75bdf98789-n2kqh  1
```

All the running proxies will be in one of the following states:

- SYNCED: The means the sidecar is updated with all the changes.

- STALE: This means there are changes, but the sidecar has not picked these changes.

- NOT SENT: This means there are no changes.

If a proxy is missing in the list, it is not connected to the Istio pilot. We can find out a proxy configuration using the following command:

```
$ istioctl proxy-config bootstrap -n istio-egressgateway-
9b7866bf5-8p5rt.istio-system
{
    "bootstrap": {
        "node": {
            "id": "router~172.30.86.14~ istio-egressgateway-
            9b7866bf5-8p5rt -system~istio-system.svc.cluster.
            local",
            "cluster": "istio-ingressgateway",
            "metadata": {
                "POD_NAME": " istio-egressgateway-
                9b7866bf5-8p5rt ",
                "istio": "sidecar"
            },
```

```
    "buildVersion": "0/1.8.0 //RELEASE"
  },
## REMOVED for BREVITY
}
```

Lastly, we can investigate the logs of the proxy to find out how it is behaving. Proxy logs can be accessed using the logs commands.

```
$kubectl logs pod/frontend-deployment-78d98b75f4-rwkbm  istio-
proxy
[2019-09-15T20:17:00.310Z] "GET / HTTP/2" 204 - 154 0 226 100
"10.0.35.28"
"" "cc21d9b0-cf5c-432b-8c7e-98aeb7988cd2" ""
"tcp://10.0.2.1:8080"
[2019-09-15T20:17:01.102Z] "GET / HTTP/2" 204 - 154 0 226 100
"10.0.35.28"
"" "cc21d9b0-tfdvh-432b-n2kqh-75bdf98789" ""
"tcp://10.0.2.1:8080"
```

Routes

Traffic routing is one of the most important features of Istio. You learned about traffic routing in Chapters 4 and 5. There will be situations when a virtual service will not work, and the associated destination rule may also fail. We can start troubleshooting traffic routes by determining the ports that the Istio sidecar is listening on.

```
$ istioctl proxy-config listeners istio-ingressgateway-
75ddf64567-jtl68.istio-system
ADDRESS      PORT      TYPE
0.0.0.0      15090     HTTP
```

The previous command summarizes the ports the proxy is listening on. To get details of how the proxy is set up for traffic on a particular port, we need more details. This can be done using the following command:

```
$ istioctl proxy-config listeners istio-egressgateway-9b7866bf5-
8p5rt.istio-system -o json --address 0.0.0.0 --port 15090
[
. . . . .
    {
        "address": {
            "socketAddress": {
                "address": "0.0.0.0",
                "portValue": 15090
            }
        },
. . . . .
]
```

The previous command shows a route name that is used for the specified port. We can find out which hosts are resolved for the route with this:

```
$ istioctl proxy-config routes frontend-v1-6549877cc8-67cc8
--name 8080 -o json
[
    {
        "name": "8080",
        "virtualHosts": [
            {
                "name": "webservice.default.svc.cluster.
                local:8080",
                "domains": [
                    "webservice.default.svc.cluster.local",
```

```
            "webservice.default.svc.cluster.
            local:8080",
            "webservice",
            "webservice:8080",
            "webservice.default.svc.cluster",
            "webservice.default.svc.cluster:8080",
### REMOVED for BREVITY
            ],
            "routes": [
                {
                    "match": {
                        "prefix": "/"
                    },
                    "route": {
                        "cluster": "outbound|8080||web
                        service.default.svc.cluster.local",
                        "timeout": "0.000s"
                    },
...
```

We can see that different web service domains and IP addresses
are resolved to an outbound address. The resolved outbound address
is configured to cluster locations, which can be determined using the
following command:

```
$ istioctl proxy-config cluster frontend-v1-6549877cc8-
67cc8  --fqdn webservice.default.svc.cluster.local -o json
[
    {
        "name": "outbound|8080||webservice.default.svc.cluster.
        local",
        "type": "EDS",
```

```
        "edsClusterConfig": {
            "edsConfig": {
                "ads": {}
            },
            "serviceName": "outbound|8080||webservice.default.
            svc.cluster.local"
        },
        "connectTimeout": "1.000s",
        "circuitBreakers": {
            "thresholds": [
                {}
            ]
        }
    }
]
```

Lastly, we can validate location endpoints for the cluster locations.

```
$ istioctl proxy-config endpoints frontend-v1-6549877cc8-67cc8
--cluster "outbound|8080||webservice.default.svc.cluster.local"
ENDPOINT                STATUS      OUTLIER CHECK
CLUSTER
172.17.0.17:8080        HEALTHY     OK
outbound|8080||webservice.default.svc.cluster.local
172.17.0.18:8080        HEALTHY     OK
outbound|8080||webservice.default.svc.cluster.local
172.17.0.5:8080         HEALTHY     OK
outbound|8080||webservice.default.svc.cluster.local
```

Destination rules are also used to configure the mutual TLS authentication on the client side. But sometimes the destination rule will not work, and the handshake will fail with a 503 error code. In such cases, we must check whether the destination rule is violating the existing configuration.

```
$ istioctl authn tls-check istio-ingressgateway-75ddf64567-jtl68.
istio-system
HOST:PORT                                              STATUS  SERVER
CLIENT   AUTHN POLICY                                  DESTINATION RULE
grafana.istio-system.svc.cluster.local:3000            OK      HTTP
HTTP     grafana-ports-mtls-disabled/istio-system      -
istio-citadel.istio-system.svc.cluster.local:8060      OK      HTTP/mTLS
HTTP     default/                                       -
istio-citadel.istio-system.svc.cluster.local:15014     OK      HTTP/mTLS
HTTP     default/                                       -
```

Summary

In this chapter, we discussed commands to troubleshoot Istio issues. We showed how to work with the Kubernetes cm command to find out the Istio configuration details. Thereafter, we looked at the proxy logs and checked the destination rules deployed in Istio. Istio is a complex distributed application, and it is hard to understand every nuance. During an incident, you can use the commands covered in this chapter to debug the configuration for root-cause analysis.

Index

A, B

Application, Kubernetes
  container creation, 18
  deployment
    configuration, 19–23
  WebApp application
    container, 19
  Web Requests Handler, 18
  YAML file, 20
Application logs, 266–270
Application monitoring, 233–235
Application setup, 195–201
Architecture, Istio
  control plane, 104–106
  data plane, 103, 104
  mixer
    adapters, 108, 109
    attributes, 109, 110
    citadel, 114
    configuration
      model, 110, 111
    galley, 114
    pilot, 111–113
    platform-independent
      component, 106
    service logs, 106
    topology, 107

Authentication
    token-based process, 281
    transport, 282
    user, 289
Authorization, 297–301

C

Circuit breakers
  cascading service, 219
  and circuit breaker, 229–231
  connection pool
    HTTP/1.1, 222
    HTTP/2, 223–228
  pattern, 56
  polyglot applications, 222
  service recovery, 220, 221
Cloud infrastructure, 1
Cloud-native environment, 78
Cloud-native microservices, 54
Cluster Discovery Service (CDS), 87
Connection pool configuration, 148
Container Runtime Interface
  (CRI), 9
Controller manager
  endpoint controller, 4
  node controller, 4
  replication controller, 5

© Rahul Sharma, Avinash Singh 2020
R. Sharma and A. Singh, *Getting Started with Istio Service Mesh*,
https://doi.org/10.1007/978-1-4842-5458-5

D

Destination rules
    connection pool, 148–150
    Kubernetes cluster, 146
    load balancing, 151
    outlier detection, 151–153
    VirtualService components, 147
Distributed architecture, 54
Distributed tracing, 81
    definition, 259
    deployed services, 262
    Envoy proxy, 260
    HTTP headers, 260
    Jagger operator, 261
    NodePort address, 263
    observability
        namespace, 261
    service mesh, 264–266
Docker installation
    Linux, 13, 14
    macOS, 15
    windows, 15

E, F

Endpoint Discovery
    Service (EDS), 87
Envoy configuration, 88–95
Envoy proxy, 307–309
External service access
    attributes, 186
    egress, 188–192
    HTTP service, 187
    mesh nodes, 184

    pod network, 183
    service entry, 185
    sidecar proxy, 183

G

Grafana
    dashboard, 251–253
    data flow, 249
    installation, 249, 250
    stakeholders alert, 253–258
    webhook channel, 254

H

HTTP filters, 86
Hystrix circuit breaker, 70

I

Istio CLI
    authentication
        policies, 124
    deregister, 124
    experimentation
        authentication, 125
        Grafana dashboard, 127
        metrics, 128
        VirtualService, 125, 126
    Kubernetes configuration,
        128–135
    register, 125
    validation, 135
Istio environment
    architecture

adapters, 108, 109

attributes, 109, 110

citadel, 114

components, 102, 103

configuration

model, 110, 111

control plane, 104–106

data plane

service, 103, 104

galley, 114

pilot, 111–113

features, 101

installation

GKE, 120

Helm, 115–118

verification, 120–122

service mesh, 99, 101, 102

services, 122

setting up, 118, 119

working, 123, 124

Istio gateway

ingress

configuration, 169

curl commands, 174

load balancer service, 169, 173

mesh, 172, 175

Minikube server, 173

sidecar proxies, 175

traffic routing, 170

virtual service, 171, 172

web service, 171

wget commands, 175

Istio Mixer, 236, 237

J

JSON Web Token (JWT), 289

K

Kubectl installation

Linux, 11

macOS, 12

windows, 12

Kubernetes (K8s)

architecture, 2, 3

autostopping

application, 41

behavior, 37

container creation, 38, 42

deployment, 30–32

framework, 82

master components

API server, 3

controller manager, 4, 5

scheduler, 4

status of deployment, 39, 40, 44, 45

terminology

deployment, 9

image, 9

Kubectl, 10

Namespace, 10

replicaset, 10

service, 10

statefulset, 10

worker

container registry, 8, 9

Kube-proxy, 5

Kubernetes (K8s) (*cont.*)
    node agent, 5
    pods, 6
    runtime container, 7, 8
Kubernetes cluster, Set Up
    Docker installation, 13
    Java, 15
    Kubectl installation, 11
    Minikube dashboard, 17
    Minikube installation, 12
    Python, 15
    Ubuntu terminal, 15
    VirtualBox, 11
    virtual machine, 16
Kubernetes logging, 268

L

Labels, 237
Language libraries
    circuit breaker, 68–71
    hands-on approach
        Java IDE, 64
        Maven project, 65
        POM file, 66
        REST controller, 67
        service output, 68
    service discovery
        Eureka server, 72, 73
        frameworks, 76
        LoadBalancer
            annotation, 75
        service registry, 74
Listener Discovery Service (LDS), 87

Listener filters, 85
Load balancing, 151
    deployment configuration,
        202–204
    least requests, 201
    random node, 201
    round-robin, 201
    weightage, 201

M

Microservice architecture
    administrator, 59
    agility, 51, 52, 58
    debugging, 61, 62
    homogeneous, 60, 61
    infinite bandwidth, 57, 58
    infrastructure, 61
    innovation, 52
    language libraries, 62
    maintainability, 53
    monitoring, 61, 62
    reliable network, 54, 55
    scalability, 52, 53
    secure network, 58
    transport cost, 59
    zero latency, 55–57
Microservices
    application setup, 32–34
    deployment, 34, 35, 37
Minikube installation
    Linux, 12
    macOS, 13
    windows, 13

Mixer subsystem
    adapters, 272, 273
    benefits, 271
    handler, 273, 274
    instance, 274–277
    plug and play approach, 271
    rules, 278, 279
    system monitoring, 271
    use cases, 272
    YAML configuration, 277
Monolith architectures
    application design, 51
    development teams, 49
    functions, 48, 49
    scaling issues, 50
    steep learning, 50

N

Naming service ports, 142
Network filters, 85

O

openssl command, 177
Orchestration platform, 1
Outlier detection, 151–153

P, Q

Polygot environment, 78
Prometheus
    custom metrics, 245–247, 249
    dashboard

Istio mesh, 240, 241
    limiting metrics, 243
    mesh request, 244
    PromQL, 242
    siege request, 241, 242
    installation, 238–240
    metrics flow, 237
Public key infrastructure (PKI), 282

R

Resiliency, 231
Retry requests
    cost of response time, 208
    end user availability, 209
    front-end service, 205
    Istio fault injection, 211, 212
    network layer, 205
    service node, 207
    VirtualService component,
        207, 210, 211
    Web App Service, 205, 206
Roles-based access control
    (RBAC), 297
Route Discovery Service (RDS), 87
Rules, 301–303

S

Secret Discovery Service (SDS), 87
Secure Sockets Layer (SSL)
    client's certificate chain, 181, 182
    HAProxy/Nginx, 176
    -HHost header, 181

Secure Sockets Layer (SSL) (*cont.*)
   HTTPS protocol, 180
   Istio secret, 179
   openssl command, 177
   PASSTHROUGH mode, 182
   pod location, 178, 179
   Kubernetes secret, 181
   TLS authentication, 181
Service-level security, 79, 80
Service mesh
   analytics, 80, 81
   definition, 77
   protocol-agnostic, 78
   sidecar pattern, 82
   TLS security, 80
   traffic control
      mechanism, 78, 79
Service mesh, Istio
   routing, 100, 101
   service discovery, 100
Service resiliency, Istio
   distributed system, 193, 194
Services
   Kubernetes
      clusterIP, 27
      ExternalName type, 29, 30
      interactions, 24
      LoadBalancer type, 28, 29
      NodePort, 27
      pods access, 25–27
      webapp, 24, 25
Sidecar pattern
   authentication, 83
   components

      CDS, 87
      EDS, 87
      LDS, 87
      RDS, 87
      SDS, 87
   envoy architecture
      benefits, 84
      cluster, 86
      filters, 85
      port listener, 85
   load balancing, 83
   routing, 83
   service verification, 95–98
spring-cloud
      dependencies, 71

T

Technical debt, 53
Timeout request, service
   siege, delay injection, 213, 214,
      217, 218
   virtual service
      configuration, 214–216
      modification, 212
Tracing, 80
Transport authentication
   certificate authority, 282
   Citadel CA, 284
   curl commands, 285, 286, 288
   destination rule, 288
   namespace level, 289
   PKI, 282
   policy, 284

rewriteAppHTTPProbers
    annotation, 287
service mesh, 283
TLS communication, 282, 283
Troubleshooting
    Configmaps, 305–307
    routing, 309–311, 313

U

User authentication
    Istio configuration, 293, 294
    JWT, 290, 294, 295
    KeyCloak, 291, 292
    OAuth token, 289

V

Virtual service, Istio
    canary release
        definition, 163
        deployment and
            validation, 166–168

    match method, 163, 165
    component, 153
    destination resolution, 145
    DNS names, 139
    Docker images, 140
    forwarding, 154, 155
    HTTP attributes lookup, 158, 159
    naming service ports, 142
    pod ports, 144–146
    Python application, 139
    rewrite, 156, 157
    routing request, 137–141
    single service, 154
    version labels, 143, 144
    webapp-deployment
        command, 140
    weighted distribution, 160–162

W, X, Y, Z

Weight-distributed
    service, 160–162
wget commands, 175

Printed in the United States
By Bookmasters